Encouraging Development in College Students

*This is a volume
in the Minnesota Library on
Student Personnel Work*

Encouraging Development in College Students

Clyde A. Parker, Editor

UNIVERSITY OF MINNESOTA PRESS □ MINNEAPOLIS

Printed at the North Central Publishing Company, St. Paul.
Published by the University of Minnesota Press,
2037 University Avenue Southeast, Minneapolis, Minnesota 55455,
and published in Canada by Burns & MacEachern Limited,
Don Mills, Ontario

The University of Minnesota
is an equal opportunity
educator and employer.

Library of Congress Cataloging in Publication Data

Main entry under title:

Encouraging development in college students.

    (Minnesota library on student personnel work;
v. 11)
    Includes index.
    1. College students. 2. College students—
Psychology. I. Parker, Clyde Alvin. II. Series.
LB3605.E537   378.1'98   78-3197
ISBN 0-8166-0839-3

Foreword

Stanley Gross wrote recently under the intriguing title of "The Importance of the Unimportance of Students." The author is concerned with students' lack of political power, their seeming inability to have any influence in changing the focus of the university from "faculty careerism and institutional loyalty" to student learning. Universities are "institutions oriented to research and scholarly production, set up to provide comfortable homes for professors and administrators." He deplores the distinctly secondary position given to students. Yet, unless they are accepted as occupying a position of major significance in the university, "the fabric which holds these institutions together unravels."

The editor and authors of this book are also concerned with the position of students in a college or university, but less with power and more with limitations in the kinds of growth provided students. They think something can be done and they are doing it, and they are doing it in a systematic, goal-directed fashion, goals derived from a selected personality theory. The contributors to the book, then, are the proponents of selected personality theories, mostly developmental theories, and the organizers of some contemporary and innovative student development programs. The book is the story of their interaction and of the research that supports both theories and programs.

Parker makes clear in the first chapter that student personnel programs, and even student *development* programs, have grown almost independently of developmental theories, and vice versa. So the attempt here is to bring the most relevant personality theories to bear upon the operation of student development programs.

This is a much needed move. Some eighteen years ago I wrote that student personnel work seldom had any philosophical basis upon which long-term goals could be developed. I used the analogy of the development of the street and sidewalk system of a rapidly growing suburb in which there was such persistent demand for streets to keep cars and people out of the mud that there had been no time to put up the street signs! So everyone moved rapidly and efficiently, but the *direction* of movement was a matter of chance beyond one-block trips. The present situation shows little change in philosophical stance except, we hope, the assumption of some combination of holism and experimentalism. More likely, what is done is unconsciously based upon rationalism and idealism; it is difficult to escape these traditional assumptions when one is a part of the academic scene.

Again these many years ago, I could find no personality theory that would cover the wide-ranging needs of a student personnel program. Rather, I selected certain elements of several psychological theory systems and arranged them into a composite. The organization of this book suggests that some composite may be the way out, but the empirical thrust of the treatments and comparisons of this book put us far ahead of my statement in 1959 — or of anything else that has been done between then and now.

A reader who considers himself or herself relatively sophisticated in the literature of the field may feel that he or she can skip over the introductory chapter of a book. Not so for this volume. It is most essential that the reader understand the background of the book and the current status of development theory and of student development programs, that he or she understand why certain writiers were selected and what instructions were given for their writing. All of this, and more, Parker gives in "Introduction: A Student Development Perspective." He also provides a succinct statement of the origins of student personnel work in American colleges and universities. There is an analysis of the apparent lack of understanding of the changing student values which led to the confrontations and demonstrations of the confusing 1960s period. Leadership was lacking from those who were assumed to be closest to student life outside the classroom. In my own experience, the "student personnel worker" has too often not been a student of student life but an administrator of institutional regulations. He or she has been less committed to student growth and the conditions that contributed to this growth than to institutional welfare demanding student conformity. Hurst, in his chapter on "Student Affairs Programming," is more explicit in stating that programming up to now has been largely the outcome of university political considerations and expediency, a given staff's interests and skills, and responsiveness to student pressure groups.

Such laissez-faire planning and seeming contradictions appeared soon after World War II. In part, the distinction between institutional and student emphases was a result of a great increase in numbers and kinds of college and university students. In even larger part, perhaps, because those appointed to institutional leadership in this field were too often general university administrators or athletic coaches already committed to the principle of student conformity to institutional regulations. Then too, many disparate functions were included under one umbrella. As early as 1951 I identified in *Student Personnel Work in College* some offices and functions of a total program as administrative in nature, giving primary service to the institution. Other functions, of course, are clearly in service of the individual students and their growth needs.

It is very pleasing to me to find that the first area considered in these theory-and-practice presentations is that of instruction. I am reminded by Parker's later quotation of my editorial comment of sixteen years ago that I have long believed that this focus upon instruction is primary. The student personnel worker of decades past, and now the student development facilitator, must stay close to the mainstream of the educational enterprise, the instructional function. I have been stating even more urgently during the past half-dozen years: "The school counselor and the college student personnel worker who maintains his or her isolation from the instructional function and from the teachers' needs is vulnerable indeed. To be useful only to the student, and then chiefly to his or her out-of-classroom needs, means that that person is dispensable in these days when budget trimming is a way of life." To be helpful to the instructional dimension of student growth, the cognitive as well as the affective and the experiential dimensions, is to be institutionally valuable in a complete sense of the term.

Every dyed-in-the-wool student personnel worker should read the Widick and Simpson and the Hurst chapters thoughtfully. It could be the stimulus of a new perception of one's professional self. Not everyone can be a Peter Madison psychologist and so skillfully blend the experiential and the cognitive (certainly *some* can), but almost every professional in this field who expects to remain on a college campus would do well to consider his or her instructional responsibility to student growth. This may be achieved within an academic, teamwork relationship or by building the student development concept into the professional function for which he or she is primarily responsible.

Illustrations of these two approaches are found in Hurst's report on the creative efforts by him and his colleagues to apply Chickering's seven vectors of development to a student affairs program. Academic teamwork is beautifully illustrated in the intervention entitled "Education through Student Interaction," and a direct application of the professional's psychological skills is the focus of the "Test Anxiety Program" and the "Math Anxiety Program." The theorists commenting upon Hurts's report were loud in their praise, but showed concern that the programs reported did not affect those factors in the university environment that caused these student deficiencies and disabilities. They wanted prevention, not remediation.

Such an overall expectation appears to me to be most unrealistic. Undoubtedly, the programs changed, to some degree, the professors who learned to refer their students to these programs. Hurst and his colleagues provided and are still providing some bright spots in an academic atmosphere largely indifferent to the areas of development proposed by Chickering. But who could possibly expect an entire university environment to be favorable to growth in such areas as "achieving competence in social and interpersonal skills," "establishing identity," "becoming autonomous," etc. I am glad indeed that Hurst and colleagues were not intimidated by a general faculty indifference, but created programs of worth wherever they could find a toehold. I have long believed that the student personnel worker should not attempt to work with an entire faculty but with departments or individual faculty members who were sympathetic to some of the goals of the student personnel staff. Teamwork can be effected here. One must take for granted that the faculty member who is preoccupied with curriculum content or department politics is not to be easily converted, if at all, to total student needs and growth. Work with those who are already inclined to march to your drum beat. They are present if you only look for them.

The next two chapters carefully design a career development model based upon Perry's stage development theory, and then test the model in a career development class. Excellent! Theory into practice, but I find also some practice into theory. Roger Myers, who has in comments on earlier chapters, pleaded for vocational development attention, seems well pleased here and sees the Perry theory as blazing a new trail for career development efforts based on developmental stages.

I have used too much space on the intentional programs. Little space left for comments on the theorists—and what a pity! These six chapters are in themselves worth the price of the book. To be highly commended also is the plan of the conference to have the "perspective" writers do their comments after they had listened to the description of "intentional programs" and after they had discussed each program presentation. That bit of creative planning makes these theories much closer to program reality than any I have formerly seen. Clearly, sometimes brilliantly written, the perspective papers carry the reader over several routes of thinking, but always realistically. Each paper is plausible. Each lives up to its inviting title!

I am grateful for several things. I am grateful to Clyde Parker for asking me to write a Foreword, which required that I read the manuscript. For I learned much about some truly invigorating programs, I learned that something *can* be done in a theory-based, goal-directed manner. And I am thankful also for becoming better acquainted with the Perry nine-stage and the Chickering seven-vector programs. I can see why they are deemed so suitable for student development planning, with, for, example, Perry's dualist-relativist scheme so easily understood and so researchable. Chickering's theory is a little more elegant in its broad sweep of areas of development. Perry contributed to me personally also in his poignantly written and highly personal "Perspective" statement. And I am grateful for understanding better Douglas Heath's carefully developed maturing person theory. I hope that I have grown more mature in years that I have become more mature in other ways — particularly I hope I have become more allocentric. Maturing is a life process, isn't it, Dr. Heath? I still have some growing to do in the years beyond age seventy-five. Whether the theory allows for it or not, I *plan* to do so!

I am thankful, too, for the possibilities given for "intentional" program planning at the University of Maryland and Colorado State University. A tip of the hat to the personnel administrators who made this possible.

If you read these pages carefully you might draw the conclusion that I am enthusiastic about this book! It is illustrative of the kind of book we should have more often. Sophisticated, operational, clearly written. Thank you, dear colleagues, for providing me with a deeply felt growth experience.

C. Gilbert Wrenn

Arizona State University
September 1977

Preface

The personality development of students has always been a goal in higher education. It has received a new emphasis in the past twenty years through extensive research and through a redefinition of Student Personnel work. An exploration of ways that research and theory can be adapted by practitioners is very much needed.

In May 1976, a conference was held in Minneapolis to initiate a discussion of such issues. The papers included in this volume were prepared in conjunction with the conference. The success of this work and of the conference is due to the thoughtful preparation and efforts of many people. Those who attended the conference provided a very important stimulus to all of us. Their reactions to the papers presented and their sharing of ideas and problems helped to shape the papers prepared after the conference.

The members of the planning committee, Lorraine S. Hansen, Pierre Meyer, James Rest, Diane Skomars, Martin Snoke, Norman Sprinthall, and Howard Williams, were responsible for the planning and organizing of the event. The funds were provided by the Higher Education and the Counseling Psychology and Student Personnel programs of the College of Education and by the Office of Student Affairs of the University of Minnesota. Without such support, it just wouldn't have happened.

Throughout the planning, organizing, and conducting of the conference, I had the very able assistance of Patricia M. King. Her steady hand and care of detail added greatly to the success of the conference. Sylvia Rosen provided the technical editing of the papers. I have come to rely on her good eye and clear head for literate expression.

To all of these good people, as well as the authors of the papers included, I say thanks for the challenge and support that has moved me another step in my own development as well as having opened up a dialogue for the readers of the present volume.

Clyde A. Parker

January 1978

Contents

Theoretical Perspectives

Encouraging Development in College Students

Introduction:
A Student Development Perspective

Clyde A. Parker

Origins

Concern with the development of students in higher education can be traced in one form or another to the beginnings of the university as an institution in modern society. In particular, in America, the early university was primarily a religious institution and its major purpose was the development of character in students. With the rise of intellectualism, an orientation borrowed from the German university, the concern of many American institutions with the development of character was pushed to one side. At the beginning of the twentieth century, however, a growing interest in providing for other than the intellectual needs of students returned to American higher education. Then it was that the first deans of men and women were appointed in universities and colleges. They were given varying responsibilities: at first, to assist the heads of the institutions with some of the student management functions and, often, to maintain order and discipline. It is to their credit that they carried out such functions humanely and with interest in the individual students as well as in the institutions' welfare.

Professional student personnel work, as most of us know it, had its real beginnings after World War I. The relative success and application of measurement and personnel procedures by army psychologists led some, notably Donald G. Paterson, to believe that many problems in higher education could be approached systematically, if not scientifically. Developments at the University of Minnesota (Williamson & Sarbin 1940) typify the movement. In

3

the early 1920s, Paterson was given responsibility for the testing program established for the Arts College; testing of freshmen had begun in 1919. Paterson, through follow-up studies, was able to determine selection procedures that reduced student mortality. These procedures led to the appointment of faculty counselors in 1921. By 1926, all freshman entrants were tested during Freshman Week. Between 1915 and 1930, the University organized a vocational guidance service for women, offices of the deans of men and women, and a testing and counseling bureau.

Dean John B. Johnston of the Arts College initiated two major changes in the organizational structure of the University to help meet the individual needs of students: a University College, to provide for students whose particular interests did not coincide with those of the major departments and, hence, required interdepartmental programs, and University Junior College (later General College), to provide a curricular program for students who did not meet the eligibility requirements for admission to the College of Liberal Arts. These two major innovations, with the testing and counseling bureau, represented what were then unique attempts to "individualize mass instruction" in a large state university.

These particular developments are important because of their many similarities to current student personnel concerns. Foremost in the minds of Paterson and his co-workers was the intent to facilitate, enhance, and stimulate the greater growth and development of students through more effective education. To them, such services were part of the activities of the regular academic faculty. A key point in Paterson's report (Paterson et al. 1928) was the recognition that such services could be carried out most effectively through the academic faculty. In fact, the idea of separating student personnel services from the work of the regular faculty was a contradiction of the basic philosophy of the services.

The vision of those early student personnel workers is illustrated by the predictions made by W. R. Harper, in 1899, in an address delivered at Brown University.

In order that the student may receive the assistance so essential to his highest success, another step in the onward evolution will take place. This step will be the scientific study of the student himself. . . . In the time that is coming provision must be made, either by the regular instructors or by those appointed especially for the purpose, to study in detail the man or woman to whom instruction is offered.

The [study] will be made (1) with special reference to his character . . . to find out whether he is responsible or careless, or shiftless or perhaps vicious; (2) with special reference likewise to his intellectual capacity; (3) with reference to his special intellectual characteristics to learn whether he is independent or original; (4) with reference to his special capacity and tastes; (5) with reference to the social side of his nature.

This feature of twentieth century education will come to be regarded as of greatest importance, and fifty years hence, will prevail as widely as it is now lacking. [Harper 1905, p. 320.]

Although, initially, it was intended for the primary work to be done by the regular academic faculty, separate bureaus were gradually established to provide individual guidance, social programs, discipline, recreation, and other services. The bureaus included the Offices of the Dean of Men and Dean of Women, the Student Counseling Bureau, and, later, the Student Activities Bureau and Student Housing Bureau. Similar developments were occurring on other campuses throughout the country; by the late 1930s, the American Council on Education (1937) considered it important to summarize these developments and to establish "the student personnel point of view" as a regular and ongoing part of American higher education. The ACE statement, which became an orientation landmark for student personnel workers, emphasized basing education upon a recognition of the individual differences of students, their systemic or holistic nature, and the need to begin instruction at their present levels of accomplishment or development. This holistic orientation of student personnel work toward both the individual student and the institution as a whole is best reflected by C. Gilbert Wrenn in the editor's introduction to Mueller (1961):

Student personnel work, therefore, once it has found itself, must quickly relate to instruction, to learning in the classroom as well as out. Its roots are here, its future is here. To be sure, it may broaden the concept of learning to include learning in the student group, in the residence hall, in the interview, in the personal budget to be made and kept. But it must always concern itself with learning, even intellectual learning. [P. v.]

Despite these beginnings in which the focus was on the individual development of the whole person in the total educational context, American institutions of higher learning allowed and encouraged the field of student personnel work to be organized as a separate field. Following the intent of the 1937 ACE statement, growth was vigorous during the subsequent three decades. By the early 1960s, almost every institution of higher education in the United States could boast of a large staff of professional and semiprofessional persons who performed the multiple functions that were then labeled student personnel work. Included were such diverse activities as health services, housing accommodations, financial aid programs, management of student activities, counseling and psychotherapy, and discipline. Increasingly, the academic faculty had shifted to these professional workers the responsibility for all student affairs outside the regular academic classroom. The typical charge to such professionals was to "meet the out-of-class needs of students," which was usually interpreted to mean the emotional, social, and recreational needs. The shift of responsibility increased the freedom of the academic faculty to engage in research and writing and to focus their teaching increasingly upon their disciplines rather than the holistic development of their students. At the same time, on many campuses, professional counselors became concerned if faculty members extended their "advising" responsibilities to interest in the personal problems of students.

As these bureaucracies grew, the personnel who staffed them became more and more identified with controlling and disciplinary functions as opposed to educational or growth-facilitating functions. In the minds of many faculty, student personnel workers were those who either controlled student behavior so that it did not get out of hand or "coddled" incompetent and unresponsive students and, thus, prevented them from taking full responsibility for their lives.

Finding themselves under attack by their academic counterparts, student personnel workers defended themselves with the doctrine of *in loco parentis*: in brief, that since most students are minors in the eyes of the law and since they are living away from home or, at least, spending many hours away from home, it is the responsibility of the institution to act "in the place of their parents." Consequently, necessary measures were taken to encourage, facilitate, and strengthen students' education, on the one hand, and, on the other, to administer just and necessary discipline to ensure that each student's behavior was "becoming to a lady or a gentleman." The doctrine was widely accepted and not often contested openly, that is, not until the mid-1960s.

The main events on American campuses during the 1960s are well known to most people. The impact on the field of student personnel work is less well known, however. With all their good intentions to be real "students of students" according to Harper's predictions, student personnel workers had become programmers, tenders of brushfires, and disciplinarians. They did not sense the growing uneasiness and unrest of the students in the early 1960s. The social unrest in the country, which grew out of the civil rights movement, the untenable war in Vietnam, and the new morality, was amplified on American campuses. No one in higher education was prepared for the sudden outbreak of bannering, strikes, barricades, and other forms of protest. The lack of preparation was especially evident among the student personnel workers who had been given the primary responsibility for student affairs and, therefore, might have been expected to be of assistance. As one campus after another was torn apart, faculty pointed at student personnel workers, and the latter pointed at the faculty in a cycle of recriminations. The more reflective persons within the field of student personnel work recognized that the promises of the 1920s and 1930s had not been fulfilled.

A reawakening and rededication to the early goals is now in progress. The American College Personnel Association (ACPA), recognizing that the philosophy of *in loco parentis* was dead, set out to define explicitly a new direction which has been labeled "student development."

If a single force behind this movement can be identified, it is the writings of Nevitt Sanford in the 1960s. Consistently, his publications (Sanford 1962, 1966, 1967) developed the thesis that institutions of higher education should have as their primary goal the individual development of each student enrolled. Outlining the characteristics of a "developmental community," he pointed out that personal development requires an environment in which the forces that challenge an individual's present capabilities are balanced by those that provide personal support. In such an environment, individuals find that while they have personal support they are also challenged by new ideas, situations, and problems; challenges that require them to develop new means of thinking, new strategies of coping, and the ability to enlarge the world in which they function. This increase in the ability to deal with an ever more complex world in ever more complex ways characterizes development, according to Sanford.

The student development movement, then, is concerned with establishing an environment in higher education that challenges and supports individuals to increase their total effectiveness, not with adjusting to or being controlled by the institution. In many ways it is a rededication to the philosophy articulated by Paterson in the 1920s and the ACE in the 1930s. But it has a new look also. Part of the new look is the attempt to build models that guide both the content and process of development.

ACPA Project: Tomorrow's Higher Education

In the late 1960s, under the leadership of the president, Donald P. Hoyt, the American College Personnel Association attempted to define more explicitly a new direction. The committee appointed for that purpose included Ronald Jackson, Dykeman Vermilye, E. Joseph Shoben, Jane Matson, and the present author. Although the committee was unable to produce a workable document, it provided the stimulus for papers (Parker 1970, 1971, 1973) that called for a revitalization of student personnel work by reorganizing existing bureaus and functions into a center for student development and by creating a theory of student development.

The suggested theory had five major elements: (1) a description of the entering student; (2) a definition of the educated person; (3) an identification of changes that are desirable and possible; (4) the identification of the forces in higher education that are capable of bringing about change in students; and (5) an understanding of how such forces can be better used. The influence of the initial paper (Parker 1970) on the content of this conference is clarified below. It is important here because several significant subsequent events led to a major restructuring of the thought, activities, and, to some extent procedures that are now followed in the field of student personnel work. An outline of those events provides an even clearer context for the conference reported here.

In subsequent years, ACPA attempted to redefine student personnel work through a project entitled "Tomorrow's Higher Education." The details of this development and its product to date are described by Miller and Prince (1976). The project has gone through three major phases. The first described the *process* of facilitating student development. This process model includes four basic steps: (1) to help the student set goals; (2) to assess current status and steps necessary to achieve the goal; (3) to facilitate growth and development through instruction, consultation, and/or environmental management; and (4) to evaluate the efforts toward the accomplishment of the goals and to initiate actions where appropriate.

In its second phase, the project identified as many programs as possible with a developmental orientation, programs which currently are being carried out in institutions of higher education. The Miller and Prince volume mentions over fifty programs and organizations that are specifically and explicitly developmentally oriented.

The third phase of the project described ways in which student affairs could be organized to facilitate student development. Since organizations are peculiar to institutions, no specific organizational model has been developed; rather, the general principles that operate in such organizations and the strategies for bringing about changes in them are described (Miller & Prince 1976).

What was not accomplished in the ACPA project was a careful examination, identification, or elaboration of psychosocial, developmental theories which can be used to guide practitioners who work with students. Independent of the ACPA effort, however, is a growing body of literature in higher education that deals with the changes in students' lives, the factors that bring about these changes, and a modicum of theorizing about what does and should happen to students in the context of higher education. It is, perhaps, too early to call most of these efforts "theories" in the usual scientific sense. On the other hand, a substantive body of knowledge now current was not available in the 1960s. Certainly, this literature is sophisticated enough to warrant a very careful examination for its potential relevance to student affairs. Most of the research and writing deals with higher education in general and not specifically with student-affairs programming. However, because of the early commitment of student personnel work to the holistic development of students in the total environment of higher education, we have been particularly interested in applications of such work to the entire context of higher education as well as to functions typically referred to as student affairs.

Unfortunately, the work sponsored by ACPA has proceeded without clear reference to developmental psychology as a discipline. The result has been the widespread use of terms and phrases like "student development" or "the development of the whole student" without definition of the key term, "development." The failure to define "development" has made it difficult to relate the general body of literature dealing with the changes in students' knowledge, values, intellectual functioning, and behaviors to "student development." On the one hand, we have no precise meaning for the term "development," and, on the other, a substantial body of knowledge of developmental psychology has been derived without particular reference to the field of student personnel work.

Conference Structure and Purpose

The context for the conference reported in these proceedings developed from the two convergent movements described in the preceding section: the change from philosophy based on *in loco parentis* to a commitment to the promotion of the development of students, and the growing body of literature dealing with student development. There was an evident need to "fill out" the ACPA model of student development by pursuing the question, Can existing knowledge (both research and theory) of how college students grow, change, and develop be useful in student personnel work?

The conference was designed to accomplish three purposes: First, to explore whether programs can be based on existing "theories" of student development rather than put together on an ad hoc basis, as has been largely true in the past.

The typical student affairs practitioner has had little guidance other than observations of others or personal creative resources in a particular situation. Mueller (1961) wrote,

The reasons why the personnel worker carries on sometimes one and sometimes another of these functions can be traced to local traditions, to emergencies to be met, to skills the particular personnel worker has developed, to techniques which come to his hand, even to ambitions that he has cherished, and certainly to the services offered in the face of the developing needs of students and the demands of parents. [P. 57.]

The conference, it was hoped, would assist practitioners to become more systematic and scientific than the picture painted by Mueller.

The second purpose was to enable several researchers to discuss the use of their work in developing activities or programs. Although some researchers have been interested in the uses of their theories (see Chickering 1974), most have been content to describe what they see as change in college student behavior, attitudes, and values. If the area of student affairs is to progress, then we must find some way to move back and forth between theory and practice.

The final purpose of the conference was to bring together in a congenial environment the practitioners "on the firing line" (persons who are currently engaged in testing applications) and "theorists" (persons who have given considerable thought to the nature of change in college students). It was expected that a group of persons so assembled in the right atmosphere would not only challenge and support each other but also stimulate a new level of thought about the relation of theory to practice.

Despite our efforts, we still do not have a comprehensive theory of student development. It is highly unlikely that any given body of research and theory can fully account for what happens to students in the college environment. Personal endeavors, observations of others, and the existing body of literature suggest that the development of individual college students is so complex that any given researcher or observer is able to account for only a portion of what happens to the individuals. Furtherance of *science* requires the focused view that a single theory provides, but the *practice* of student personnel work depends on the practitioner having a much more comprehensive view and understanding of students in their environment. This paradox can be overcome only by some form of systematic eclecticism in which different but complementary theories are brought together to round out the picture of the whole student. At this time, a case cannot be made for any particular set of complementary theories, but the areas or types of theories that must be included in such a set can be specified.

The five questions advanced by Parker (1970, 1973) as the concerns of an adequate theory of student development are still relevant today. Developmental psychologists are searching for the relative importance of the nature of the environment, on the one hand, and the nature of the person, on the other. Most of them would agree that both are important and that the interaction of the two is what stimulates development, but one still finds different emphases. Developmental psychologists appear to be consistent in their concern with changes that result in the organization or pattern of thought and behavior over time; what is considered development, as opposed to learning, is characterized by systemic change more than the accrual of bits of behavior or knowledge. It is change in the interrelations of the parts that enables the person to respond to more complex situations effectively. These changes often are referred to as *structural changes*.

In addition, developmental psychologists are concerned with the regularity of change across individuals in order to be able to anticipate or describe changes occurring in all persons and the sequences in which those changes take place. The four characteristics of change—interaction between person and environment, the systemic or holistic nature of growth, regularity and sequence, and the universality of patterns of change (at least within a given culture)—seem to be the main defining variables of developmental psychology. Developmentalists disagree about the relative importance or best definition of each characteristic.

Student personnel workers, by contrast, have been more interested in facilitating or supporting change that "should be" taking place in students during the college years. Their "theories" rarely have been verbalized and the changes they seek most frequently have been isolated and fragmentary. Thus, one of the major tasks that confronts the field is to select a set of complementary theories that not only can describe the course of development but also suggest the direction and means for change.

In working with college students and, more recently, in attempting to find an adequate theory to explain and describe college student behavior, it has become apparent that five different types of theory are needed to fully account for what happens to the students. At present, developmental psychology can be divided roughly into theories assuming (1) that development is discontinuous and occurs in stages, or (2) that behavior is continuous and progresses in smooth, if uneven, development. Cutting across these two different ways of thinking about development is the question of whether the stimulus for change comes primarily from within or without the person. Theories that adhere to the exogenous position emphasize environmental characteristics and cultural tasks as requirements for successful participation in the culture. Theories that emphasize the importance of the internal stimulus look to the nature of the individual to explain change. Although a clear-cut distinction cannot be made between the two positions, we can characterize them as "task developmental" and "stage developmental." The stage theories tend to emphasize those characteristics of the person which are inborn or biological in origin. Developmental task theories, in contrast, tend to emphasize the characteristics of the environment (either the physical or social environment) that require different modalities of coping as the individual progresses through the normal life span.

Because they are focused on the regularities and universals of development, neither stage developmental nor task developmental theory really takes into consideration the individual differences that seem so apparent to a careful student of human behavior. Although people differ on many dimensions, only the differences in rate or nature of development concern us here. Theories that focus on those individual differences are important to our understanding of what happens to a student in the college environment — that is, why some students develop in a given environment and others do not, or why some develop faster than others. These questions have led to the inclusion, in our set, of those theories that are particularly concerned with typologies or temperaments, even though they are traditionally thought of as not being within developmental psychology.

If the matter is pursued further it becomes clear that, although both stage developmental and task theories look at the individual in progress, neither speaks to the "ought" question as directly as do those theories that have attempted to describe the mature personality or to deal with the fully educated person. Such theories give us an ultimate sense of direction as we attempt to design programs to facilitate development.

Granted that a fully adequate developmental theory will be universal in its descriptive power, still the college environment has special characteristics that demand special consideration. Also, we have become sensitive to the highly differential impact of different college environments. Thus the inclusion of theory that is directed specifically to college environments is an important addition to our complement.

The five types of theory are necessary to account adequately for what has been observed in large numbers of existing research studies. They are task theory, stage developmental theory, temperaments or typologies, theories of the mature person, and person-environment interaction theories. The latter three are not usually included in developmental psychology but, because the development of the college student (and probably of all other persons throughout the life span) cannot be adequately addressed without consideration of all five, they are included here. It is highly unlikely that a single theory can address such a wide array of concerns and data, but effective practitioners must cover that broad a range.

In organizing the conference, we wanted to include representatives of each of the five types of theory. We were also interested in focusing the discussions of the conference around specific, applied programs that would illustrate the utility of theory in practice. The conference was structured so that persons whose work had been primarily in research and theory building could freely interact with persons whose work was primarily in application and practice. Obviously, these distinctions are not clear-cut; persons in each group necessarily have spent parts of their professional lives in both kinds of activities.

We were particularly interested in focusing attention on the broad scope of student development, to include programs in both the student affairs area and the regular academic classroom. To oversimplify, we wanted to have examples of the application of task theories to both the student affairs area and the classroom and, also, applications of stage developmental theories in both student affairs and academic areas. We wanted to see analyses of and reactions to these attempts at application. Therefore, we selected as reactors a representative of each of the five types of theories.

The conference organization was unusual in that we asked the "theorists" to write reactions to the applications of theory, as presented in the papers of the four "practitioners," before the conference. We also asked them to delay preparing their formal presentations until they had spent two days in dialogue with other conference participants. Thus they were able to include ideas gained at the conference in their discussions of the utility of their particular theories in higher education. There is ample evidence in the papers presented here that the format "worked" because the theorists' papers, in one way or another, reflect the work of the other conference participants. With the inclusion of these written reactions, the volume presents a dialogue in which the reader can take part.

Obviously, the papers do not duplicate other works of the participants. Rather, their work is extended and given specific application to higher education. Each paper reflects the author's basic orientation in a general context that is readily apparent. Because of the unusual organization of the conference and this volume, a "reader's guide" is presented for ready reference.

Overview of the Volume: A Reader's Guide

Before discussing each of the papers, it may be well to highlight the six issues that emerged as the conference progressed. Not unexpectedly, each issue is a continuing one in developmental psychology and has been the focus of discussion at other conferences and in other volumes. These issues are as follows.

Is development sequential in nature? Stage theory presupposes recognizable, sequential patterns in a person's behavior which can be identified. Development consists of moving from one stage to another, and stages are qualitatively different from each other. Nonstage theorists tend to believe that although development is uneven it progresses in some continuous manner, such that changes are not always easily observed and are best described as quantitative rather than qualitative in difference. A stage usually refers to a pattern of behaviors that is distinctly different from the patterns of other stages: "the whole is more than the sum of its parts." The individual so orients toward life that his or her responses have a particular recognizable consistency (e.g., Loevinger's conformity stage).

A related and separate issue focuses on whether development is continuous or discontinuous *if* it is sequential. That is, does change from one stage to another take place all at once so that sudden differences can be observed, or is behavior change a continuous flow so that stages gradually emerge?

Another issue emerged in the discussions of the various attempts to use developmental theory in student programing. It can best be described as the "is to ought" question in student development. That is, most persons would agree that theories of development are descriptive in nature. The issue arises over whether they can be prescriptive in nature and, more specifically, whether the descriptions of what happens to students *in general* can be used as a basis for organizing programs or other forms of engagements with students to promote their development. Such change should be in the direction of movement described by the theory. A more complete discussion of these issues was stimulated by the conference and can be found elsewhere (Parker 1977). A second part of this issue is the ethics of consciously planned, induced change. An often heard question was, Does one person have the right to try to set conditions to change another?

Are developmental theories universal in their descriptions of human behavior, or are they more cultural, subcultural, or even ideographic in nature? This question becomes particularly important when one begins to think about the "application" or use of theory in the design of programs for persons and settings, environments, or cultures different from those in which the original data were collected.

Another issue is a specific example of the question of universality. Are there factors that are sufficiently peculiar about the college environment to justify a set of theories that deals with college student development as distinct from human development in general? Stated more boldly, the issue is, If we have a good theory of life-span development, is there anything unusual or different about the college environment that would cause us to consider that environment specifically in our theory?

The last issue is more subtle but, nevertheless, an important consideration in relation to the special nature of the college environment. It might be a rephrasing of the heredity versus environment question. More specifically, it focuses on the question, Does development proceed *primarily* from the environment? Basic to this issue is one's view of people as "machines" to be acted upon or persons who act upon their environment.

Although these six issues were rarely addressed specifically during the conference, much of the dialogue and, particularly, some of the comments in the papers presented here grew out of an implicit recognition of their importance and immediacy.

DEVELOPMENTAL THEORY IN THE CLASSROOM

The conference included two examples of the ways in which the development of college students can be promoted directly in the classroom. These examples are in keeping with the long-term commitment of student personnel work to make the total college environment a setting for the promotion of student development. Widick and Simpson's paper exemplifies the use of stage development theory (Perry's work) to structure the content and procedures of a history course. A psychologist and a history professor taught the course together, the historian focusing on the discipline content and the psychologist, on what was happening to the students personally. The worth of history as an area of human knowledge was explicitly recognized but, at the same time, the education of the whole student was promoted.

By contrast, Madison, a clinical psychologist, has been able to combine the best of clinical and academic knowledge in the teaching of his "Personality Laboratory." It is an excellent example of how knowledge can be personalized and, conversely, how personal experience can be abstracted into theory. In this case, rather than drawing on specific theories of college student development (Madison at one time had created his own), Madison chose to draw upon his extended knowledge of clinical psychology, both theory and practice, to assist students to understand the broader scope of human development by using each student as a specific example. His classes are neither therapy groups nor abstract theoretical discussions; rather, they seem to combine the best of experiential and didactic instruction to personalize learning.

DEVELOPMENTAL THEORY IN STUDENT AFFAIRS

Hurst's paper is an ex post facto description, in theoretical terms, of a series of highly creative developmental programs at Colorado State University. The staff of the counseling center at Colorado State were among the first to employ student development concepts in the creation of a total program. Their work has been a benchmark for student affairs in research and evaluation as well as practice. The three programs described in Hurst's paper can be adequately reinterpreted in Chickering's developmental vectors. Further, Hurst proposes that Chickering's vectors are a useful "content" addendum to the developmental processes cube that originated at Colorado State. His paper suggests an encompassing method of mapping out a total student development program.

Before developmental theory could be used in specific career development programs, it was necessary to translate a general developmental theory into vocational terms. Knefelkamp and Slepitza make the translation in their paper. Like many such adaptations, it is a very enterprising and creative project. But they do not stop at the theorizing stage. Their co-workers in the Student Affairs Office at the University of Maryland (Touchton et al.) take the theoretical propositions and create a curriculum for career development around them. Like the Widick and Simpson application of Perry's theory to the curriculum, the model originated by Touchton and her colleagues relies heavily on the Sanford concepts of challenge and support. Their attempts at evaluation include not only student satisfaction, but a test of the utility of the Perry model in such work.

THE THEORISTS THEMSELVES

A brief note about each theorist whose paper is given here will help the reader entering the dialogue among the conference participants.

William Perry is the director of the Bureau of Study Counsel at Harvard University. His work, *Forms of Intellectual and Ethical Development*, was the basis for three of the applications presented. His scheme was developed after extended interviews with two different groups of students over a period of four years each. The scheme is basically a stage model of development and describes the student's progression through nine "positions" or "stages." The scheme describes college students specifically and has been readily adapted for the specific programs described here.

David Hunt, working primarily with adolescent students, had developed and worked with a conceptual-level scheme that has many of the same properties as the Perry scheme. Much of Hunt's experimental work has been devoted to testing the utility of his conceptual-level model in classroom teaching in the public schools. That work has led him to raise a fundamental criticism of attempts to use theoretical models as a basis for practice. His major contribution to this conference was to draw the attention of the participants to the complexities in applying the general and abstract to the specific and concrete. His position is not cynical. In his creative paper he describes in detail the necessity for a model of whole persons so interacting with one another that each takes responsibility for what happens in the interaction, each contributes to that interaction, and all are at once both theorists and practitioners. His notions that personal constructs supersede abstract theories and that the former rather than the latter are the basis of personal action have become an extremely stimulating idea in the search for models of application.

Roger Myers, a former director of a counseling center, is currently the chairman of the counseling psychology program at Columbia University. He was trained in the tradition of differential psychology and is thoroughly conversant with vocational and career choice. Because of his identification with career development and career counseling, he served as an excellent representative of task development theory; in this case the specific task is making career choices and decisions. His perspective is much broader than the task, however; and from his unique vantage point as both practitioner and professor he helped the participants to examine the utility of attempts to apply theory.

The extended and comprehensive research of Douglas Heath, beginning with his work at Haverford College and extending to crosscultural samples, has provided him with an unusual basis from which to compose a general theory of maturing. His belief in the importance of models of life-span development and in the continuous testing of his model was a provocative stimulus which forced the participants to think beyond the immediate setting toward the identification of end goals for students. His is the more complex of the models presented and one of the better researched. (Some of his earlier works are cited in his paper.)

The recognition of individual differences in the way students develop was a distinctive contribution of Roy Heath. Heath first proposed his model of the "reasonable adventurer" about twenty years ago. Since then he has expanded the model to show how individual differences in temperament affect the flow and processing of information. In this paper, he shows how different types of students develop at different rates and, in particular, how the nature of that development differs among individuals. Unlike other developmental theorists, his emphasis on those individual differences provides an important perspective to our consideration of the issues of human development.

With our concern for the uniqueness of the college environment, it was important that a representative of the person-environment-interaction theorists participate. Ursula Delworth, who was then associated with Western Interstate Commission on Higher Education (WICHE) and its project on mental health on the college campus, provided a broad knowledge of a variety of such theories. Her own work has centered around the "ecosystems" model developed at WICHE, but in her interaction she drew heavily from Barker, Pervin, Holland, and Pace and Stern. Recognizing the importance of questions on cultural and subcultural differences, she asserts that, while development is organismic and may proceed from the nature of the individual, it is also dependent upon the environmental milieu in which the individual lives.

The conference papers are given here in the general order in which they were presented at the conference. The "application" papers are presented first and are followed by the specific reactions of the six theorists to them. Then follow the six papers which were prepared after the conference by the theorists in response to the conference. Although the application and theory papers can be read as discrete units, the reader is encouraged to proceed through the papers in the order in which they are presented here in order to follow the issues as they were developed and reacted to.

The reader should be alerted, however, to one particular difficulty in using the volume in this way. As will become abundantly clear, the interaction of theory and practice in the material is intimate and obscures the separation of one from the other. It was equally difficult in presenting the material to decide which should come first—the theory papers or the applications. In either case the reader would suffer to a degree from not having the context in which to understand some of the comments. In making the decision to follow roughly the format of the conference there is risk that the reader will not fully understand the theoretical basis of the application or some of the theorists' reactions to those applications. In most cases the potential problem was anticipated by the author or minimized by the editor.

There are a few places that deserve special consideration. Two sets of applications (Widick and Simpson, and Knefelkamp and Slepitza) are based on Perry's work at Harvard. Widick and Simpson present a brief overview of his model in the beginning of their paper. Knefelkamp and Slepitza extend that model to make it adaptable to career decision making. A careful reading of these sections is essential to understand the remaining portions of those two sets of papers. The interested reader may wish to spend additional time with the original Perry work.

The model of maturing presented by Douglas Heath in his paper in the second half of the book is referred to in several of his comments to the specific application papers. The model is two dimensional, quite complex, and uses vocabulary which will be new to many. Readers who are unfamiliar with his work may wish to read his longer paper first in order to more fully understand his comparisons, contrasts, and critiques of other theoretical positions and the applications of those theories. Since none of the applications used his theory directly, understanding how his work is similar to and different from other theories will enlarge one's grasp of the field.

David Hunt's reactions to several of the applications will not be fully appreciated until one has read his longer paper. If one does take the time to read that first, it is likely that all of the applications will be seen from a different perspective and that his particular comments will take on new meaning in conjunction with the applied papers.

And one last note about the theories and applications. Hurst draws heavily from Chickering for an analysis of the programs at Colorado State. Delworth makes frequent reference to Chickering's work in her critiques of the application of theory to emphasize the importance of institutional characteristics as support factors to the particular programs discussed. Other than Hurst's brief discussion of Chickering's seven vectors, there is no elaboration of Chickering's work. His is one of the few attempts to present both a theoretical model of student development and a discussion of the implications of that model of institutional organization to promote the development of students. At this point, we can only encourage the reader to refer to his work directly.

The reader is encouraged to keep in mind the six issues which emerged during this conference, and thus engage in a dialogue that, I hope, will be fruitful in expanding knowledge and awareness of the issues and in increasing the ability to resolve some of them.

REFERENCES

American Council on Education. *The student personnel point of view: a report of a conference*, Series I, 1937, 1(3).

Chickering, A. *Education and identity*. San Francisco: Jossey-Bass, 1974.

Harper, W. R. *The trend in higher education*. Chicago: University of Chicago Press, 1905. Quoted in K. H. Mueller, *Student personnel work in higher education*. Boston: Houghton Mifflin, 1961.

Miller, T. K., & J. S. Prince. *The future of student affairs.* San Francisco: Jossey-Bass, 1976.

Mueller, K. H. *Student personnel work in higher education.* Boston: Houghton Mifflin, 1961.

Parker, C. A. "Ashes, Ashes . . ." Paper presented to the convention of the American College Personnel Association. St. Louis, March 1970.

————. Institutional self-renewal in higher education. *Journal of College Student Personnel,* 1971, 12, 405-449.

————. With an eye to the future. *Journal of College Student Personnel,* 1973, 14, 195-201.

————. On modeling reality. *Journal of College Student Personnel,* 1977, 18, 419-425.

Paterson, D. G., et al. The Minnesota student personnel program. *Educational Record,* Supplement no. 7, 1928, 9, 3-40.

Sanford, N. *The American college.* New York: Wiley, 1962.

————. *Self and society: social change and individual development.* New York: Atherton, 1966.

————. *Where colleges fail.* San Francisco: Jossey-Bass, 1967.

Williamson, E. G., & T. R. Sarbin. *Student personnel work in the University of Minnesota.* Minneapolis: Burgess, 1940.

Encouraging Development through the Curriculum

Developmental Concepts
in College Instruction

Carole Widick and Deborah Simpson

In the past decade, many educational analysts have focused on the limitations of undergraduate education and expressed particular discontent with instruction in the college classroom (Arrowsmith 1968; Bell 1966). Although many factors contribute to the dissatisfaction and conflict that pervade discussions of the teaching-learning process, the concerns center on three basic questions: (*a*) What is the purpose of classroom instruction? (*b*) What are effective instructional methods for achieving that purpose? (*c*) How does one interest college faculty members in learning and using effective approaches in their teaching?

This paper presents the history and current status of our particular efforts to respond to those questions. First, we briefly outline our assumptions about the goals of classroom instruction, then we describe a model for developmental instruction, and third, we present two different applications of our model.

The Purpose of College Instruction

Students' purposes for attending college generally fall into three categories: knowledge acquisition, personality development, and career preparation. Controversy has followed attempts to decide which goal is most important or appropriate to higher education (Barzun 1968; Sanford 1967).

As with most student personnel practitioners, our values bind us to the liberal arts tenet that students should learn more than facts in a classroom; we believe that they should also have experiences

27

that help them to formulate a humane value system, integrate a world view, and develop a broader understanding of self and others. In an increasingly complex world, an accumulation of facts simply is not sufficient; a "developed" individual is needed to use those facts.

Until recently, the idea of the classroom as a developmental agent has been a rhetorical goal; we have not had a sufficient understanding of development to guide an instructional program. During the past few years, however, knowledge of adolescent and adult development has grown by quantum leaps. The research-based models that now exist provide causal connections between learning and development. By drawing upon and trying to use that knowledge base systematically, we believe it is possible to take an integrative approach to college teaching, an approach that fosters both subject-matter mastery and student development.

A Model of Developmental Instruction

Acceptance of the notion that college instruction can and should focus upon both learning and personal development is quite a step from designing a course that actually does so in an explicit, systematic manner. One must consider what kind of development is possible and feasible in a college classroom, what psychological processes are involved in development and in subject-matter learning, and what methods of teaching stimulate the processes of learning and development. Our efforts to develop a suitable model were guided by available theories and empirical data.

EGO-IDENTITY THEORIES: A GUIDE TO CONTENT

A primary source for understanding development, particularly of the traditional college-age student, is the group of theories described as ego-identity models. Erik Erikson (1968) provided the foundation for student development efforts in his description of psychosocial stages. His foremost contribution rests in his discussion of the developmental tasks facing the young adult: the resolution of identity and achievement of the capacity for intimacy.

Many other theorists who have built upon the Eriksonian foundation have focused more intensively upon students in the eighteen to twenty-five age range. Chickering (1969) proposed a model of development in which the task of achieving identity is divided into seven "vectors"; and Farnsworth (1966) and Keniston (1971) identified similar sets of tasks facing the young adult.

The ego-identity models provide general developmental goals. Given Erikson, a developmental teacher would attempt to foster identity resolution. Chickering is more specific in suggesting that the classroom can encourage growth along dimensions, such as intellectual competence and autonomy, which contribute to identity attainment. The goals seem valid, yet the models are descriptive and global in focus; they simply do not explain the process of psychosocial development in ways that relate to specific instructional practice.

What the ego-identity models offer for instruction are guidelines for the selection of content. We have little doubt that Erikson and Chickering accurately captured the central concerns of most young adults. In this sense, they identified "developmental content"; for example, various subject matters, such as personality theory, that deal directly with identity issues may speak most effectively to the young adult. With increasing study of development across the life span, a range of "developmental contents" may be specified for nontraditional students. It is possible that all fields have some content, particular issues, theories, or methods, which can be used in a course to converge with the learners' psychosocial realities.

PERRY'S COGNITIVE DEVELOPMENTAL MODEL: A GUIDE TO GOALS AND INSTRUCTIONAL METHODS

Cognitive development theories describe the ways that thought processes develop and the influence of those processes on other aspects of personality development. The theories provide a functional model of the learner that allows developmental status to be related to learning processes; that is, they suggest ways that a teacher can organize and structure instruction to better fit the student's readiness to learn.

The work of Perry and his associates (1970) is the basis of our instructional approach. Perry's scheme describes intellectual and ethical development as occurring in a generally irreversible sequence of stages in which each stage represents a qualitatively different structure or set of assumptions about knowledge and values. Individuals who are at different stages of development have different views of the nature of knowlege and, to some extent, reflect those differences in their ways of learning. According to this scheme, students pass through nine developmental stages or positions. In a general sense, individuals move from a simplistic, absolute stance vis-à-vis knowledge and values to a complex, pluralistic perspective. There follow the three basic divisions of the scheme.

Dualism. The first three positions represent a dualistic structure for viewing knowledge and values. The dualistic learner assumes that all information can be classified as either right or wrong and that uncertainty is an error of some sort. For the student at these positions, learning is a matter of finding and knowing right answers. In moving from position one to position three, the student successively alters his or her explanation for uncertainty, increasingly accepting its legitimacy.

Relativism. In the movement through positions four, five, and six, absolute right and wrong conceptions of knowledge and values are displaced. In position four, multiplicity, the student perceives uncertainty to be legitimate and pervasive; yet, it exists in an unordered diversity. In position five, all knowledge is seen as contextual and relativistic; at this point, concern with the nature of knowledge interacts with the student's personal life. The student seems to generalize relativistic assumptions to the realm of self and is faced with many vantage points from which to consider his or her own identity. At stage six, the individual seems to recognize that his or her identity will be "created" by acts of commitment.

Commitment in Relativism. In contrast to the earlier positions, the changes defining the last three positions are affective rather than structural. Movement through these positions involves the individual's recognition that affirmation of identity/commitment is a process which will demand continual attention.

Developmental Goals for Instruction. The Perry scheme provides a conceptualization of student development that describes and explains the interweaving of intellect and identity. As Perry (1970) stated, "The students' endeavor to orient themselves in the world through an understanding of the acts of knowing and valuing is therefore more than intellectual and philosophical. It is a moral endeavor in the most personal sense. . . . [The students'] realizations confront them repeatedly with reworkings of the issues of competence, loneliness, community and self-esteem" (p. 54). The nine positions define a relevant set of developmental goals for collegiate instruction. The ultimate goal, the affirmation of identity through choice, is a bridge to Erikson's concept of development. However, the scheme, like other cognitive developmental perspectives, outlines steps along the way—intermediate goals—and suggests the importance of cognitive conflict in moving students along the steps.

Developmental Positions as Individual Differences. Perry's construction of the scheme focused upon the internal cognitive structures rather than their behavioral or affective manifestations. Yet, certain behavior patterns reflecting different developmental positions have been suggested from interview data. Students who think in dualistic ways show the following characteristics. (1) Encounters with uncertainty or diversity are often very stressful; one could assume that an "open" classroom would not be a very happy place for these students. (2) Interpretive tasks (e.g., essays) pose great difficulties; it is quite hard to "compare and contrast" an issue when one does not recognize that a variety of legitimate viewpoints exist. (3) Learning occurs at the direction of the instructor, the authority who has the "right" answers; independent approaches to a course are a decided exception. (4) Evaluation may take on an overwhelming importance; students may be confused about the criteria for giving grades and may pay excessive attention to procedural detail (e.g., numbers of pages).

Perry's data showed that students at relativistic positions respond differently to academic demands and classroom instruction. The following characteristics seem to be most appropriate for them. (1) In early stages of relativism, they turn the idea of pluralism into academic license, emphasizing the value of intuition. (2) They appear to manage their studies more efficiently and effectively; in particular, they are capable of performing complex, analytic tasks with some skill. (3) For them, learning has become more internalized, and they seem more able to use "freedom to learn." (4) In general, they express less concern about pleasing the teacher and evaluation procedures.

These developmental differences are obviously relevant to instructional planning. Moreover, they are supported by other cognitive models of development (Hunt 1970, 1972; Loevinger & Wessel 1970), models of student development (Heath 1964; Marcia 1966, Sanford 1962, 1967), and empirical studies of college instruction (Domino 1968, 1970; Siegel & Siegel 1965; Stern 1962). An essential commonality pervades these models. Certain students, variously called "authoritarian," "foreclosed," "conforming," and "low in conceptual level," are externally directed and view the world in categorical ways. They are less skilled at complex learning tasks and tend to be most comfortable in highly structured environments. Other students, conversely identified as "rational," "moratorium students," "independent," and "high in conceptual level," interact with their environments in complex, integrated, and self-directed ways. These particular students tend to be more autonomous in their approaches to learning.

The very redundancy of these findings bestows validity on the learner differences. Yet, the cognitive developmental models, particularly the Perry scheme, are especially important because they subsume those findings under a developmental umbrella that explains why the differences occur.

ADAPTING INSTRUCTION FOR DEVELOPMENTALLY DIFFERENT STUDENTS

The basic differences noted in students at dualistic as compared to relativistic positions suggest that they require different instructional environments in order to learn and develop most effectively. Thus, developmental instruction would seem to demand the design of instructional approaches that "match" the learner's developmental status (Hunt 1972).

The Perry scheme does not prescribe particular instructional components for students at different developmental levels. Hence, a psychoeducational design process (Snelbecker 1974), a translating of various theoretical ideas and empirical facts into a coherent "matching model," is necessary.

Dualistic Positions. An instructional environment that optimally matches students at dualistic positions fosters movement (or creates readiness to move) to relativism, aids subject-matter learning, and allows the students some degree of comfort in the process of moving from one position to another.

Some form of cognitive conflict or dissonance is a necessary component of development. Perry's descriptive data stress the importance of students being confronted with pluralistic viewpoints. Other theorists (Chickering 1969; Sanford 1962; Schwab 1969) have emphasized this same factor as a method of fostering cognitive complexity. Both Sanford and Schwab extensively discuss the value of selecting and patterning content to reflect such diversity. Heath (1964) found that conflicting themes in literature provide a powerful catalyst for growth in students whose characteristics are similar to the dualistic stage of development. For dualistic thinkers, it seems to be important for subject matter to be selected, sequenced, and presented to explicitly guide the student through relativistic intellectual operations. Such guides allow the students to practice relativistic skills and, also, to stretch their subjective paradigm for perceiving the world.

It has been noted that the structure of subject matter can be too elaborate or complex, inhibiting rather than facilitating learning (Ausubel 1968). A similar reaction has been demonstrated in attitude change processes: influence attempts that are too alien to an individual's belief system are ineffective. Indeed, satisfaction data from various developmental models show that dualistic-type students are disturbed by "liberal" teachings (Henry & Renaud 1972). Thus, steps to moderate or gradually introduce diversity appear to be a necessary functional element in a dualistic instructional program.

Many theorists (Erikson 1968; Henderson 1970) have reemphasized the importance of direct experience in learning and development, particularly for dualistic students who think in concrete ways and have difficulty with abstract, hypothetical tasks. Sprinthall (1973) found that high school students at developmental stages corresponding to dualism require experiential, role-taking tasks for growth to occur. Learning activities that provide a direct, immediate personal experience of the relativistic world may be a necessary augmentation of the structure of subject matter to foster dualistic student development and academic performance.

A number of studies support the finding that dualistic students are either incapable of acting or extremely threatened when instructional processes allow great individual latitude. Jacob (1957) concluded that, "The more a student is in need of direction and respects authority the less will he respond to a course which in content or method of instruction stresses individual responsibility for value judgments" (p. 129). The results of subsequent studies have consistently confirmed Jacob's conclusion (Hunt 1970; Stern 1962).

In explanation, Munsinger and Kessen (1964) reported that individuals prefer the degree of uncertainty or ambiguity that matches their ability to process information. Unguided learning activities exceed dualistic students' capacity for uncertainty, particularly if the subject matter is offered as a pluralistic mosaic.

Certain approaches that control and limit uncertainty have been studied in regard to student differences. Schulz (1968, p. 137) found that students whose cognitive-processing orientation is similar to the dualistic stages were best able to learn when guidance was provided by "advance organizers," a framework providing the cognitive map for subsequent learning. Without such a framework, students with dualistic structures may be overtaxed, whether the task requires either mapping a particular content or a plan for one's learning. Dualistic students seem to need specified and externally directed learning activities and only a few demands for self-direction.

Relativistic Positions. For relativistic-thinking students, the instructional environment should provide challenges and supports that foster movement to commitment, subject-matter mastery, and student enjoyment of the course.

Piaget (1952) suggested the existence of within-stage development—"horizontal décalage"—a process by which a person's capacity to use his or her highest stage of cognitive operations is gradually expanded to include a wider range of "content" areas. It appears that, in some cases, there is a particular order in which cognitive operations are applied to different realms.

It is plausible to expect students who have attained relativistic reasoning to be unable to employ that reasoning consistently. Indirect support for this idea is provided by a study of high school students' use of formal operational thought (Higgins-Trent & Gaite 1971); of the students classified as in formal operations by Piagetian tests, less than half employed those intellectual operations on a situational task. Thus, relativistic students may be in need of extending and more consistently using relativistic cognitive operations and assumptions.

Perry asserted a developmental goal: that relativistic students learn how to make intellectual and personal commitments. Schwab (1969) argued that college students are ignorant of what is involved in responsible decision-making and choice processes. Henry and Renaud (1972) interpreted their preliminary findings as an argument for "moratorium" (a classification roughly parallel to relativism) students to learn to assess their efforts critically and make thoughtful choices, and to direct their investments to more challenging and long-term tasks. They suggested that the curriculum could facilitate this process by providing a wide range of alternatives and allowing for experimentation without "failure." Relativistic students may need the subject matter to be organized in a pluralistic mode to emphasize further analytic skill development while focusing upon issues of commitment.

Relativistic students appear to be able to learn with more satisfaction in an environment that allows them latitude to direct their own learning (Mann et al. 1970). Moreover, the process of taking responsibility for one's own learning provides what Schwab labeled a chance for "rehearsal of consequences," an important preliminary to commitment. For these students who are less bound to concrete ways of responding to events and are more secure and skilled in hypothetical modes of thinking, direct experiential modes of learning would be less imperative, although they might be preferred. Thus, a variety of learning activities would allow relativistic students to achieve academic mastery; however, those activities that require self-direction may be both preferred and facilitative of development.

One additional component is involved. For all students, development and learning can be risky ventures. Our knowledge of how people cope suggests that students need an instructional atmosphere that encourages such risk taking. Thus, an environment characterized by a high degree of trust between students and teacher and an attitude of cooperative learning would seem to be very important.

Developmental Instruction: A Matching Model

A functional model for college teaching can be graphically represented as shown in Figure 1.

First Application: The Themes in Identity Course

Our initial effort to apply the developmental instruction model occurred in 1974 (Knefelkamp 1974; Widick 1975). The goals were to foster academic mastery, using performance on three tasks that required different levels of cognitive complexity; and student development, which was conceptualized as movement along the Perry scheme. Our approach was experimental. Two classes of freshman and sophomore students were taught; in one, an instructional approach matched to students at a dualistic developmental level was used; in the other, the approach matched relativistic-thinking students. Since the students selected which class to attend, both classes were expected to include dualistic and relativistic students. This factor, although not experimentally pure, allowed us to examine the effects of matched and mismatched instruction.

CONTENT OF COURSE

The course was interdisciplinary and included two basic content areas, literature and psychology, to illustrate themes in human identity. The literary content was drawn from nineteenth- and twentieth-century novels and plays, and personality theories provided the basic psychological content.

The two contents were chosen as the course subject matter in the belief that their different conceptualizations of the resolution of identity could serve as important stimuli to development. Four particular units addressed the needs of the freshman population and were consistent with the nature of the disciplines: identity as reflected through significant others, one's relationship with society, career, and the purpose for existence. An outline of one of the units follows. Unit I: Identity as reflected in relationships with sig-

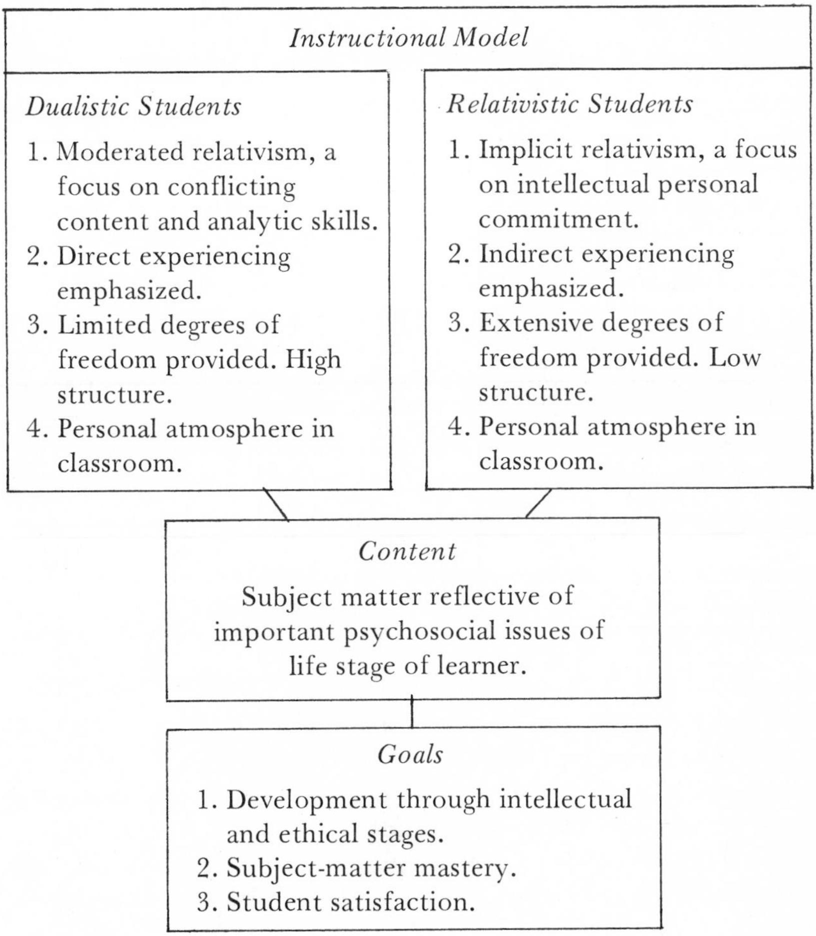

Figure 1: Matching model for developmental instruction

nificant others. Thematic content: the nature of love, the nature of trust, and the nature of sexuality. Literary content: *Zorba the Greek*, Nikos Kazantzakis; *Who's Afraid of Virginia Woolf*, Edward Albee; and *Atlas Shrugged* (excerpts), Ayn Rand. Psychological content: Three distinct approaches to the nature of man were emphasized: the psychoanalytic (Freud), the humanistic-existential (Frankl), and the behavioral (Skinner).

Instructional Approach, Dualist Treatment. The instructional pattern was designed to provide both challenges and supports for dualistic students, that is, we included elements which could induce or allow the student to use his reasoning abilities and apply those higher-order skills to this course content, or which create a manageable level of cognitive conflict leading up to development of more complex modes of thinking.

Two general instructional components were used to provide learner challenges: (*a*) emphasis on relativism of viewpoint and (*b*) experiential learning modes.

Relativism in viewpoint was operationalized in both the selection and presentation of the readings and in the instructional activities designed for the class. The focus was upon conflicting or paradoxical themes within a given book. For example, the book *Zorba the Greek* was viewed in terms of the conflicting views of life provided by the main characters. Also, emphasis was placed upon the conflict in perspectives from book to book. Psychological theories provided significantly different explanations for different identity issues.

The instructional procedures also emphasized alternative perspectives. In the didactic presentation of issues and guidance of discussion, the teachers stressed relativistic views. The dominant instructional statements were "Are there other ways to explain that?" and "Does anybody view it differently?" In-class activities were constructed to identify, in concrete terms, the divergent viewpoints among the writers, students, and instructors. For example, class debates were held; students were asked to pair up with others who viewed an issue in a different way and to discuss it.

The course included both didactic and experiential modes of

learning. The role of experiential learning was major in the treatment for dualists. In-class forms of experience were constructed to foster empathy with widely divergent points of view and a wide range of personalities—characters in novels, authors, psychological theorists, other students in the class, and the instructors. For example, one activity asked students to imagine themselves as three different characters in a novel.

An out-of-class, direct experience was included as part of the dualistic curriculum; for individuals who think in dualistic ways, concrete experiences serve as a bridge from an event to the ability to analyze that event. The students were assigned the roles of psychologist and journalist to interview a series of people about major issues in their lives. In all modes of experiential learning, reflection and discussion in class through a journal were central.

Two types of support were provided for dualistic-thinking students: (*a*) a moderate to high degree of structure to the class and (*b*) a personal atmosphere in the classroom.

In the dualistic treatment, the instructors took full responsibility for planning the class; moreover, expectations about performance requirements were conveyed consistently and in specific terms through handouts, study guides, and the provision of guidelines and due dates for papers and assignments.

Based on the assumption that learning does not best occur in a high-stress and or high-anxiety environment, activities were conducted to create a nonthreatening classroom. Early and continuously, activities were used which build trust by allowing individuals to talk with each other. The class was divided into small groups frequently, and one small-group arrangement was fairly permanent, giving students a sort of home base. Particularly, the instructors reacted to students personally by extensive dialogue carried out through student journals.

Instructional Approach, Relativist Treatment. The relevant instructional process for relativistic students included helping them to extend their capacity to think in complex ways and to make both intellectual and personal commitments. For the relativist treatment, the challenges derived from a number of sources: (*a*) demands for commitment amid relativistic, diverse content, (*b*) indirect experiential learning, and (c) a low level of structure in the instructional process.

The approach stressed the importance and necessity of intellectual commitment and the drawing of conclusions. In content and instructional process, the instruction identified and recognized the existence of conflicting viewpoints yet focused upon their resolution in a commitment process. For example, authors and major characters were examined in terms of basic approach to life or assumptions about man. Activities were constructed to bring out the issues of commitment. For example, students were asked to boil down the message of a play to a one-line quote. Students were asked which psychological theory best described a certain character, in contrast to the dualistic treatment that asked students to analyze a character by three different perspectives.

The use of experiential learning was similar to the dualist class with the exception that experience included only the vicarious nature of the literature and the in-class laboratory experience. These students, it was assumed, would be sufficiently complex in their thinking to grasp "experiences" provided by simulations or through literature and to be capable of empathy, even though the specifics of a situation were markedly unfamiliar to them.

The class was designed to be less structured than the dualist treatment. Fewer guidelines and fewer due dates were employed; all assignments were negotiable, with independent projects allowed. The instructors planned and directed a smaller percentage of class time. Students were given responsibility for a percentage of class time. Expectations were minimally prescribed and left for student interpretation and initiation. The classroom group was used to generate more of the structure for the units; much of the overall framework was arrived at inductively through discussion. A more ambiguous course structure created a situation in which the students needed to decide how to respond to the class and confront the consequences of their decisions. For example, journals were to be turned in three times during the quarter, "when" was left up to the students.

For relativistic students, the demand for commitment could be a challenge to the way in which they typically structure knowledge. Students at these stages may need certain supports to make intellectual commitment a possibility to be considered. For this course, two elements served to moderate the curricular demands: (a) the existence of diversity in the content and (b) the personal atmosphere of the classroom.

Diversity of the content existed in the readings. This component was assumed necessary; for students operating from a relativistic framework, diversity in viewpoints would match their perceptions of the world. At high-stress points, these students could seek shelter in the knowledge that alternatives really do exist and delay confronting the issue of commitment to a singular perspective.

The other ingredient of support came from the atmosphere of the classroom. The approach to creating a high-trust level was identical to that of the dualistic course.

THE IMPACT OF THE COURSE

Developmental Progress. Based on ratings of before and after responses to a projective measure assessing developmental status on the Perry scheme, definite stage change occurred. Table 1 shows the amount of change for students in both treatments (taken from Knefelkamp 1974).

Table 1. Amount of Stage Movement by Instructional Treatment

Stage Movement	Dualist Treatment			Relativist Treatment		
	D*	M†	R‡	D*	M†	R‡
No movement	...	2	1	...	...	...
+1/3 stage	...	1	2	...	2	1
+2/3 stage	...	2	...	...	6	1
+1 full stage	...	5	...	...	2	...
+1 1/3 stages	2	1	...	...	...	...
+1 2/3 stages	1	...	...	2	...	...
N	3	11	3	2	10	2

*Students who began as dualists.
†Students who began in transition from dualism to relativism, i.e., multiplicity.
‡Students who began as relativsts.

In general, the changes conform to developmental theory that assumes a sequential pattern; thus, one would not expect to find movement larger than 1 2/3 stages. The greatest change occurred in individuals rated at the strict dualistic positions. Interestingly, a large number of the students taking the class were rated as multiplicity students, those in transition from dualism to relativism; the treatments seemed about equally effective for them. As one might expect, movement in individuals at higher stages was less. The college classroom may be too restricted an environment to have a major impact on life commitments, as we have observed. In another sense, these students are not ready for such a move; they have the cognitive complexity to cope with the demands of a relativistic world but they simply need more time and experience before the making of commitments will be realistic. The course may have helped to create a readiness for making those commitments when the time is right.

Academic Performance. Three types of tasks were used to assess mastery of the subject matter: an essay requiring analysis, application, and evaluation of the course content; a short-answer objective examination requiring rote knowledge; and the keeping of a journal. For the journal, the instructions were to enter into it whatever seemed "interesting, appropriate, and memorable." The writing of the journal was a task in which the student had to decide how and what to include, what format to use, and how to organize the entries. Given the characteristics of developmentally different students, we assumed that on the more complex essay and journal tasks, relativistic students would be at an advantage, regardless of instruction; however, students who were in a matched instructional treatment would outperform their developmental counterparts in the mismatched instruction section. On the objective examination, a direct interaction effect was expected. For purposes of analysis, students were categorized as either dualists or relativists; thus, those students at multiplicity were divided: those who were more complex in their thinking were grouped as relativists, those less complex, grouped with the dualistic students. Table 2 provided a descriptive summary of student performance. In general, the impact was not strong but seemed to tend in the expected direction.

Satisfaction. It was assumed that those students in sections matched to their developmental status would simply enjoy the

Table 2. Mean Scores and Standard Deviations for Task Performance of Students
Categorized by Perry Scheme and Instructional Treatment

Category	Section I: Dualist Treatment		Section II: Relativist Treatment	
	Mean	SD	Mean	SD
Task 1: Midterm analytic essay:				
Dualists.	72.80	12.34	75.38	13.11
Relativists	62.92	20.86	80.08	6.40
Task 2: Short-answer essay:*				
Dualists.	80.07	6.61	65.36	10.64
Relativists	75.35	15.90	88.30	6.20
Task 3: Journal writing:				
Dualists.	111.55	55.68	93.38	38.70
Relativists	113.58	32.26	117.33	36.40

*Significant interaction effect, $P < .05$.

course more. Questionnaire results were difficult to discriminate; all students rated the course in extremely positive ways (which was, of course, delightful). Time and space do not allow an extensive rendering of the results. Perhaps the most interesting satisfaction finding was an unobtrusive measure. A rater counted the number of unprompted comments that students wrote on the satisfaction questionnaire, and 82 percent of the dualist students/ dualist section, 63 percent of the dualists/relativist section, 33 percent of the relativists/dualist section, and 67 percent of the relativists/relativist section added that the course had been enjoyable or meaningful to them. It is interesting that the highest percentage of those responses came from students in the matched treatments.

Clinical Analyses of Student Journals. At the outset of the effort, it seemed that the scores on the performance tasks might not reflect different responses to the tasks and different approaches used to complete them by students with different developmental characteristics. Raters clinically analyzed the student journals. From their ratings, it appeared that dualistic and relativistic students approached the journals differently; moreover, an in-depth view of the journals provided a richer picture of the students' responses to the course and their own development. Some of the more central observations about the journals follow:

Those students rated as relativists simply wrote more than those rated as dualistic thinkers. One would expect individuals who think in terms of alternatives and hypothetical situations to take more words to express themselves, and this was definitely the case. Some dualistic students appeared to have little to say; one student expressed it this way, "I view the log as something very difficult to write in. I just couldn't get into it."

Relativists included themselves more in their logs. They seemed more able to use the journal as a vehicle for self-reflection and clarifying ideas; one relativist student stated it this way, "the log was one of the best ways to experiment without fear of missing the point." In contrast, this comment was made by a student rated as more dualistic, "I really thought the log was stupid at the beginning of the class but after a while I just decided it had to be done so I started, after a while I decided it wasn't quite so dumb."

Dualists and relativists both had trouble with the journals, but the difficulties were different. Dualistic students expressed concern that they were not "meeting expectations." After turning in the log twice, one student rated as more dualistic wrote, "I tried twice to write in this journal what you guys wanted. And it didn't turn out so hot. So this time I'm going to write what I want!"

For some dualists, the task seemed very complex and they did not know where to start or what to write.

For relativists, the journal posed the problem of integration, making a coherent order out of complexity. An eloquent statement of the dilemma follows: "I used to think that by defining something such as love or what has meaning in life, you immediately put limits on it, but in the past few months, I've discovered that by not being able to clarify my own thoughts, feelings and reactions, I really put the limits on. Everything is scrambled deep inside, and so lately I've attempted to write down, even verbalize my reactions to experience." This relativistic thinker has so much to contend with that getting it articulated is a tough job.

In another sense, students who approach the world more pluralistically appeared to fear the journal as a narrowing force. In this sense, what the student writes becomes his identity—often a frightening prospect. As one student put it, "In a previous attempt to write a journal for a course I found it extremely difficult to express my reactions and feelings on paper, mainly because it seems too permanent."

In general relativists acknowledge responsibility for their own learning while dualists emphasized external motivators. Students were asked to indicate if they had done any independent study for the course; 16 percent of dualists and 75 percent of relativists indicated independent activity. (It may be that relativists, being less bound by "truth," are much more flexible in their definitions of "independent" and "study.") One student rated as dualistic responded to the inquiry about independent activity by saying, "I heard nothing about wanting outside books, reading. We should have been informed that we could do special projects." For dualists, tasks were less linked to a quest for understanding and more bound to what was expected or required. Independent activity does not appear to emerge without internalization of the goals of learning.

The results from this study warranted optimism. In general, all of the student in both sections of the course performed the academic tasks at a fairly high level of competence. Matching had some effect on performance. In addition, satisfaction was uniformly high. A major facet of the program of instruction was the fostering of student development, that is, progression along the Perry scale. The results of this aspect of the study were strongly positive.

As one examines the teaching procedures that we employed in the "themes" course, one becomes aware that the content and range of techniques (role playing, lectures, discussion) were not particularly novel. In fact, a standard course in literature or psychology might look quite similar. Yet, it is our belief that developmental instruction is somewhat different; it involves a systematic and explicit effort to diagnose and respond to individual differences which takes into account the nature and processes of development.

Reality Testing: A Second Application

Our original intent was to develop an approach to college instruction that could be used by faculty members in a variety of fields.

Yet, the extensive investment of time and the range of diagnostic and counseling skills employed in the teaching of the themes course raised a series of important questions. What does this developmental approach to teaching offer to those faculty members in large universities who daily teach to an auditorium packed with 200 or even 500 students? Even with classes of human size, can the teaching assistant in sociology or the professor of philosophy use the developmental instruction ideas? Or, is collaborative effort between subject matter and student development specialists required, and, if so, what form should it take?

During the past year, we have explored applications of the model of developmental instruction that respond to those questions. The particular application described here was an attempt to infuse developmental concepts into a more traditionally taught discipline-based course.

The Initiation of the Project. In a faculty member who conducts a large freshman/sophomore survey course, "United States History from 1865 to the Present," we found a colleague willing to sponsor our efforts. He described his goals as follows: "Like every other teacher I want to try to help students frame questions and try to help them develop the means of solving problems." Yet, he expressed doubts about reaching those goals, "What they [the students] expect from a lecturer is an outline of the reading material, so they don't have to read it, so they know what they have to know for the exam to get a particular grade. Two-thirds of the students are in the course because they have to fulfill some kind of university requirement. They come in and find out that it [the course] is not like what they have had in high school; they react negatively and there is a very real problem."

Upon finding a theory that makes sense out of experience, one always runs the risk of making subsequent experiences fit the theory; yet, it seemed quite possible to relate this faculty member's concerns to the developmental model. The course goals and evaluation procedures emphasized the students dealing with history as a complex of themes, as a relativistic subject matter; however, many of the students expected categorical knowledge, and they reacted negatively to what they perceived as "unnecessary" ambiguity. In this sense, the improvement of performance in the course, which was desired by the teacher, is identical to the fostering of development. To improve students' abilities to analyze and synthesize seems to require helping them to alter their assumptions about the nature of knowledge and values.

The course was taught in a fairly traditional lecture/discussion section format. The lecture was used to convey basic content and demonstrate analysis of the issues. Discussion sections were hypothesized to complement the lectures, to provide a place where students could ask questions, pose problems, and "become actively involved in the learning process." Typically, discussion sections were used to amplify the lecture material through a standard recitation approach. To us, those discussion sections seemed an unmined source for developmental impact. If the discussion section could be structured as an environment that (*a*) helped the students to relate course content to their own lives and (*b*) stretched their ways of perceiving history and the nature of the world, then it might have a distinctive impact on development and academic performance. Inspired by such possibilities, we undertook the design of such a discussion section.

THE DESIGN OF THE DISCUSSION SECTION

Course Content. The content of the course consistently addressed the issues involved in the relation of individual and society; for example, late-nineteenth-century industrial expansion and the rights of the worker; prohibition, the societal legislation of individual morality; and the depression's economic constraints colliding with individual aspirations. Many of the issues have corollaries in certain dilemmas facing students today; for example, the current economy and dwindling job prospects may effectively limit a student's "freedom" to define his identity. As has been noted, identity resolution and adoption of an integrated value system require recognition of self in the context of societal pressures. In this sense, it seemed that the course content had the potential to connect with the students' personal concerns or, at least, to help bring those concerns to consciousness.

The following general topic areas for the discussion section were necessarily defined to parallel the lecture content: (1) The

Nature of History; (2) The Impact of Industrialization; (3) The Progressive Era; (4) The Prohibition Era; (5) The Depression; and (6) The 1960s: Society and Marijuana. In addition to the required readings for the lectures, literary works were selected for use in the discussion section. These works were chosen to create a sense of times past and a certain universality in the way societal issues were expressed, which could potentially help students to make connections to their own lives; the works included Sinclair's *The Jungle*; excerpts from *Ragtime*, by E. L. Doctorow; *This Side of Paradise*, F. Scott Fitzgerald; and *Main Street*, Sinclair Lewis.

The Instructional Approach. Based on the faculty member's description of "typical" students in the course, and an initial examination of responses to the developmental instrument used in the themes course, application of the approach matched to dualist-thinking students seemed more appropriate. Employing the rationale stated in previous sections of the paper, we were guided by these functional components: moderated diversity, experiential learning modes, a high degree of structure, and a "personal" atmosphere.

As with the themes course, we attempted to employ these components consistently throughout all aspects of the instructional process: the treatment of content, the behavior of instructors, the purpose and demands of various tasks, and evaluation procedures. We tried to so design the instruction that the functional variables permeated all levels of instruction from the molar view, the course taken as a whole, to the molecular, a particular question on an essay examination.

The following basic teaching techniques were selected to focus on the various content areas: (1) The Nature of History: student essay on "most significant historical event"; guided group discussion; (2) Impact of Industrialization: a role-play activity, "The railroad comes to Possumtrot and Dogwalk"; (3) Impact of Industrialization: value-clarification activity examining the morality of characters in the novel, *The Jungle*; (4) Prohibition: a role-play activity, "A legislative hearing in Ohio to ratify the Congressional prohibition resolution"; (5) The Depression: oral history interviews; (6) The Nature of Historical Analysis: a group problem-solving activities involving evaluation of historical essays; (7) The 1960s: student research project surveying current attitudes of various social groups about marijuana. Teaching techniques, such as role playing and value-clarification procedures, seemed particularly useful with historical subject matter; yet, they require a specific design for learners who are more dualistic in their approach to history.

Obviously, space does not permit an extensive description of the class; the following two examples convey how the instructional techniques were operationalized and give a flavor of the class:

A Role-Play Activity. Role playing is often thought to be artificial and not successful in conveying the immediate reality or integrating experience and conceptual knowledge. To be effective, role playing requires that the student engage in extensive hypothetical thinking and have extensive knowledge of the context in which the role is to be enacted; moreover, it requires that the student be relatively unconcerned about appearing foolish.

Specific attempts to incorporate diversity, experiencing, and structure and to create a nonthreatening atmosphere in role playing can improve the effectiveness of activities for students who approach learning in dualistic ways. The following task used those elements to increase learning and provide developmental prods.

The Instructional Task: Student groups were given the prohibition resolution submitted to the Ohio legislature by the United States Congress. Acting as individuals living at the time, student groups were asked to present a "substantiated, coherent, and convincing" argument before the Ohio state legislature on the prohibition issue. Students were appraised of the fact that the legislature panel would listen and question their ideas.

A. Diversity of viewpoint and practice in relativistic reasoning.
   1. Roles were explicitly chosen to convey the divergent perspectives of different societal groups and individuals within the same social groups. Roles included feminists, WCTU members, business executives, clergy, farmers, and members of a minority race.
   2. The task allowed for creativity (and a certain zaniness) but required students to provide evidence that they (in their

roles) would have taken such a stand. This requirement engaged the students in historical research.

3. During the legislative hearing, the instructors explicitly challenged each group to consider alternative perspectives. The sequence of student group presentations was geared to provide a series of conflicting interpretations of the prohibition issue.

B. Experiential modes of learning.

1. By definition, role-play activity is a fairly close approximation to the experiencing of an event.

2. To create a more direct experiencing of the issue, various media aids were used to set the context. A multimedia slide presentation, using readings from Carry Nation's biography, pictures of prohibition rallies, and descriptions of the evils of saloon life, were used to start the class session.

C. High structure.

1. Through handouts and verbal instructions, the instructors gave an explicit description of the task.

2. Students were given an explicit series of steps for getting into their roles.

3. Student groups were given procedural guides and direct help by instructors for preparing their presentations. Particular emphasis was placed on guiding students in ways to find evidence and build logical arguments.

D. Personal atmosphere: In general, effort was made to create a supportive classroom environment. The instructors tried to take facilitative roles in working with students. The task was constructed so students could work cooperatively. Basically, the activity was fun; the "ham" in everyone was invited to enter the classroom.

Oral History Interviews. Creating opportunities for students to talk with people who had lived through a particular historical event would seem to have particular developmental and learning potency, it allows the communication of the complexity of particular issues in human dimensions. Yet, learning from such interviews requires a student to be able to ask relevant questions and to relate the interviewees' responses to a broader, more abstract analysis of an historical event. The design and implementation of such activities can be aided by developmental notions.

The Instructional Task: In this course, the Depression was a major content area. Students have a tendency to view the Depression in stereotypical ways—for example, the bread line as a universal experience. To help students grasp the complexity and range of impacts of the Depression, they were given the task of conducting oral history interviews with individuals who had lived during that time. The interview activity was structured for "dualistic" learners as follows:

A. Diversity of viewpoint and practice in relativistic modes of reasoning.

   1. Interviewees were selected who had divergent socioeconomic and/or cultural backgrounds. The nine interviewees included a black cook in a sorority house on campus who had lived in the South during the 1930s, a woman whose parents were Lithuanian immigrants, a woman who had married a doctor and moved to an affluent suburb during the Depression, and a Catholic priest.

   2. Students were given a task that asked them to identify explicitly the similarities and differences in both life-style and perceptions of the Depression among the interviewees.

   3. In discussion groups following the interviews, students were asked to compare and contrast the lecture interpretation of the Depression with the interviewees' experiences.

   4. Students were then asked to write a paper in which they summarized the conflicting interpretations of the Depression.

B. Experiential modes of learning: The interview process provided a direct experience with "historical" figures.

C. High structure.

   1. The task was explicitly structured to help students to develop good interview questions and to link their observations to the course conceptual content. The instructors

provided each student with a biographical blurb on the nine interviewees, an explanation of the task, and a schedule.

2. Instructors structured and guided preparation for the interviews. Students were given sample interview questions and four general topic areas that needed to be covered in the interviews and related to the lecture content.

3. The instructors provided specific guides for writing the comparative paper.

D. Personal atmosphere.

1. The nature of the activity focused upon the experiences and feelings of "real" people. The task encouraged both an intellectual and emotional involvement with the interviewees.

2. Instructors tried to create a tone of joint exploration in the classroom. Cooperative small-group learning was employed, which allowed for students to share responsibility and excitement; the instructors tried to facilitate the work of those groups.

3. In discussions following interviews, instructors expressed and drew out personal reactions to the experience.

The two activities, role playing and oral history interviews, were the core of the developmental instruction. Unfortunately, it is impossible in this discussion to convey the sense of fun, interest, and discovery that pervaded the class.

THE IMPACT OF THE DEVELOPMENTALLY DESIGNED DISCUSSION SECTION

The "developmental" discussion section was implemented during winter quarter, 1976. It was taught collaboratively by a graduate student in history and the second author of this paper, a graduate student in the student personnel studies program. A quasi-experimental design was used to assess various process and dependent variables. The developmental section was compared to two control sections or, more accurately, two comparison sections, since control treatments were not specified.

Process Variables. Each discussion section was audiotaped for rating on the developmental instruction dimensions, and students were asked to rate instructional processes. These measures were included (*a*) to assess the actual implementation of developmental treatment according to the plan, and (*b*) to compare the three discussion sections on the actual teaching-learning processes employed.

The preliminary analysis of the student ratings suggests that the sections differed in some aspects and that the developmental treatment created an environment which was characterized to some extent by diversity, experiential learning, high structure, and a personal atmosphere. The supporting data are presented in Table 3.

Table 3. Percentage of Students Responding "Very Often" and "Quite a Bit" to a Series of Behavioral Items

Item	Developmental Section	Control Section A	Control Section B
1. The instructor presented more than one view on the same issue.	85%	59%	65%
2. The instructor has a good grasp of the material.	100	88	100
3. The instructor explains assignments so you know what is expected.	95	81	91
4. The instructor presented material which helped you understand what it was like to live at the time.	100	63	70
5. The instructor seemed to be concerned with you as an individual.	95	47	53
6. The instructor makes you feel that your comments are good and/or worthwhile.	79	76	90
1. I compared and contrasted different ideas and facts presented in discussion section.	67	56	55
2. I found material discussed in section was relatable to my own life.	63	24	37
3. I left class unsure of what my assignment was.	10	11	14
4. I talked with my teaching assistant after discussion section.	47	31	10
5. I grinned, chuckled, or laughed during discussion section.	74	56	43
6. I found the discussion section to be enjoyable.	84	44	58

Outcome Measures. The study used the same basic outcome variables as those used in the themes course: developmental progress, subject-matter mastery, and learner satisfaction. In general, the same methods were used to assess outcomes in this study.

Table 4. Amount of Stage Change per Class (%)

Stage Movement	Section 1 (Treatment) (N = 19)	Section 2 (N = 14)	Section 3 (N = 14)
No movement	37	43	60
+1/3 stage.	32	29	33
+2/3 stage.	16	. . .	7
+1 stage	16	7	. . .
+1 1/3 stage.	. . .	21	. . .

The results seem to indicate that all three sections had students who gave evidence of increased complexity in their reasoning about values and knowledge (see Table 4). The treatment section had the greatest number of individuals showing stage movement: 63 percent as compared to 57 percent in section 2 and 40 percent for section 3. In contrast, section 2 had individual students showing the greatest amount of change. Interestingly, the history instructor who taught in the treatment section also taught section 2; analysis of classroom tapes indicated that he increasingly used "treatment" methods in section 2 as the quarter progressed. While the results are not clear-cut, students in the treatment section showed a pattern of consistent small changes in their ways of viewing knowledge, this pattern seems congruent with our current understanding of development.

Descriptive findings are available on the academic performance measures. Academic performance was assessed by a midterm and final essay examination, both of which focused on comprehension, analysis/synthesis, and evaluation of the course material. Two graduate student instructors used a blind-scoring procedures to grade the examinations. The mean performance scores of the three discussion sections are presented in Table 5. Scores on the final examination were found to be significantly different (P < .01). The developmental approach seems to have a positive effect on subject matter mastery.

Table 5. Mean Performance Scores on Two Examinations

Examination	Developmental Section*	Control Section A†	Control Section B‡
Midterm essay	75.0	69.6	71.0
Final essay	82.4	77.5	74.8

*$N = 23$ on midterm; $N = 22$ on final exam.
†$N = 21$; $N = 20$.
‡$N = 25$; $N = 23$.

Perusal of student satisfaction ratings indicates that the developmentally designed class was a positive experience for most of the students. When asked about the value of the course, students made comments such as the following: "The personal interviews were great. It was a fine opportunity to learn history from people who actually experienced it, not just a text." "I really got into the prohibition role play and enjoyed it, mostly because I was learning in fun ways, and partly because I was learning about people's feelings in the past and how people think and why."

Although all analyses of the data have not been completed, the positive effects of the developmental model appear to be established. One instructor (the second author) observed that student behavior in the class was not typical of other history discussion sections; students in the developmental section knew each other, seemed almost excited to come to class and talk to each other, and even set up their own group-study sessions to prepare for the final exam. This evidence is compelling when one considers that the discussion section met only twice a week for fifty-minute classes.

We believe that it is possible to productively employ the developmental instruction ideas in the context of a large freshman/sophomore survey course and, furthermore, that a developmental framework can add an important dimension to the concept of a discussion section.

Discussion

One aspect of the design and instructional process—that is, the adaptations required in the developmental instruction model—deserves particular comment.

Emphasis was given to structuring confrontations with diversity, helping students to master the complex analytic skills of relativistic thinking, and fostering an immediate, experiential sense of history. For a number of reasons, less stress was placed on students' relating the content (issues of societal conflict) to issues of autonomy and morality in their own lives. In this course, students simply did not examine their own lives in the way that students did in the themes course. The content, although theoretically relevant, appeared rather abstract to connect easily with the student's psychosocial concerns. Interestingly, student expectations about what is appropriate in the college classroom came into play here; although instructors tried to emphasize the personal meaning of the content, the students seemed to feel that it was unnecessary, personally risky, or even a threat to their doing well in the course. To encourage such personal reflection would have required extensive instructor modeling, more time to build a climate and alter student expectations, and the use of various media to minimize the risks involved (e.g., a log allowing student-instructor dialogue). In traditional subject-matter courses, attempting to foster cognitive development along the Perry scheme is a significant effort; explicit attention to students' psychosocial concerns may not be feasible.

A second observation has implications for future efforts. As we designed the course, we became quite excited by the possibility of developing a manual of "developmental techniques" which could be used by teaching assistants in charge of discussion sections for the history department. With some modification, the discussions of the developmental use of role playing and oral history techniques reported here are examples of the content for such a manual.

Yet, the manual idea had drawbacks. During the course, we became aware once again that the developmental instruction model is a sort of scientific road map that restricts the description of the instructional effort to directions and pathways but omits the topography and the give and take of a classroom. The use of theory requires a parallel artistry: a counselor's intuitive sense and capacity to listen, empathize, and respond at many levels. Certainly, a part of that responsive capacity comes from an extensive knowledge of developmental psychology which can provide necessary knowledge for the realization of the limits and uncertainties that must accompany the use of terms like "dualism" and "relativism" when a classroom of students is viewed. The collaboration between the historian and the student personnel worker who were employed to teach the class was effective because it allowed the particular skills of each instructor to be maximized. This factor was perceived and apparently appreciated by the students.

For college teachers who are interested in improving their teaching and responding more effectively to student needs, the developmental notions may have a strong appeal. Yet, providing those teachers with a manual of developmental guidelines would probably not be enough help, and it might even lead to the rigid application of the concepts. A manual or set of instructional directions would need to be supplemented with on-going training programs. In fact, some sort of faculty development effort seems to be an important and challenging next step in our work.

Where are we now? We have used developmental theory to design and teach courses at the college level, and the evidence indicates that those theory-guided efforts can have a strong impact on several areas. In an environment which provides cognitive challenges and a variety of supports, students do seem to develop along the path that Perry described; they incorporate more complex ways of thinking about knowledge and values. While this is not the only important type of development, it does seem to be a crucial foundation for the kinds of learning and self-analysis that comprise an examined life. Students also show ability to master the subject matter and to enjoy and invest more in courses taught using developmental concepts. These results suggest that attention to student development need not detract from academic learning; indeed such efforts may complement and augment knowledge acquisition. Moreover, the model can be adapted for a variety of course contents and structures. Yet the use of developmental ideas results in costly teaching, teaching which seems to require student-teacher interaction, much time and effort spent in creating a distinctive educational environment. If we are seriously concerned with helping students learn and develop, we can expect to find few instructional shortcuts.

REFERENCES

Arrowsmith, W. The future of teaching. In A. C. Eurich, ed., *Campus 1980.* New York: Dell, 1968.

Ausubel, D. P. *Educational psychology: a cognitive view.* New York: Holt, Rinehart, & Winston, 1968.

Barzun, J. *The American university: how it runs, where it is going.* New York: Harper & Row, 1968.

Bell, D. *The reforming of general education: the Columbia College experience in the national setting.* New York: Columbia University Press, 1966.

Chickering, A. *Education and identity.* San Francisco: Jossey-Bass, 1969.

Domino, G. Differential prediction of academic achievement in conforming and independent settings. *Journal of Educational Psychology*, 1968, 58, 256-260.

———. Interactive effects of achievement orientation and teaching style on academic achievement. *Journal of Educational Psychology*, 1970, 62, 427-431.

Erikson, E. *Identity: youth and crisis.* New York: Norton, 1968.

Farnsworth, D. L., *Psychiatry, education and the young adult.* Springfield, Ill.: Charles C. Thomas, 1966.

Heath, R. *The reasonable adventurer.* Pittsburgh: University of Pittsburgh Press, 1964.

Henderson, A. *The innovative spirit.* San Francisco: Jossey-Bass, 1970.

Henry, M., & Renaud, H. Examined and unexamined lives. *Research Reporter*, 1972, 7(1), 5-8. (The Center for Research and Development in Higher Education.)

Higgins-Trent, A., & Gaite, A. J. H. The elusiveness of formal operational thought in adolescents. Paper presented at the 79th Annual Convention of the American Psychological Association, Washington, D.C., 1971.

Hunt D. E. A conceptual level matching model for coordinating learner characteristics with educational approaches. *Interchange*, 1970, 1, 68-72.

———. Matching models for teacher training. In B. Joyce & M. Weil, eds., *Perspectives for reform in teacher education.* Englewood Cliffs, N.J.: Prentice-Hall, 1972.

Keniston, K., *Youth and dissent.* New York: Harcourt Brace Jovanovich, 1971.

Jacob, P. *Changing values in college: an exploratory study of the impact of college teaching.* New York: Harper, 1957.

Knefelkamp, L. L. Developmental instruction: fostering intellectual and personal growth. Ph.D. dissertation, University of Minnesota, 1974.

Loevinger, J., & Wessel, R. *Measuring ego development.* Vols. 1 & 2. San Francisco: Jossey-Bass, 1970.

Mann, R. D.; Arnold, S. M.; Binder, J. L.; Cytrnbaum, S.; Newan, B. M.; Ringwald, B. E.; Ringwald, J. W.; & Rosenwein, R. *The college classroom: conflict, change, and learning.* New York: Wiley, 1970.

Marcia, J. Development and validation of ego-identity status. *Journal of Personality and Social Psychology*, 1966, 3(5), 551-558.

Munsinger, H., & Kessen, W. Uncertainty, structure and preference. *Psychological Monographs*, 1964, 78(Whole number 9).

Perry, W., Jr. *Forms of intellectual and ethical development in the college years.* New York: Holt, Rinehart, & Winston, 1970.

Piaget, J. *The language and thought of the child.* London: Routledge & Kegan Paul, 1952.

Sanford, N., ed. *The American college.* New York: Wiley, 1962.

———. *Where colleges fail.* San Francisco: Jossey-Bass, 1967.

Schulz, R. W. The role of cognitive organizers in the facilitation of concept learning in elementary school science. Reported by D. P. Ausubel in *Educational psychology: a cognitive view.* New York: Holt, Rinehart, & Winston, 1968.

Schwab, J. *College curriculum and student protest.* Chicago: University of Chicago Press, 1969.

Siegel, L., & Siegel, L. C. Educational set: a determinant of acquisition. *Journal of Educational Psychology*, 1965, 1, 1-12.

Snelbecker, G. *Learning theory, instructional theory, and psychoeducational design.* New York: McGraw-Hill, 1974.

Sprinthall, N. A curriculum for schools: counselors as teachers for psychological growth. *School Counselor*, May 1973, 361-369.

Stern, G. Environments for learning. In N. Sanford, ed., *The American College.* New York: Wiley, 1962.

Widick, C. An evaluation of developmental instruction in a university setting. Ph.D. dissertation, University of Minnesota, 1975.

Comments on Chapter 2

William G. Perry, Jr.

Comedy consists in the encrustation
of life by the mechanical.   Henri Bergson

So does tragedy.   Bill Perry

The case reports gladden my heart. I have been scared by the rash
of sudden "applications" of developmental theories and measures
to students. Higher education, having been set back on its heels, is
eager to justify itself. Many faculties have begged me for a nice,
quick, pencil and paper instrument that would measure their success in pushing students along the road to maturity. But I do not
like the idea of "applying" such theories to people, perhaps because I had good old nineteenth-century "character development"
applied to me.

I am not afraid that the applications of such a theory would
work, mind you. My experience proves that students' souls are
safe against even being saved. If students were to feel pushed, they
surely would dig in with their heels and give us the responses—the
new catechism, according to Knefelkamp and Slepitza—which we
yearn to hear. I am not even scared of that.

My nightmare takes the form of a specter (of straw, I hope)
that is highly educated in the tradition in which I was educated.
He is the product of two thousand years of scholastic tradition
and a science that put essence before existence. I mean that he

thinks that theories "govern" events; that categories, by necessity, are bigger than the particulars we put "in" them; and that the higher and more abstract the concept the greater the truth, which leads him upward toward eternal verities. For him, as for Plato, the concrete instance is dross and imperfect; thus he speaks of the "merely" applied. When he stoops to "apply," he uses his concept (Latin: *concipio*, to grasp) to strangle life in the name of truth, goodness, and beauty. For him, the present exists only to be improved upon, and its value is judged only by its outcome.

Have we, with our developmental theories, only added to the armamentarium of this monster? He lives, alas, in all of us; I find mine pillowed smugly among my best intentions.

The catch, of course, lies in the ambiguities of "application." I know how to apply Wildroot hair tonic to my bald head or a tourniquet to a patient, but what does it mean to apply a theory of personality development? To what do we apply it? *To* our students? Do we teach our students to apply it *to* themselves? Do we apply it *in* our teaching? Or *in* our thinking? Or *in* our ways of seeing? The differences can be those that distinguish love from murder.

The authors of the case reports all use the term "application," and because their address to students is unambiguously humanistic, what they mean by the word comes through without a formal definition. Widick and Simpson, moreover, seem to echo my concern in their feeling that, somehow, developmental teaching as they do it is not after all readily exportable in a manual.

I would like to spell out briefly some of these humanistic assumptions which exorcise my specter. (*a*) Existence precedes essence: the humanist's cry over centuries. To me it means that the particular is prior to the general, the general being an abstraction from *aspects* (never the whole) of particulars. The same is true for your experience, your life. What you experience is legitimate *in that you are experiencing it*, not *because* "lots of people feel that way" or because "I'd feel the same in your shoes," or because the *cause* is clear. (The degree to which your feelings or reading of your experiences are to be deemed "appropriate" is another matter entirely and not the justification of your reality.) (*b*) Any event, no matter how small, is bigger than any category or theory which may be used to enlighten our understanding of it. Because categories illuminate aspects of events and do not contain them, events require complementary theories to enlighten them, but the enlightenment can never be complete. Even physics, queen of sciences, had to concede this one (Bohr 1923) and fell through the ice to join even humanistic psychologists, a muddy and messy lot at best. (c) The present is all we have, informed as it must be by our experience of the past and our visions of the future. (d) Interpersonally, I undertake to prize your particularity here and now, even as I would have you prize me. (e) (corollary to d) If in prizing you and otherwise providing you with nutriments of growth, I may hope to "foster" your growth, I will remember that this is a very different matter from "getting you" to grow.

Widick and Simpson have given us a model of the best uses of developmental theory in education. They used a descriptive theory to suggest action for "fostering" development. The theory remains descriptive, not prescriptive, and they intend their actions to invite students, intrigue them, and support them. Their language makes it clear that the rest must come from the student.

I am not surprised that the relativistic students did not move so quickly into the commitments to which they were invited. Presumably, they had only recently arrived in this great complex world and needed to explore, to enjoy a lot of horizontal décalage before risking that illusion of "narrowing" that commitments bring. I have some thoughts also about the losses of such "developments" which I will share by the end of this conference.

I welcome, too, the distinction Widick and Simpson make between the "identity" course and the "history" course. The first involves the student unavoidably as subject matter. Relevant as it is to our identities, history *can* be held at arms' length *qua* "History." So, even when it is taught to invite and provide personal relevance (e.g., role taking), the invitation is easier to decline.

The authors' final comments raise issues I would like to see faced. They concede that much personal attention and special skills (as well as a special outlook?) are requisite for developmental teaching of the kind which they demonstrate to be so successful. I think I know what they mean. As I write these comments, there lie beside me in a pile the weekly "letters" from the students in my class. They write from the care and pain and joy of the bitter sweetness of rapid change. It will take me hours to "answer" them. And it will take more of me to do it than my time. Right this minute, I am not sure I will make it.

How do we disseminate this sort of thing? A manual might convey the theory, the principles, and a few techniques. But when I sit down to help a new staff member to learn how to answer these letters (or logs or thoughts in progress) it is a long hard learning— and even one short letter, where concern is deep, can take an hour to answer.

We must face the reality of the authors' last sentence: "Yet the use of developmental ideas results in costly teaching, teaching which seems to require student-teacher interaction, much time and effort spent in creating a distinctive educational environment. If we are seriously concerned with helping students learn and develop, we can expect to find few instructional shortcuts."

Indeed.

REFERENCE

Bohr, N. The roots of complementarity, as quoted by Gerald Holton in *Thematic origins of scientific thought: Keppler to Einstein.* Cambridge, Mass.: Harvard University Press, 1973.

Ursula Delworth

Both applications described by Widick and Simpson are creative, serious, and well-developed attempts to operationalize Perry's developmental concepts for work with students. It is significant that this kind of work is being done collaboratively by academic faculty and student personnel staff. I concur with the authors' concerns about producing a manual that may give too "technical" a set to instructors. However, I hope that they go ahead with the idea of using a manual in conjunction with an ongoing training program for faculty and graduate teaching students.

The emphasis on personal atmosphere in the classroom echoes one of Chickering's conditions for impact: positive interaction with faculty and administration. He listed four general conditions that were conducive to productive relations among students and faculty: accessibility, authenticity, knowledge, and the ability to talk with a student. Chickering hypothesized that the presence of these conditions contributes to intellectual competence and a sense of competence, autonomy, purpose, and integrity. Although Widick and Simpson did not give a great deal of information, it appears that they produced these conditions, at least to some extent, in their two applications. The authors also seem appropriately concerned with facilitating the conditions (especially ability to talk with a student) in their proposed training program.

There is some evidence from Barker's work that students in smaller behavior settings (small schools) show greater cognitive complexity than students in larger settings. This finding has implications for class size in trying to teach developmental concepts. The two applications indicate that a good deal of student activity occurred in the setting but the size of the setting (number of students) was not reported. It is interesting to speculate on how large such a setting could become and still have students show growth in developmental levels.

In looking at the authors' applicatons from the point of view of person-environment fit theorists, I am struck by their statement that students "simply need more time and experience before the making of commitments will be realistic. The course may have helped to create a readiness for making those commitments when the time is right." It would seem then, that the actual making of commitments might well be either facilitated or cut off by elements in the larger environment of the university. These elements would include students' experiences in other classes, size of the university, and general student culture, among others. In order ultimately to facilitate the achievement of higher developmental goals in a reasonably large number of students, we may be faced with no less a task than more thorough assessment and the systematic redesign of large elements in the college environment. To do less may seriously limit the potential impact of such applications as those described by Widick and Simpson.

David E. Hunt

That colleges and universities should attempt to enhance the personal development of their students is generally agreed, but where such enhancement should occur and the degree to which it should be an explicit goal in courses is less clear. The case studies by Widick and Simpson provide valuable information on these issues by demonstrating the opportunities in and difficulties of incorporating a developmental perspective into day-to-day instruction.

Widick and Simpson conclude that incorporating a developmental view in teaching requires a "parallel artistry: a counselor's intuitive sense and capacity to listen, empathize, and respond at many levels"; and I found their emphasis on this "parallel artistry" the most important point in their studies. For the past several years, I have been working with junior and senior high school teachers in "applying" a developmental theory to their classroom practice. Contrary to what I expected, the theory is much less important than the teachers' capacity to adapt to students through what I have called "reading" and "flexing." A theory may serve as an exemplar or metaphor for such adaptation (if it coordinates student differences with different educational approaches), but it cannot be "applied" directly. As Widick and Simpson observed, even a step-by-step manual will not guarantee success. When I work with teachers, I try, first, to discover their "theories" and concepts of development, then I build on their personal ideas, rather than laying on a theory; therefore, I agree completely with Widick and Simpson that there are no shortcuts.

I find it helpful to distinguish between explicit and implicit matching. The matching model, Figure 1, is a good example of *explicit* matching since it guided the teacher's adaptation of instruction (that students were not assigned to classes according to the model is unimportant for the moment; the point is that the teachers taught differently according to explicit instructions and without regard to individual student pull). The second application they describe involves more *implicit* matching because, although a guide was given, the discussion leader attempted to "tune in" to each individual student (as indicated in Table 3). Implicit matching, therefore, refers to the minute-by-minute, spontaneous adaptation which teachers make to individual students. It is the parallel artistry of reading and flexing. It should be noted that the teachers in the Knefelkamp and Widick studies also may have been implicitly matching, but it was not prescribed (and from a strict experimental view would have compromised the design). The distinction is useful because it opens the question of how explicit matching affects implicit matching or, put another way, if teachers can acquire the parallel artistry of implicit matching through experience with an explicit matching model.

I applaud the use of multiple criteria (stage change, variety of performance scores, and satisfaction) to index program effects in Widick and Knefelkamp's matching applications. I found the interactive effects in the short-answer essay tests impressive because in most matching work with which I am familiar matching effects are found in preference and satisfaction but not, usually, in performance. Having tried developmental criteria in our work, I wonder at the use of stage change in relatively short-term intervention studies. I realize that if we are attempting to enhance development, we must have some evidence of developmental growth but, as we know, meaningful development requires time; hence, even with the best of measures a student may not manifest measurable growth as a result of a three-month intervention.

I suggest that we attempt to characterize the effects of such programs by (a) specifying the stage-specific goals for specific students and measuring how well these stage-specific skills were acquired, and (b) describing more individual students to indicate effects. Developmental studies do not lend themselves to the traditional designs, method of measurements, and statistical analyses employed in contemporaneous studies, and we must create new characterizations for the effects of such developmental studies.

Finally, a brief comment on self-matching. I think that matching work should include the student, and it should proceed toward the student's self-matching as much as possible. This inclusion requires that students learn more about their own developmental stages and styles as well as the instructional approach that is more appropriate for them. The case studies provided by Widick and Simpson are a good basis for including students in the matching process.

Douglas H. Heath

The imaginative use of Perry's cognitive stage model for identifying the interaction between instructional mode and cognitive style represents a needed direction for educational research. The attempt to specify contrasting types of modes (e.g., high vs. low structure) and then to establish them to determine their effects represents an advance over much developmental research. Failure to find the predicted interactions raises numerous questions about the assumed validity of the stage model used, the adequacy of the research strategy for studying change, and the appropriateness of the altered instructional conditions.

I have not been persuaded of the utility of a cognitive *stage* approach, particularly for understanding college students or adults. A stage model usually implies qualitatively distinct and universally sequential landmarks, so to speak. In my longitudinal studies of development from age seventeen through the early thirties, I have never found such a stage concept to be operationalizable with enough specificity to be useful for organizing the developmental process throughout the life span. I prefer to conceive of the personality as an evolving system that may mature on five interrelated dimensions as it seeks to fashion an optimal relation between its systemic needs and the demands of the environment. Thus I prefer to think of cognitive development dimensionally, examining how the cognitive skills and concepts of students are increasingly articulated (symbolization); analytic, judgmental, and logical (allocentric); differentiated and relational (integration), stabilized and resilient (stable); and mobile and transferable (autonomy). What may seem to be a distinctive "stage" is, for me, more likely the result of societal or educational demands for certain types of adaptations at different periods in one's life. I have expanded these ideas in my chapter later in this book.

Restriction of our understanding of student development primarily to cognitive development may distort our efforts to affect cognitive maturation. By abstracting cognitive development out of the maturing personality (self-concept, values, personal relationships), we may ignore other major effects of a liberal education upon a student. The authors make a number of noncognitive assumptions about the differences between their dualists and relativists that imply a more comprehensive personality model of development. Increased cognitive relativeness (allocentric and integration cognitive skill) seems to be directly related to increasing identity (stability and, possibly, integration self-concept), autonomy (autonomy of self-concept and values, and interpersonal relations). A more comprehensive model of maturing might suggest a host of other characteristics that covary with allocentric cognitive maturation—for example, increased symbolized, allocentric, and integrated self-concept and values; increased allocentric and integrated personal relationships. In other words, we might discover that increased allocentric cognitive skill development is closely related to many facets of psychological maturity, as I have defined it. If so, then we might seek a much wider range of effects of our educational interventions than just a few cognitive ones measured by the essays and journal writings. I am suggesting that we may unduly limit our understanding of the effects of a course or college education if we confine our study to too narrow a domain of cognitive effects. For example, the accompanying table summarizes very crudely, and only suggestively (certainly not definitively), the ranked orders of effects of three quite different colleges. Note that cognitive skill change represented only a small portion of the principal types of effects found, effects, incidentally, that correspond quite well to what many educational philosophers claim should be the effects of a liberal education.

Given the complex effects of a liberal education, it seems judicious as a research strategy to measure as comprehensively as we can. If we had controlled for scholastic aptitude of the dualists and relativists and redefined them as less and more allocentrically mature, and then asked if high versus low structure facilitated their maturing differentially, we might have discovered that degree of structure facilitates a range of different effects other than just allocentric cognitive growth. More change may occur when a person is being educated than we are aware of, just because we do not have a comprehensive mapping of all of the likely possible changes that could take place.

I appreciated the ingenuity of the authors in specifying a priori the characteristics of their instructional modes and then seeking to implement them. I have no systematic and precise way to identify the types of developmental learning conditions that may be appropriate for specific types of growth in the classroom, although I

Rank Order of Effects of Three Colleges on Their Students

Dimension of Maturing	College		
	1	2	3
Symbolization of:			
Cognitive skill	12*	12	13
Self-concept	9	2	6
Values	4.5	15.5	7
Personal relations	6	4	5
Allocentrism of:			
Cognitive skill	4.5	7	3
Self-concept	16	19	15
Values	11	10	10
Personal relations	10	5	11
Integration of:			
Cognitive skill	8	1	8
Self-concept	17.5	8	17
Values	14.5	9	14
Personal relations	1	3	2
Stability of:			
Cognitive skill	14.5	18	16
Self-concept	13	6	12
Values	3	15.5	4
Personal relations	2	14	1
Autonomy of:			
Cognitive skill	20	17	20
Self-concept	17.5	13	18
Values	19	11	19
Personal relations	7	20	9

*Rank of 1 indicates greatest effect.

have written about the institutional types of factors that may affect maturing. My research and teaching experience suggest that cognitive maturation in college may be best facilitated by high motivational involvement and faculty expectations, extensive modeling of alternatives, and close monitoring of very frequent student activities requiring the specific cognitive skills being assessed, with frequent detailed feedback about progress. Given Piaget's emphasis on the relation of interpersonal reciprocity to the development of reversibility, extensive use of small self-teaching groups (which the authors did in one phase) requiring considerable oral interpretative explanations might be emphasized. My hunch is that few courses, no matter how effectively organized, are going to have lasting effects on cognitive maturation (though not necessarily on value or self-concept development). The more powerful factors are likely to be the quality of the college's intellectual atmosphere, the degree of classroom dialogue, high faculty expectations for certain types of cognitive skill maturation (and not just mastery of information for multiple choice tests), and the intellectual discussions and arguments that take place outside the classrooms with friends and roommates who share different perspectives. It will not be just one or two of these factors that have identifiable effects; it is the consistency of the psychological context, including all of these factors, that will have the predicted effects.

Roger A. Myers

Widick and Simpson have synthesized the relevant parts of adult development theory, grappled with the central question of how to design instructional experiences for students at different developmental stages, offered some excellent examples of their efforts at design, and reported their attempts to investigate the consequences of practicing what they have come to preach.

I found the theoretical portion of their paper extremely useful and their settling on Perry's scheme an intelligent choice. I am, however, less ready than they are to conclude that the descriptive theories which they considered and the single theory which they chose have brought us to the place of "adapting instruction for developmentally different students." In the best of all possible worlds I would have hoped for more empirical support for the trusted theories in smaller, better controlled experiments before putting them to the test in a natural setting. But we do not live in that kind of world, and Widick and Simpson apparently had promises to keep.

Considering the state of the art, the authors did a remarkable piece of work in both designing the themes course and modifying the discussion section for the history course. They appeared to use all that was useful from the literature in deciding what manner of learning experience would best enhance the development of what kind of student. The power of their logic is strong and, more important, their skill at adapting what was presumed to be ideal to what was in fact possible was truly admirable. Their course designs look good enough to stand alone, regardless of the results of their very stringent efficacy tests.

Throughout their discussion of this matching problem I was frequently reminded of the parallels between their effort and the similar attempts to design differential learning environments (i.e., treatments) for different kinds of learners (i.e., clients, patients) in the research literature on counseling and psychotherapy. The two spheres of activity obviously have similar elements: the relatively gross nature of adult development theories, the faith in the process of interpersonal influence, the belief that curriculum is the best guide for directing interpersonal influence, a tradition of assuming helpful outcomes without convincing evidence, and so on. (For the moment, permit me to argue, without arguing, that theory is to psychotherapy what curriculum is to teaching.)

Two themes from the past interest me in this context. The first is the general concept that differential diagnosis should lead to differential treatment, which was hotly debated for some time. The patently obvious notion that people with different life circumstances, needs, and impediments were best served by different therapeutic experiences was not accepted by all therapists and counselors. Rogers, for example, argued that (a) the way to help people grow through and beyond their present difficulties was relatively standard for most people because the source of the difficulties was the same for most of them; (b) the diagnostic activity itself became a barrier to the treatment because of its external and depersonalizing nature; and (c) for all of the hue and cry, differential treatments seldom resulted from differential diagnoses anyway. Although that debate has lost its vigor by now, one can fantasize the same sort of argument should Widick and Simpson seek to have their way outside of a few experimental classes at their university.

The second theme from the counseling and psychotherapy literature that seems relevant is represented by the studies on constituting therapist-patient pairs on some strategy presumed to maximize the potential for influence. We all remember the early enthusiasm and later skepticism about A- and B-type therapists and the kinds of patients they were supposed to help best, the hopeful attempts to match the pairs on value and personality dimensions, the beginning work on matching cognitive style, and the harsh lessons learned about not matching on race and socioeconomic status. In general, the progress on this front has been mixed, to take a charitable view, and hardly encouraging to the Widick-Simpson effort. The same observation applies to an influence process that is much less complicated than the teaching of a college course.

I seem to be suggesting that, persuasive as Widick and Simpson are and successful as they seem to have been, they have set themselves a difficult task, one that has not been marked with remarkable success, even under easier conditions.

It is a bit difficult to know precisely what the empirical checks on the outcomes of the Widick-Simpson courses tell us about whether schemes brought about the intended changes. Their Table 1, which reports on stage movement during the themes course, is beclouded by a number of interpretation problems. The authors recognized that the strict dualists changed the most, although I am not sure that they would have predicted as much change in the relativist treatment as in the other. The puzzling issue is the small number of students who could be classified as either dualists or relativists: an unfortunate accident or an important finding? Nowhere can I find what the authors expected as a base-rate distribution.

Conclusions may be fostered by reclassifying the subjects so that the multiplicity people are spread a bit better. Failing that, an internal analysis of the multiplicity subjects may be helpful.

The data in Table 2 look a bit more encouraging, but I am not sure of the nature of the significance test; if I were Widick and Simpson, I would take a close look at the distribution of those journal-writing ratings.

I, too, am pleased that all students liked the courses so well that they rated them positively. Nevertheless, no effects are no effects, and that is how the game is played.

Since not all of the relevant data on the history course are available, we should reserve judgment about the outcome there. And, as I have said before, the authors have put their work to a very severe test, indeed.

One must be encouraged, over all, by the news that Widick and Simpson are at work. They have based their efforts on good theory, designed a very impressive innovation to instruction, and pursued a sensible research effort in a setting where research is not easy. I hope they are encouraged enough to keep on with it.

Laboratories
for Student Development

Peter Madison

Although my task is to present a case study, I must refer to some aspects of my activities as a theorist as a prelude to explaining student development laboratories and personality laboratories, the two types of structures for student development that I have been using in my teaching.

In 1949 I arrived at Swarthmore College fresh from graduate school. I was armed with the theory and method described in Henry A. Murray's *Explorations in Personality* (1938) and steeped in the sociocultural theory that Talcott Parsons and Clyde Kluckholm were developing at the time. Murray's theory, broadly psychoanalytic in its focus on early developmental influences and on the subtle continuation of such structures into adult life, merged with a Lewinian attention to the interaction between such personality structures and the environment. The Parsons-Kluckholm analysis of how personality and social systems were intertwined complemented the Murray-Lewin view. Through Robert W. White's tutelage at Harvard, I also was equipped with Murray's method of studying persons, the "diagnostic council" (Murray 1938). The method involved using multiple interviewers from a variety of backgrounds and an array of tests and clinical interview techniques to study the single person, followed by a description of the individual's personality formulated by the group.

When I was asked to teach a course on personality, I turned the class into a diagnostic council. As a group we studied student volunteers, much as Murray, White, and the other authors of *Explorations in Personality* had done. This application of theory and

74

method to understanding student personality and to teaching began a cycle of interaction between theory and application in which I have been involved every since.

Studying students led me to feel that the personality theories I knew did not fit students in some respects, and I was stimulated to reformulate the Freud-Murray-White type of concepts with which I began. Eventually, I published a synthesis of what I knew with ideas from the Gestalt psychology I was exposed to at Swarthmore (Köhler 1947), Robert Leeper's perceptual view of personality, and some developments of my own (Madison 1969). The effort represented a theory of student development in the sense that it showed, through illustrative case history examples, how a particular synthesis of concepts that were widely current among personality, learning, perception, and sociocultural theorists, together with a few suggested innovations of my own, could be used to formulate the facts of student development in college at a case study level. It represents the outcomes of a close and intensive interaction between theory and application in which each modifies the other.

Over the intervening years, the interaction of theory, the study of students, and teaching led me to the development of two teaching programs that represent applications of personality theory to college teaching. I will describe the two types of student development laboratories, the first of which I call "student development laboratories" and the second, "personality laboratories."

Student Development Laboratories

The student development laboratory, as a teaching method, grew by small degrees out of my interest in theory. I do not claim that the development of method was guided by the theory because, at the beginning, I did not see it as a special approach to teaching. It grew out of the practical necessity of having to teach courses on personality, my observations of the effects of intensive personality studies on the students, and direct suggestions from students as to what they wanted. I liked the Murray-White type of theory and their way of studying students through repeated interviews over long time periods. When I was faced with my first classes in personality, I proposed that as a class we study some student volunteers as a more interesting way of learning about the topic than just reading the text. Both the class and the students studied found the experience highly involving.

A few years later, five graduates of one of these classes proposed a follow-up course. They wanted to turn the diagnostic council method upon themselves as subjects rather than studying out-of-class volunteers. They wrote autobiographies, descriptions of their lives on campus, took a lot of tests, and exchanged copies of all data; then, as a group, we formulated the personalities of each class member in turn. To ease the potential threat, each person presented his or her self-formulation before the rest of us entered in. The students were wildly enthusiastic; "the best course in four years of college" was the consensus.

My theoretical, clinical, and teacher selves were all intrigued. I noticed the often-loose fit between the facts of personality and the theories we used to formulate student lives. In time, it led me to develop my own synthesis of theoretical concepts. Clinically, I liked the insights into themselves that students developed and the special intimacy we all shared. As a teacher, my ego was flattered by their enthusiastic endorsement and I asked the department if I could repeat the course, this time with ten students.

When the same exciting results occurred, I decided to propose the method to the department as a permanent course offering. Their unexpected resistance gave me my first inkling that I was proposing an unorthodox innovation in teaching. All but one of the faculty objected to students being privy to intimate data about one another's personalities, and several expressed fears that I would precipitate some sort of harmful reactions.

Over several repetitions, I noticed special effects on both me and the students which were not true of my other courses. Lab groups became very close. Ten students, each sharing written autobiographies, college histories, and test data in class were not just a class; we were a group as intimate and involved as any therapy group, although our task was manifestly a cognitive one—to understand each person in terms of concepts used in personality. They became special to me, I to them, and each to one another.

The effects of sharing private aspects of personalities had consequences well known in therapy groups: Everyone felt more "normal," more human, to discover that one's dread secrets were, in
fact, generally shared experiences that had set one off as a bit
strange simply because the individual never knew that he or she
was not unique.

Graduates of the course often visited my office and spontaneously wrote follow-up histories. I began to see the value of restudy-
ing graduates of this sophomore course during their junior and
senior years, and, eventually, after college, much as White (1952)
did. I noticed some phenomena that existing theorists said little
about. For instance, in some cases, college friends and roommates
had a surprisingly strong influence on development. The frequency
of intense, self-limiting crises in rapidly developing students was
another surprise. I have described other findings in my book (Madison 1969).

The lab student's relation to theory and to psychology was
sometimes visibly affected. Students reported that they now knew
how to *use* theory in living rather than just for passing exams.
Their insights of how much their choices of major, friends, and careers were a product of specific childhood and family experiences
seemed to free them to question their choices more openly. For
instance, "Steve," who entered the lab in the midst of a crisis over
whether to continue in engineering, came to see that he was cling-
ing to an unsuitable major for fear of losing his father's support.
"Trixie" reported that she spontaneously observed, in the course
of writing her autobiography, that she chose male friends, in part,
on the basis of their teasing, lack of consideration, and commitment elsewhere—characteristics of her relationship to her father.

I gradually developed the lab into a systematic teaching method
and took it to Princeton with me in 1960. It proved to be equally
effective and popular there. In 1963 I brought it to Arizona where
it finally became a "student development laboratory."

During an extended leave at Nevitt Sanford's Institute for the
Study of Human Problems at Stanford University in 1964-66, I
studied what was by now a vast collection of student histories
and wrote *Personality Development in College* (1969) as a text for

the lab type of course. After that, lab groups studied their own and one another's personalities by formulating their lives in terms of my version of theory.

DETAILS OF THE STUDENT DEVELOPMENT
LABORATORY METHOD

As I teach the course, the student development laboratory consists of eight to twelve students and the instructor. We meet weekly for a three-hour lab session and two-hour theory class. In class, we study whatever theory we are going to use. At different times, I have used most of the theories summarized in Hall and Lindzey (1970). The clinically based theories, such as Freud and Murray, are easiest to use on case histories. My version of personality theory fits student data well because it was developed specifically for that purpose. The theory in White (1952) is also easy to use for similar reasons. An instructor can use any theory which he knows how to apply to case-study type of material.

For the lab, I wrote a manual (Madison 1966) which students follow in the production of the vast quantities of data each collects on herself or himself and re-produces so every member of the lab has a copy. During the first five weeks lab students are asked to write their precollege autobiographies and their college histories outside of class, following the comprehensive instruction in the manual. During the period that students are doing this extensive homework, class meetings center around discussion of college journals. For the first lab session, each is asked to bring multiple copies of a written college journal, which is a descriptive account of the most emotionally involving event of the preceding week. They are distributed and each student gives an oral version to the lab group; then he or she is asked to expand on the personal meanings of the event described, and a general discussion follows.

As instructor, I ask whether anyone sees what was described as illustrating any theoretical concept and I point out any relation that I see. The exercise trains students to begin thinking of their lives in terms of psychological concepts; and the experience leads to sharing intensely meaningful experiences and to a rapid development of group feelings of trust and closeness. The experience provides the kind of emotional ventilation that occurs in therapy groups with much of the same relief of anxieties and expressions of support from lab members. The journals show that some students are doing emotionally risky things which they consider to be everyday events in their lives. A girl may describe a conflict with parents over living with a boyfriend, and a boy might tell about his difficulties in choosing to quit taking money from home in order to feel independent. A suicide of a friend, experiences with drugs, flunking important tests, breaking up with a lover, a clash with a roommate, or an exhilarating ski trip are examples of what may be reported in the weekly college journal. The academic purpose of the task, which is to provide raw data for theorizing, appears to encourage a feeling of freedom to talk about whatever is important. Freedom to talk is further encouraged by everyone's adopting a code name which is used exclusively, in both written material and addressing one another in the lab. Rules of confidentiality are adopted. Students are told that they may discuss what happens in labs with intimate outside friends but that they must use code names only. Codes also protect against the inadvertent loss of data. At the end of lab, all copies of data are returned to the student who produced them. After the course is over and grades assigned, students who are willing to contribute their data to research bring them in voluntarily. Any material kept by the instructor is understood to belong to its author, who may withdraw it from the instructor's research files at any time.

After the fourth week, the lab group begins working with the autobiographies and college histories which have been distributed. Each lab member schedules himself or herself for a future diagnostic council session. On the appointed day, the lab assembles, each having read all the data on the student whose personality is to be formulated. This student begins with a summary of the most important developmental events in his precollege history and suggests ways in which what happened may be formulated in theory. Then we all enter with our ideas. The instructor acts as chairman-mediator-group-leader as well as chief theorist to whom more difficult questions of theory are referred. The experience is exciting and sometimes trying to the student on the hot seat for the day; typically, however, he or she receives much understanding and warm support.

The students' college history is then reviewed. The focus is on relations between his precollege past and his course through college up to now and on his developments as a person. Next, his collection of weekly journals is reviewed to see how his personal tendencies are entering into his management of daily life on campus. Themes that run through all three types of data are given special attention. What the student is trying to do with his life and how he is coping, or blocking himself, come to light.

Finally, we turn to the student's relation to us. He is asked how he perceives each member of the lab and we talk about instances in which his personality, as inferred from all the data and discussion, displays itself in his perceptions of other lab members. Each of us describes our perceptions of the subject in turn and these are discussed. The student typically leaves the lab full of ideas about himself, emotionally charged, and feeling highly positive.

It has always impressed me how understanding and supportive students are of one another in this kind of exercise. Sensitive feelings are readily perceived and dealt with gently. If there are fears and distress, warm understanding and support flow generously.

Following the presentation of his data and the group formulation of his personality, the student is asked to incorporate the fruits of the diagnostic council discussion into a term paper, which becomes the basis of his course grade. The paper summarizes the important events of the precollege past, college history, semester's collection of weekly college journals, and the student's account of how he responded to the lab group and we to him. Themes that thread their way through all four types of data are especially focused on. How the student has developed over time, his typical coping mechanisms, and what influences are shaping him in college are of special interest. The student is asked to use as many theoretical concepts as possible in his formulation and to suggest new theoretical ideas based on his own data.

By the time the lab is over, the members have become intensely involved with their experience and quite expert with the theory. They often become a cohesive group on campus and meet to talk over what is happening to them. Annual reunions with the instructor are requested by some groups at which each reviews what has happened over the year and focuses on understanding the changes.

As a practicing group therapist, I am aware that the developmental lab provides everyday students with strong experience of a kind that ordinarily we find only in therapy and growth groups. I see the same kind of developmental impact as in any good group. At the same time, the student learns a great deal of theory in a highly usable form. He knows how to use theory after experiencing its value and helping to apply it to eight to twelve classmates. Students tell me that there is no course like it and that they feel much personal benefit. In anonymous course evaluations at Swarthmore, Princeton, and the University of Arizona, students regularly rated it the best course in the department, or among the top courses. Absences are unheard of, except for dire illness. Students in crises who drop all their courses typically hang on to the lab course as the one meaningful academic activity remaining. The only criticism students make of the lab is about the amount of work involved. Generally, the term paper, autobiographies, college histories, college journals, tests, and other data that students voluntarily add runs to 100 typed pages; even 200 pages is not unusual. Although students protest the work, it is in the tones of an author who complains that his work has become so engrossing that he does not have time to eat. They add childhood and high school diaries as appendices to their papers and collections of poems they have written; and they spend unasked-for hours persuading other students to write descriptions of their personalities, taking tests that are optional, and so on. It is a turned-on way to learn and to teach.

One of the frequently expressed concerns of other faculty and departmental chairmen concerns the possible dangers of such a course. After the early conflict with the Swarthmore faculty, I instituted elaborate precautions, such as submitting the prospective class list to deans and to the college psychiatrist for screening. For several years at Arizona I had agreements with the college health service, counseling service, and our psychiatric consultant to the clinical program to see anyone who became disturbed. But nothing ever happened and I relaxed after a while. If anyone is distressed when the bell rings, which rarely happens, I ask whoever is free to stay with me and the student and we talk until the student feels alright. As a clinical psychologist, I am aware that students who are psychotic or suicidal occasionally enroll in labs. I find that other students relate to them as persons rather than as psychiatric cases, and I do the same, much to their benefit. Nothing untoward has happened in fifteen years of teaching such labs.

Personality Laboratories

I greatly enjoy teaching student development laboratories and regard them as the best teaching I have ever done. Recently, however, I have been exploring some new formats, one of which I call a "personality laboratory." It looks promising enough to describe here. Personality laboratories grew out of student development laboratories, as a direct result of my becoming a part-time group therapist at Southern Arizona Mental Health Center in 1965. As I developed group skills, I began to pay more attention to the interpersonal relations of group members in student development labs. Up to then we had focused on (a) the student's precollege history, as seen in his autobiography, (b) his college history, and (c) his daily response to campus life, as seen in weekly journals. The task was to detect consistencies and differences in all three types of data and to formulate them in theoretical terms. But as the semester wore on and reactions among group members intensified, it became clear that these immediate here-and-now perceptions of and responses to one another often had a close relationship to what was evident in the other data. So we added a final focus. Having conceived of each person's personality on the basis of the three types of data we had been using, we now asked, Do our reactions to each other make sense in terms of our formulations? Indeed they did. Students found it electrifying to turn their formulations on this immediate datum. Sometimes the considerable discrepancies between the student's self-image as portrayed in his autobiography, college history, and weekly journals, and his response to us in group added an exciting new dimension. The analysis was scarier because our responses to each other were less subject to censorship, but the sense of dealing with a real kind of personality data that had not been filtered through the group member's own censorship added intense excitement.

Inevitably, my interest turned to the possibilities of going beyond understanding personality to what could be done to change those students who were or became dissatisfied with themselves. My theory was concerned with change as it happened naturally on campus, and it had many implications for the kinds of experience a student could expose himself to if he wanted to develop rapidly. Much of the discussion in student development labs centered on changes taking place naturally, and the lab experience supported such changes. But my theory was not geared to *producing* change directly in labs and I turned to psychotherapy for ideas and methods to try out. My original clinical training had been loosely psychoanalytic but I had adopted a modified Rogerian style after a seminar with Carl Rogers. In 1972, I began an intensive program of attending workshops and institutes in Rogerian groups, transactional analysis, gestalt therapy, and assertive training. As I learned each approach I began to adopt features for lab use, a process I am in the midst of just now.

My present interest is to develop ways of teaching the psychology of personality so that students not only learn the textbook theories but may elect, voluntarily, to attend laboratories in which they choose to apply concepts and methods directly to themselves for their own self-understanding and, when they wish, self-change. My colleagues (Robert L. Wrenn, Reed A. Mencke, William H. Thweatt, and Richard Coan) and I have experimented with such a conception for the past four years. We have developed four new courses toward this end, one of which is described here.

Theories that Are Usable in Personality Labs

Personality-laboratory-style teaching poses a severe test to any theory being considered for use: Can it be applied to the everyday lives of students? To be applicable, the terms of a theory must have a connection to everyday events, without elaborate intervening assumptions. Much of Freud's developmental theory is excluded, for instance, because the chain of inference from present observable behavior to psychosexual stages is long and tenuous. On the other hand, Berne's (1961) concept of ego states is tied to observable cues which are evident in words, voice, posture, and gestures.

Further, has the theorist developed usable *methods* for applying his concepts to the tasks of self-understanding and change? Again, Freud's interpretation of dreams is an extremely difficult method to teach and use. But Perls's (1969) use of psychodrama to act out dreams can be readily taught to students. Freud's way of dealing with resistance through interpretation requires long analytic training, but Perls's methods of identifying ways we stop ourselves and of dealing with these blocks by exaggerating them is relatively simple.

Fortunately, we have some teachable and usable theories of personality. In my program I use Rogers (1970), Berne (1961), Perls (1969), and behavior theory (Cotler and Guerra 1976). My criterion leaves some cherished theories on the shelf: Freud, neo-Freudians, Jung, Murray, Lewin, Allport, Goldstein, Sheldon, Cattell, and existential psychology, for instance. Most have concepts that might contribute to self-understanding, but they all fall short on theory and method which students could use to *change* themselves.

My own theory of student development (Madison 1969) went with the rest — I quit using it as a text in 1974. Its conceptual applicability to student life is excellent. Students regularly report finding themselves in the cases and theory. It was designed as a text for use in student development labs and serves that purpose well. A student who applies the concepts to his autobiography, college history, and college journal will come out with a good understanding of how he had developed his precollege personality, how those personal tendencies interacted with the college scene and guided his selection of and response to college major, friends, lovers, roommates, instructors, and his continuing relations to parents. He can see how the way his personality was organized his freshman year led to developmental crises and to change, and he understands that anxiety is a healthy aspect of challenge and response. But if he asked, "Now that I understand myself, how can I change what I don't like about me?" he would find no specific answers. I suspect the same is true of the other theorists we are considering at this conference.

Students as Lab Leaders

Until a few years ago, I used labs only in special small courses enrolling ten to twelve students, obviously a luxury in a 30,000 student state university. In our large personality courses, which normally enroll eighty to 100, I usually taught the same theories but left it to the student to apply the concept of himself as best as he could. I did offer options other than taking examinations to facilitate the task, such as a term paper applying the concept to the student's life (in which case the student carried out the project described previously). Several years ago, Reed Mencke, associate director of the Student Counseling Service, experimented with using students as lab leaders. Thus he was able to break up the class into lab-size subgroups of about ten students for one of the three weekly meetings of the course. Students in the lab groups were so enthusiastic that the rest of us soon followed suit. Today, five of us use personality labs in teaching our large courses. The usual weekly arrangement is for the whole class to meet for two one-hour meetings with the instructor: for the third meeting the students are divided into subgroups of ten that meet for one two-hour session.

Selection. As yet our selection of lab leaders is unsystematic. Mostly it is a matter of self-selection plus interview. Lab leaders usually speak enthusiastically of their experiences to like-minded friends who then come and ask about the program. We also describe the opportunity in our large personality courses and hold a meeting for all interested students just before preregistration. At the meeting, the four or five instructors using labs describe their particular programs, and students fill out and submit applications to whomever they choose to lead for. A selection interview follows. I suspect that the best clue to selecting leaders is to ask members of lab groups to rate each other on leadership potential sometime after midsemester. We have not tested the idea but we do ask student leaders for recommendations of prospective future leaders in their groups. Most of us also require a grade of B in the basic personality course in which the students are enrolled as a qualification.

Training. We train leaders in somewhat different ways. I do it by asking them to enroll in a course on group leadership. The heart of the course is a three-hour lab in which, for two hours, we become a lab group ourselves with me as leader, and we carry out the same lab that they will do with their ten student members later in the week. Such direct modeling, as Bandura (1969) has shown, is a powerful form of teaching. The third lab hour is devoted to discussing the lab we just finished; I point out less obvious leadership aspects and the students bring up leadership problems with their own groups. We role play such problems as much as possible. A student plays the problem student and I model how to deal with the incident or issue.

The balance of the course consists of readings on the theory and method being used. If I use transactional analysis, for instance, I ask the student leaders to read an additional book on the topic.

I have students lead in pairs as a training device. Students who have been leaders during a preceding semester act as the senior leader and are paired with an assistant leader who is new to lab leadership. The next semester, the assistant is in charge of his or her own lab group and he or she trains someone in turn. When possible, I use male-female pairs on the assumption that it is better for each sex to participate in the leadership. Co-leaders are asked to hold a strategy session before meeting their lab group.

The above format has proven adequate but all of us feel that more could be done. This year we introduced a course on group leadership, theory and practice. Reed Mencke and I expect to experiment with training leaders more systematically before they start leading labs. This semester Mencke is giving his students intensive training in listening and responding skills, using the Gazda (1973) model followed by specialized training in a particular approach, such as TA, Gestalt, assertive training, and the like.

Effects on Student Leaders. Student leaders are enthusiastic about their experiences. Becoming a leader puts them into an active learning situation in which the responsibility invariably proves to be intensely motivating. After two semesters as leaders (the limit), they leave the program regretfully with the highest praise for the experience. Those who have a helping profession as a career objective find that being group leaders gives them a realistic taste of what counseling and psychotherapy will be like. The rest constitute a trained pool of citizens with facilitative interpersonal and leadership skills. We train upward of 100 such paraprofessionals a year, a spin-off from the program that has much value in itself.

Content of Personality Labs

What we do in labs depends upon the theory and method we are studying in the parent course. My illustration is from the "Normal Personality" course I taught fall semester, 1975-76. I am still experimenting widely with content variations. For this round I chose transactional analysis and Gestalt psychology. On other offerings I have included Carl Rogers, George Bach, assertive training, human sexuality, and parts of my own theory in various mixes.

I chose Berne and Perls because they offer theories that are of current interest and have high applicability to student life and classroom teaching. Their methods can be easily adapted to a laboratory format. The two theories also fit well together. Berne has rescued the best from psychoanalysis and cast it in an easily understood language. His theory is strong in understanding development but somewhat weak in how to bring about change. Perls's interest is specifically on how we prevent our own development. He specifies ways of working on such developmental blocks which are helpful to lab students. We start with Berne (1961) or James and Jongeward's *Born to Win* (1971) as a text and focus on development during the first half of the semester. We use Fagan and Shepherd (1971) for Perls's theory. Contracts such as those used by Berne offer a bridge between TA and Gestalt theories. After formulating their own development using TA, students write contracts for changing anything they are dissatisfied with in themselves. At that point, we go on to Perls, who offers special ways of working on contracts.

Such a fusion of TA and Gestalt is now widely used. Robert Goulding, director of the Western Institute for Group and Family Therapy in Watsonville, California, is a leading exponent of the synthesis (Goulding 1972) and has long trained practitioners in summer workshops at his institute.

Laboratory Methods. Since personality labs are intended to exemplify the particular theoretical approach being taught in the parent course, the procedures used are derived from the theory. In the case of TA and Gestalt, these procedures are either found in writings by Berne and Perls or their followers, or they were used in TA and Gestalt workshops which I attended over the past four years. Most have been adapted by me to fit an academic laboratory setting. The TA and Gestalt laboratory methods have been written up in first-draft form in a laboratory manual (Madison 1976). The lab manual, sold to students through the bookstore, is used as a text by my laboratory sections of the "Normal Personality" course. What follows is a brief summary of the lab procedures.

Transactional Analysis in Labs. Transactional analysis is customarily divided into structural analysis, transactional analysis, game analysis, and script analysis; I follow these subdivisions in teaching and in labs with several modifications. I treat contracts as a separate, special topic, and I divide script analysis into two parts, following Steiner (1974). Steiner considers the usual procedures taught under script analysis to represent what he calls "structural analysis of scripts," in which the focus is on understanding how the person developed as he did. How to bring about change is called "transactional analysis of scripts"; it includes the TA theory of stroking.

Structural Analysis. The purpose of the unit on structural analysis is to acquaint students with those consistent patterns of feelings, experience, and behavior that Berne (1964) called "ego states." They appeared to him to be grouped into three broad categories which he named Parent, Adult, and Child, each thought to have different origins and characteristics. Berne assumed that each person responds to a specific stimulus in different ways because of each ego state. The Child ego state is further subdivided into an impulsive, emotional component (Natural Child), an intuitive creative, manipulative part (Little Professor), and an accommodating one (Adapted Child). The Parent ego state has two aspects, a Critical and a Nurturing Parent.

Berne's ego state concept is easy to use in labs because the subdivision of personality to which his terms refer are defined in observable and readily recognizable ways that play a meaningful part in everyday activities. By carrying out the exercises suggested in the lab manual, students can directly experience enough aspects of each ego state to easily relate them to their daily experience.

Beyond teaching identification of aspects of one's own personality, the unit on structural analysis is designed to allow lab members to judge the degree of comfort or discomfort they experience when functioning in each ego state. Thus, students discover that it is easy to criticize (Critical Parent) but harder to nurture (Nurturing Parent), and particularly difficult to nurture oneself, a deficiency that leads to low self-esteem and depression. Others are weak on factual, rational, and planning functions used in dealing with external reality (Adult), leading to poor organization of academic studies and degree programs. Long service in the educational system has left most students submissive, obedient, and oriented to pleasing (Adapted Child) to the point of self-denial, although a few are openly rebellious (a component of Natural Child) to the point that any requirement to adapt to the campus authority structure keeps them fuming and ineffective. Most students who have survived the system necessarily have a strong manipulative component (Little Professor) that is useful in "psyching out" the faculty and administration.

The ego states scheme provides concepts the student can use to assess the strengths and weaknesses of his or her personality. Spontaneous expressions of surprise are common: "I'm all Adapted Child; I know how to be good but I can't let myself play." "I can never ask for anything for myself without feeling guilty" (low self-nurturance).

Transactional Analysis. It was Berne's insight that two persons can relate to one another in parental, adult, or more childlike ways, and as long as both are on the same wavelength (adult to adult or child to child) the interaction can proceed. Crossed transactions lead to disruption. In lab, students practice sending messages to other group members from a particular ego state. The receiver learns that he can either reply from the same ego state or "cross" the transaction by coming back from a different ego state. The exercise leads to insights of how interpersonal arguments develop (an

Adult message is responded to from Child or Critical Parent), and how to stop an impending fight (reply from your Adult to messages from the other person's Critical Parent or Natural Child).

Structural and transactional concepts provide useful conceptual tools for the analysis of male-female relationships on campus. Students compare their personal programming to the cultural one in which women are high on Nurturing Parent, low on Adult, and high on Adapted Child and Little Professor (intuition), as compared to men who are programmed to be low on nurturance, high on rationality, and low on intuitive skills. Both sexes have an overabundance of Critical Parent and Adapted Child and are low on Natural Child. Lab members develop a perspective on their opposite-sex relations when they see that some of their differences, which had appeared as personal deficiencies, and some of the male-female complaints against the other, which they had supposed were peculiar to their own opposite sex relations, are built-in structural characteristics widely shared in our culture.

Game Analysis. Berne (1964) showed how we can use Freud's concept of unconscious motives to understand a wide range of otherwise puzzling behavior. By pointing out that everyday transactions commonly are double-layered, with a conscious, socially acceptable motive covering an ulterior, unconscious intention, he showed that it was possible to understand many otherwise puzzling relationships between students and teachers, students and parents, and students with one another. His clever labels poke fun at our foibles and allow lab members to laugh at themselves when they look at the psychology of the student who habitually baits professors or the administration, teachers who allow themselves to fall into seductive relations to students, or students who compulsively cut others down. In lab, such common campus games can easily be role played with much humor and insight.

Structural Analysis of Scripts. Classical script analysis provides interesting reading, lectures, and discussion but is not so easy to bring into the lab because its premise is the idea that each of us made momentous childhood decisions that still guide our lives, as though we were blindly following the scripts of plays. Although TA theorists insist that such decisions can be consciously remembered, my experience has been that the unitary and transparent scripts implied by the theory are infrequent among college students. I ask students to fill out the Life Script Questionnaire in the manual and to work out their own scripts as I lecture in the main course. Students who feel that they have a clearly understandable script are encouraged to volunteer to present it in their lab group.

Transactional Analysis of Scripts. "How to change your script" has been called the "transactional analysis of scripts" by Steiner (1974). He offered some particularly important applications to living that lend themselves to lab exercises. Berne incorporated into his theory of "stroking" the everyday concept of love along with technical notions, like reinforcement, primary and secondary drives, and Freud's "instinctual derivatives." The primary stimulus hunger of infancy, which needs direct touching for satisfaction, becomes transformed by social learning into recognition hunger, which is satisfied in basically social ways. The lab units center on Steiner's concept of the "stroke economy," the idea that society's need to socialize and control its members has led to unrealized limitations on our freedom to freely give and receive strokes, leaving most of us in varying degrees of chronic stroke starvation.

A first exercise is to assess the lab group's stroke economy by having lab members record the strokes they would like to receive and compare them with what, in fact, they are receiving from their present group. Students compare how others see tham against how they would like to be seen. The exercise can lead to some jolting surprises, but usually it gives a favorable boost to students' self-images.

Steiner's suggested exercises for breaking down the stroke economy lead to lab members' practicing giving strokes to other lab members, asking for strokes, and stroking themselves, all of which prove to be surprisingly difficult to do. Some students are amazed to discover that they would rather die than ask for a simple compliment; others find that they regularly discount every good thing said to them so that they are habitually undernourished. Some discover that, unknowingly, they have been subtly discounting others in just about every statement they make. Steiner's observation that we are thoroughly brainwashed to respond in such ways becomes a tangible reality and leads to more honest give and take.

Gestalt Psychology in Labs. Frederick Perls fits the campus zeit-geist well, possibly because his thinking has helped to shape it. Be-cause much of his writings are disorganized, I prefer to use a paper-back collection of readings by Fagan and Shepherd (1971). The ideas are easy enough to present in the large lecture part of the course, but the lab adaptation had to overcome Perls's style of working on stage as a dramatic one-man show. Obviously, we could not train undergraduate lab leaders to do gestalt groups as Perls did. Fortunately, both the original Perls, Hefferline, and Goodman book (1951) and Stevens (1971) contain numerous ge-stalt "experiments" which are already adapted to classroom use. I have excerpted some especially usable ones having an unambigu-ous relation to gestalt theory in the manual.

Awareness. The exhortation to "know thyself" traditionally stamped on the entrance gates to the campus comes alive in Perls's hands. He has transformed Freud's free association method from a hidden, esoteric clinical procedure to a simple exercise. Lab mem-bers learn to tune in to their stream of consciousness and to talk it while experiencing it. What seems so simple to describe proves dif-ficult and enlightening. Students discover how much they censor, how much they are habitually attuned to inner or outer sensations, whether they are aware of feelings or of more impersonal facts, and how much they block themselves from knowing. The aware-ness training is preliminary to learning to use the method as a tool in self-discovery in succeeding lab units.

Experiencing versus Looking for Causes. An early application of the awareness exercise is to have students examine their interac-tions with one another in the lab group. They find out how much time they are spending asking questions, giving advice, and making interpretations of others' behavior, and they learn to tune in to their direct experiences instead and to report them. The students discover that reports of direct experiencing of others are valued and that they are a far more useful type of information than the usual interpersonal fare.

Introjection. The idea that, as children, we take on as our own behaviors and characteristics modeled by significant others which may not fit very well with our more basic self-feelings is found in many theories. In my studies I found that college students typically spend their first three semesters getting rid of what Perls called parental "shoulds" (introjects), after which they are free to select their own majors, friends, and life-style. Perls's famous top-dog/underdog exercise quickly tunes a lab member into his "shoulds." The student only has to begin speaking to an empty chair, in which he imagines himself seated, with as many sentences as he can muster that begin with "You should. . . ." The parade of shoulds typically includes studies neglected, laundry undone, parents unwritten to, diets ignored, and an endless list of other self-improvement programs gathering dust on the student's personality shelf.

By shifting chairs and replying to his "shoulds," the lab member develops some clues about how he resists all his shoulds, much as he once did parental pressures as a child. Motivations for procrastination and poor academic performance surface for discussion.

Projection. Projection, in the pathological, defensive meaning Freud gave it, is relatively rare among students, but Wundt's apperception is part of the most ordinary percept. Perls fused both into one concept with simple apperception at one pole and defensive disownment at the other, making it possible to demonstrate his concept with simple but convincing illustrations. Thus, in "object identification," a lab member is asked to "become whatever object in the room most represents an aspect of yourself, and to speak as though you *are* the object: 'I am the door. I am wide and allow you all to come in easily, but I protect everyone in this room against intrusion and make it cozy here.'"

The transparency of the speaker's personal qualities in this simple exercise is striking to lab members. They readily recognized a correspondence between what they already know of the speaker with the qualities attributed to the object; and usually they are able to detect some further free personal information beyond what the speaker has already disclosed. With training, the method

lends itself to exploring the personal meanings of almost any aspect of one's existence. If one dreams of an oak tree standing on a
hill, one simply "becomes" the oak tree and speaks from its perspective, and the resulting flow of feelings suggests a rich array of
possible meanings which simply thinking about the tree symbol is
unlikely to bring up. "Becoming" a rosebush, one of the identification exercises described by Stevens (1971) reveals surprising
depths of feeling which, on examination, the lab member is usually able to relate to his or her life with illuminating consequences.

With practice, the method lends itself to the investigation of
one's tendencies to blame, reject others, and feel jealous. The assumption is that when a person strongly blames, feels jealous, or
feels rejected, he may be doing what he accuses others of doing.
In the exercise, one proceeds by first blaming and then investigating the blame as a possible projection by experimenting with saying, "And I do it myself." Similarly, for one who feels rejected, he
is often *also* rejecting.

Unfinished Business. One of Perls's best insights was his perception that we feed our own present-day angers by carrying over
grudges from the past in the form of resentments that spill over into our current lives. If these resentments originated in childhood
and adolescence, they may be petty yet keep students and parents
from feeling or expressing their love for one another. Perls suggested that we can all become more human if we face these grudges,
and he dealt with such "unfinished business" by using Moreno's
(in Stevens 1971) psychodrama technique of speaking directly to
the persons at whom we are angry by imagining them seated in
empty chairs in front of us as we state a series of sentences beginning with, "I resent. . . ."

Perls did not leave matters there, of course. After the resentments were all stated, he asked the speaker to shift chairs and "become" the parent and to reply.

The exercise is performed in pairs or triads; students become
worker and observer in turn and give each other feedback and support. Invariably, students report feeling more reconciled and lov-
ing toward their parents. Sometimes, following the exercise students call or write parents to say, "I love you."

Lab members need not be angry to use unfinished business. If they do not feel resentful they are asked to imagine any significant other from their past and start with, "There are some things I have felt about our relation that I have never told you."

Perls discovered that, by speaking from each position in turn, a different perspective emerges. The other becomes more understood and attitudes that start out in strong opposition mellow and move toward the center.

In my own longitudinal studies of students, I have noticed that they commonly have difficulty seeing parents as persons until late in college. Perls's method looks like a way to speed up this natural developmental process.

Retroflection. The most usable idea on repression since Freud has been Wilhelm Reich's (Lowen 1975) insight that repression does not take place unnoticed within our heads. When we shut off feelings, Reich observed, we commonly tense our body musculature in ways that are visible to others and, with training, to ourselves. Tensing chest muscle and slowing down breathing are common and visible aspects of supressing or repressing feelings. The concept has given rise to strong interest in body "language," as in bioenergetics. Perls incorporated Reich's concept into his theory with the concept of "retroflection" (Perls 1969), in which one turns impulses intended for others back on oneself, typically through a muscular tension or action. Thus, I may twitch my shoulder, supressing a motion to strike out and, with it, repressing anger. In a sense, I hit myself instead of you. The concept is illuminating to students but I am still in an early stage of developing usable laboratory procedures.

Implications of Personality Laboratories

Labs are, first and foremost, a superior way to teach psychology as a subject matter. No experimental, physiological, learning, perception, or comparative psychologist would consider teaching his topic without labs for the simple reasons any physical scientist would support: Concepts that are disconnected from the actual materials with which a theory is concerned would be empty teaching. After all, a science consists of both concepts and *methods* to deal with its materials. In personality teaching, concepts frequently have been divorced from method, as in the usual adjustment courses in which students learn ideas but are not taught how to use them in living. In personality, a substantial body of what naturally belongs to our method has been fenced off from everyday use in teaching and living by labeling it "psychotherapy" and "counseling," and treating it as knowledge that is too dangerous for any but trained clinicians to use. A groundswell movement to recapture the citizen's right to know how to use psychology for his own benefit without recourse to "therapy" has rallied under George Miller's banner of "giving psychology away to the people" because it is the person's birthright to have free access to whatever is known about ways to improve the human condition (Miller 1969). I see labs as a part of this movement.

Personality Labs and Student Development Theory

In my career, I started out thinking of myself as a personality theorist but gradually I changed my self-image to that of a student development psychologist. I now find myself, once again, a personality theorist, albeit with a difference: I am thoroughly committed to an interest in students and to finding ways that psychological theory and method can be useful to them. What has happened to my theoretical side is that I saw that my theory of student development was not different but a particular synthesis of personality concepts. I see student development theorists as psychologists interested in personality development in a particular setting during a particular phase of life. In that sense, I am a student development psychologist. I like to think of myself as scouring every area of psychology for good ideas and methods to bring to students for their use. Right now, I am trying out concepts and methods from counseling and therapy. I feel that they are a rich source and I am busily mining them and feeding the results into the curriculum.

REFERENCES

Bandura, A. *Principles of behavior modification.* New York: Holt, Rinehart, & Winston, 1969.

Berne, E. *Transactional analysis in psychotherapy.* New York: Grove Press, 1961.

———. *Games people play.* New York: Grove Press, 1964.

Cotler, S. B., & Guerra, J. J. *Assertion training.* Champaign, Ill.: Research Press, 1976.

Fagan, J., & Shepherd, I. L. *Gestalt therapy now.* New York: Harper & Row, 1971.

Gazda, G. M. *Human relations development: a manual for educators.* Boston: Allyn & Bacon, 1973.

Goulding, R. L. New directions in transactional analysis: creating an environment for redecision and change. In C. J. Sager & H. S. Kaplan, eds., *Progress in group and family therapy.* New York: Brunner/Mazel, 1972.

Hall, C. S., & Lindzey, G. *Theories of personality.* New York: Wiley, 1970.

James, M., & Jongeward, D. *Born to win.* Reading, Mass.: Addison-Wesley, 1971.

Köhler, W. *Gestalt psychology.* New York: Liveright, 1947.

Lowen, A. *Bioenergetics.* New York: Coward, McCann, & Geoghegan, 1975.

Madison, P. Instructions for the student development self-study course option. Manuscript, 1966.

———. *Personality development in college.* Reading, Mass.: Addison-Wesley, 1969.

———. A manual for personality laboratory students and leaders. Manuscript, 1976.

Miller, G. A. On turning psychology over to the unwashed. *Psychology Today*, 1969, 3, 53-55, 66-74.

Murray, H. A., collaborators. *Explorations in personality.* New York: Oxford University Press, 1938.

Perls, F. S. *Gestalt therapy verbatim.* Moab, Utah: Real People Press, 1969.

Perls, F.; Hefferline, R. E.; & Goodman, P. *Gestalt therapy.* New York: Dell, 1951.

Rogers, C. *Carl Rogers on encounter groups.* New York: Harper & Row, 1970.

Steiner, C. *Scripts people live.* New York: Grove Press, 1974.

Stevens, J. O. *Awareness.* Moab, Utah: Real People Press, 1971.

White, R. W. *Lives in progress.* New York: Dryden, 1952.

Comments on Chapter 3

William G. Perry, Jr.

In the light of the concerns outlined in my comments to Widick and Simpson, I would like to highlight three aspects of Madison's report. They express for me the power of that dialectic which Madison developed in creating a fruitful interchange of the general and the particular, the objective and the phenomenological. It is through this dialectic, with all its paradoxes, that I see him to have maintained the ideals of the scientist in himself, and at the same time, transformed the specter I have described into the servant of life.

Madison insisted, explicitly in *Personality Development in College* and implicitly here, on his "two-faced" theory. One face looks at student development from the outside, objectifying and conceptualizing it through the observer's experience. In asking his students to master these concepts, however, Madison does not ask them to experience themselves in such terms. Rather, Madison gives them a second "face" of theory—concepts and metaphors in the language of their phenomenological experience. Then, as I read him here, he encourages them to translate from one to the other, mastering objective theory as a subject matter and allowing this learning to enrich and confirm the primary meaning and loyalty they accord their lives as subjects.

In keeping with this stance Madison offers students certain models of other students in the act of "applying" psychological concepts to their lives. The distinctive feature of each of these models, which is carefully underlined, is that the students involved have found the concepts illuminating "up to a point." Beyond that point, the particular experience is larger than the concept (e.g., "Thomas" on reintegration in more than one modality; "Michelle" on seeking out challenging situations; "Patty" on intense investment in other than transference figures). In each case, the experience does not have to be reduced to fit the concept but the concept requires revision and expansion to fit them.

Returning to the dialectic between theoretical subject matter and subjective growth, Madison makes it clear to his students and us that they will be graded on their mastery of the first. This focus befits an academic course in a university, even a course that sets out to provide not only conceptualizations of growth but exercises intended to promote it. The excellence of the design of Madison's courses makes it hard to believe that any student could go through a course without significant growth. The ingenuity of students and clients in such matters is worthy of the highest respect. And Madison gives it.

He has indeed, then, exorcised my murderous specter. Clearly his students have found it lifegiving to learn to give psychological meaning to their experiences. But, even as a psychologist, he has conveyed to students that psychological meaning is only one meaning. He has left them aware that, helpful as it is to conceptualize the mechanics that might otherwise encrust their lives, it is harder to conceptualize the life that transcends the mechanics, that "gets it all together."

Roger A. Myers

My first and predominant affective reaction was one of admiration for Professor Madison. I admired the psychosocial base that could produce an impression of a loose, unself-consciously aware, pragmatic, yet modest intellect. Only once before have I encountered one who admitted to making a living by stealing ideas—not at all a rare occupation. Seldom, although more than once, have I been permitted to hear from a psychologist who focused on his or her concern with the developmental processes of students being taught with more acuity than was devoted to hard issues, such as grades,

GRE scores, certification exams, and other rites of passage. Finally, I cannot help but notice the nearly (no one is perfect) total absence of shibboleths and taboos in the thinking of a psychologist conducting his business of teaching.

Since I am a middle-level academic administrator, my second reaction was one of wonderment for the settings that rendered student development labs and personality labs feasible from an economic point of view. There was no wonderment about the enthusiasm of the included students; that seemed as natural as snow in Minneapolis. "Who wouldn't be enthusiastic about such an elegant learning experience?" Then I listened and imagined that, indeed, there may very well be some students who would not be thus enchanted. In fact, many students I have known in these Northern Plains and in the concrete canyons of Manhattan would not have volunteered, endured, or permitted such intensive and exhaustive mingling of the form and the essence of the educational experience. Who are they, I asked, and what are their stripes? Although I have some hunches, it is more important to ask if Madison is not describing a very special set of experiences (a differential treatment) for a very special cohort of students, selected, or self-selected, in a very special way (differential diagnosis)?

Wonderment also does not describe my reaction to the news that Madison's faculty colleagues resisted the innovation he proposed. Psychology faculty are not widely known for their concern for student development. I find quite typical, for example, the faculty unease with the notion that academic concepts should relate directly to the self-understanding of the students who are learning those concepts, let alone the panic one observes when "learning" is suspected of leading to self-regulation of self-stimulation. Worse yet, the radical departures Madison proposed probably evoked the worst kind of professional fear: of inconvenience. Enough berating my brethren, on to other reactions.

A minor, and somewhat delayed, reaction was amazement that such emotionally rigorous and meaningful learning environments have not produced a single case of psychological casualty to date. I do not think of myself as an alarmist in such matters, but I am concerned with the potential for psychological casualty in the human potential movement, various outreach gestures, and other intense experiences which therapists call quasitherapeutic. The apparent safety of Madison's labs reveals both a skillful selection procedure, no matter how inexplicit, and Madison's impressive resources as a clinician.

Yet another reaction was my pleasure at Madison's artistic combination of the best of the therapeutic enterprise and the best of the teaching enterprise. For a long time I have been secretly pleased with an insight I thought only I had, that psychotherapy is far and away the best way to learn about how individuals grow and develop; unfortunately it is one of the worst ways to influence that growth and development except for a very few carefully selected adults (in New York, notably, unemployed actors and suburban matrons). The labs combine the best of "getting to know" with the best of "how to influence" in a way so sensible that one wonders why so few academicians have tried it. I am also pleased that the labs make such prominent use of the process of universalization to dispel feelings of uniqueness among college students. Although group experts have long recognized its potency, the process is strangely underused in natural settings such as classes and associational groups.

It pleases me that Madison sees that students in his therapeutic classes learn a great deal of theory as they learn about themselves and each other. Once again, the insights of therapy have been diverted to didactic gain. Patients in therapy learn theory and grammar in the process of getting cured; in fact, some people say that learning to speak and theorize like one's therapist becomes the operational definition of the cure. But no one I know has ever looked at the other side of the coin and tried to capitalize on the fact that theory and grammar can be taught that way. More's the tribute to Madison.

With my concern for vocational development, I am forced to be troubled by Madison's apparent neglect of his students' concerns about the anticipation of, preparation for, entry to, conduct in, and reflection upon their work roles. There are rare hints of focus on choice making in the labs, but such issues are clearly subordinate to the sexier aspects of the lives of young adults. Elsewhere it seems to be quite generally accepted that vocational development is an important and inextricable aspect of human development;

yet it gets only passing nods in the description of the labs. It is not clear, for example, that the various approaches to thematic analysis of student lives even recognize the possibility that identity issues for young adults are closely intertwined with issues of patent social roles outside college, especially work roles as they are anticipated, played, or avoided. The descriptions of the labs suggest to me a general deficit in preoccupation with the future, while "past is prologue" is writ large in much of what goes on.

In discussing the personality labs, Madison refers to the scarcity of usable theoretical schemes and laments the great theories that are left on the shelf, therefore. We learn that Freud, the neo-Freudians, Jung, Murray, Lewin, Allport, Goldstein, Sheldon, Catell, and the existentialists have been excluded. One notices, timidly, that Super, Holland, Roe, Bordin, and Tiedeman, whose theorizing is considerably less venerated, are also gathering Arizona dust (sand?), even though they might meet the criterion of usefulness, especially for college students. One hopes that, when all the resources of Hall and Lindsey have been exhausted, someone might take a look at Osipow.

Finally, and still in role, I feel enriched by theoretical insights which Madison has culled from his vast experience with the student development and personality labs. It is valuable to find further verification of the importance of peers to development in young adulthood; theorists in vocational development will welcome that support. It is equally valuable to be awakened to the frequency of self-limiting crises and to speculate about their meaning to vocational development.

I find it especially useful that Madison provides data to tell us that college students usually spend three semesters expunging their "shoulds" before they are free to select majors and, one presumes, career goals from autonomous self-relevant bases.

Finally, it is intriguing to hear how well the theories and techniques of Eric Berne and Fritz Perls work with normal young adults. It is even more intriguing to speculate on how these theories might influence intervention in the service of enhancing vocational development.

Douglas H. Heath

The methods used by Madison to further student maturation within a college setting are highly innovative and they reflect a deeply systematic understanding of the complexity of personality development. His approach provokes three issues: (*a*) How shall we conceptualize the principal effects of his methods? (*b*) What are the principal conditions that further such effects? (*c*) How generalizable are his insights for furthering student development in other settings and courses?

PRINCIPAL EFFECTS OF METHODS

No systematic rationale or mapping is presented of the principal types of effects predicted or found from the use of student development laboratories. However, Madison presents some anecdotal examples (ones I have also found in similar experiential types of teaching) that illustrate the principal types of growth noted during the college-age period. Clearly, a principal purpose and probably effect of his methods is increased ability to represent accurately not only one's self and values but also one's relationships with other persons (symbolization self-concept, values, personal relations). Madison provides examples of how students increase in cognitive skill, as well, to symbolize their personal experience, a potentially powerful attribute of ego strength (e.g., "to use the method as a tool in self-discovery"). Another principal effect that can be induced from his report is what I call the allocentric maturing of the students' self-concepts (e.g., "everyone felt more . . . human"), values and personal relationships (e.g., "how understanding and supportive students are of one another"), and of cognitive skills (e.g., "speaking from each position in turn, a different perspective emerges").

Another important developmental trend that college enhances is the progressive integration of a person's cognitive skills, self-concept, values, and personal relationships. Madison reports examples (e.g., students learn "how to *use* theory in living"; assessment of how similar themes emerge in different facets of personality and class interactions, "group feelings of trust and closeness").

Increased stabilization and autonomy of cognitive skills, self-concept, values, and personal relationships had been found in other studies not to be so prominent types of growth during this age period. Madison does not provide as many examples of these types of effects although he alludes to the persistence of close group relationships over time and increased autonomy of the lingering effects of "specific childhood and family experiences." Since the lab exercises heavily stress self-autonomy and responsibility for one's growth, I assume that if systematic studies were conducted of their effects, many students would show considerable maturing in autonomy.

CONDITIONS FURTHERING MATURING

Implicit in Madison's account are numerous insights of what stimulates maturing, conditions also found in other studies of student development. Critical to the initiation of growth is the experience of disequilibrium. By radically altering traditional student roles and creating teaching conditions that personally involve students in issues of central value to them, Madison creates tension, frustration, and the need to learn how to adapt differently (e.g., "exercise can lead to some jolting surprises"). The astute use of various methods to encourage symbolization (e.g., autobiographies, content that is self-referent, game analyses, and specific awareness training) provides students with the reflective and analytic tools by which to make sense of the adaptive dilemma in which they are immersed. The heavy reliance on small, supportive, mutually self-educating sustained groups is a powerful learning condition that, I believe, represents the direction in which education will be moving increasingly in the future. Its primary effect is to further allocentric development. Madison also uses a variety of methods that further the integration of the students (e.g., Perls's methods of encountering projections, the interweaving of theory and experience that integrates different types of cognitive processes, etc.). Stabilization of cognitive skills is probably enhanced by extensive self-reflective writing, of self-concept and values by the semester focus on self, and of personal relationships by the maintenance of close small-group interactions over time. Finally, autonomy is enhanced by Madison's explicit expectation that students will become more self-determining, and by his use of theorists, like Perls, who emphasize self-responsibility, and methods like contracts and students as teachers.

GENERALIZABILITY OF APPROACH

My research and similar types of teaching experiences confirm the potential maturing effect of Madison's approach. I do not question his assessment of the students' sense of involvement, excitement, and growth. Madison's dilemma is that he has so tied his methods to specific psychological content (and to a very limited range of personality theories, at that) that it is not clear just how general a model his approach is for learning other types of content, particularly nonpsychological, as well as for institutional and faculty policy changes. The emphasis on the content is too pointedly psychological and requires too much clinical expertise on the part of teachers to make the program useful on a broader scale. My hunch is that 99 percent of most faculties would claim that not much in his report would be directly useful to them, a claim I would dispute, however. Therefore, we may have a potentially powerful type of course that furthers maturing but does not have much potential for influencing the teaching practices of most other faculty, and which many faculty would claim is not suitable for an "academic" education anyway.

However, I think contained within Madison's approach are assumptions on and insights of what could make for more powerful, liberally educating and maturing language, history, and literature courses. But such potentials have not been made explicit. The challenge of such a student development approach is to identify such assumptions and findings, create more general type of methods, and demonstrate their usefulness in courses whose content is not so specifically psychological in scope. What I found most paradoxical about the entire conception of the Madison approach was that the assumptions implied were *seemingly* not implemented in the teaching process itself (e.g., teacher role remained that of establishing course goals, framing in great detail the sequences of the course, lecturing didactically, and evaluating student performance by grades). That is, the process of teaching did not seem to be quite consistent with goals like furthering student autonomy, probably an inevitable inconsistency when one teaches large numbers of students. The consequence might well be little transfer of most of the maturing effects found in the course to student behavior in other courses and situations, except for the behavior of the student teachers who are securing experience that can help to stabilize and make more autonomous their growth. If a student development approach is not to be confined to a few faculty in one department, then it must provide a more powerful generalizable model that is transferable to a wider range of teaching situations.

Ursula Delworth

The labs developed by Madison and his colleagues are an exciting and worthwhile intervention. Such efforts are especially essential in a large college, like the University of Arizona, if we take Barker's theoretical formulations and research seriously. Often, students are seen as (and feel) "redundant" in large campus settings. That is, there are more of them than are needed to play active roles in curricula and student affairs. Only the "best" are chosen and others lead "marginal lives," in that they have less opportunity to actively explore their interests and abilities and to develop a repertoire of appropriate and satisfying behaviors. Madison's labs provide an active, exploratory behavior setting in which each student is needed for his or her contribution.

The materials provided to prospective students and those students beginning the labs is also impressive in terms of giving students information to "route" themselves into and through the environment. Students are clearly seen as responsible persons, able to make choices and act, from the time they are introduced to the labs.

Madison and his colleagues have made considerable strides in presenting students with material and methods to use to better understand and take control of their lives. The individual change methods discussed sound solid and potentially effective. It would be exciting to see the labs so extended that students could better assess their own "fit" with the campus environment and focus on changes needed in the environment as well as in themselves. Student development staff long have been engrossed in changing students to fit into various campus environments. Madison has developed a scheme in which students have control over this change and actively decide what is to be changed and how. However, one can easily think of situations in which student efforts might more effectively be directed toward change in some aspect of the environment, rather than toward change in themselves. An example might be an unsatisfactory study situation in residence halls. Individual students can focus on finding other places to study or on ways to lessen their distractability. As an alternative, they could direct their attention to the environment and to ways the residence halls could be organized to provide maximal study situations for students desiring them.

Two of the person-environment-fit theorists provide ways to move in this direction: Holland (Walsh 1973) makes the assumption that people may be characterized by their resemblance to one or more personality types. Six basic personality types are described: realistic, investigative, social, conventional, enterprising, and artistic. People generally possess characteristics of all six types, but Holland suggests that each individual behaves in a manner reflecting one or two orientations more strongly than others. Holland further suggests six model environments that correspond to the personality types. He developed methods to determine both personality and environment types, and some research suggests that congruent personality-environment types tend to be associated with stability, satisfaction, and achievement.

A second approach is that of Stern (Walsh 1973), based on Lewin and Murray's formulations. Behavior is seen as a function of the transactional relationships between the individual and the environment. The needs of persons and environmental presses are measured by separate instruments, and the results are compared to determine congruence.

The use of such approaches as Holland's or Stern's might be adopted in the labs to enable students to look at both themselves and the campus environment. Their understanding of the impact of the college environment on their lives could be enhanced and the possibility of change in the environment as well as themselves could be offered.

Students are, clearly, strongly influenced by their precollege experiences but Madison wisely insists that the students explore and attempt to understand the impact of their current college experiences as well. The approaches developed by Holland and Stern could enhance this understanding and possibly bring about productive change. Little has been done in this latter area; the theoretical formulations remain largely descriptive. It would be beneficial for us all if such a talented and productive group as Madison and his associates were to tackle the problem of how to use these concepts more effectively in assisting students to bring about change.

REFERENCE

Walsh, W. B. *Theories of person-environment interaction: implications for the college student.* Iowa City: The American College Testing Program, 1973.

David E. Hunt

I experienced some initial uneasiness at the thought of being a "theorist" who would comment on the work of "practitioners," and when I read Madison's case study, I knew why. His study illustrates at once that good practice never comes directly from "theory" but from practice itself: reflecting on it and developing theory *from* practice. In this sense, Madison exemplifies the kind of theorist needed in the world of practice.

The explicit content of the case study is very impressive; it ranges from the most general level ("the subject matter of personality is persons, and since we are persons, the study of ourselves") to the specific (the use of person-specific time codes in the writing of autobiographies), and from the first undergraduate course to the Ph.D. program. As I read Madison's description of the strong, "electrifying," and indelible effects on his students, I begin to ask myself why they happened. It was then that I realized the importance of an implicit feature so important that it is not discussed explicitly: every psychologist is a person. As Madison demonstrates, the psychologist must relate to students as a person rather than as an expert only in order that students can experience these positive effects. With his background in clinical psychology and part of his current time devoted to group therapy, Madison manifests his sensitivity to this point on almost every page. However, I want to give the idea that psychologists are persons some additional emphasis because it is probably the most critical feature for someone who wishes to try to use such a program. Put another way, an instructor might attempt to adopt this program by following it page-by-page and sentence-by-sentence, but unless he or she accepted the fundamental fact of his or her being a person, the program would fail.

When the instructor of a psychology course explicitly accepts being a person, it permits the establishment of a climate for considering the psychology of persons. As Madison's descriptions indicate (especially in his training of leaders for the personality labs), the psychologist does not completely abandon being a psychologist—that is, the psychologist's professional experience in reflecting on issues about persons and himself. However, the psychology instructor must blend these orientations of psychologist-as-person and psychologist-as-psychologist so that the student can experience the instructor as nonarbitrary, authentic, and trust-producing. As Madison demonstrates, it is in such climates that (a) interpersonal trust can begin, (b) one's intuitions and common sense can be acknowledged, (c) psychological ideas can be considered in relation to one's personal knowledge, and (d) the events between instructor and student, and among students, will illustrate one of the most central phenomena in psychology, persons-in-relation.

These changes in relationships and climate in the classroom occur as much because of the psychology instructor's underplaying his role of unquestioned authority as it does to the instructor's accepting being a person. These changes also transform the nature of the teaching-learning process to a much more reciprocal experience in which procedures like diagnostic councils and peer teaching become appropriate. In this reciprocal climate, students and instructors can consider psychological theories in terms of how much they add to understanding persons in real life. Such courses as those developed by Madison and his colleagues will not only facilitate student development but enrich psychological theory.

Encouraging Development through Student Affairs

Chickering's Vectors of Development and Student Affairs Programming

James C. Hurst

Traditionally, student affairs programming appears to have been influenced by a nonsystematic process that was dependent upon three major determinants. The first determinant was the interest and/or orientation of the staff members comprising the student affairs division. If a newly hired staff member had or developed an interest in marital enrichment workshops for married students, for example, the institution soon had a marital enrichment program for their students. Occasionally, staff orientation and interest was congruent with current student needs and the programming served a legitimate function. Often, however, there was little relation between the two, but the programming was maintained anyway because there always seem to be willing students if an opportunity to participate exists.

The second determinant that has played an important role in student affairs programming is responding to student requests and demands. This process is deceptive in its apparent validity. After all, what could be more legitimate than to listen to what students demand and then to respond appropriately? One major weakness in relying on this process is that the programming result usually is remedial and reactive rather than proactive, preventative, and/or developmental (Morrill, Oetting, & Hurst 1974). The failure of student affairs programming during the turmoil of the late 1960s and 1970s seemed, in large measure, to result from this reactive rather than a proactive stance. Another weakness is the difficulty in determining the extent to which the views of a student pressure group or publication represent those of larger student populations.

One major university appeared ready, in 1969, to accede to students clamoring for the removal of the ROTC from the campus when a systematic survey revealed that the overwhelming majority supported the presence of the ROTC (Hurst & Hubbell 1971). A third weakness is that this process assumes that students are both capable of systematically identifying all of their needs and describing and communicating them to the appropriate place for action. The track record in higher education refutes this assumption. Finally, this process predisposes a programming emphasis on the student, with the environmental component either overlooked or ignored (Creager 1968).

A third determinant that has traditionally influenced student affairs programming is political considerations and expediency. This factor has inhibited the growth of programming that had great potential, has fostered programs with little relevance or impact, and, occasionally, has led to the creation of appropriate and effective program interventions, all for irrelevant or noncritical reasons (Hurst, Weigel, Morrill, & Richardson 1973). A sexuality workshop, which is popular with students and empirically valid, is discontinued because of the discomfort of a key administrator; a minority student support program flounders as the result of inept leadership, but no change is made because a few minorities will oppose the decision and perhaps disrupt the administration; and an orientation program that fails repeated attempts to validate its impact on students is retained because it *appears* to be effective to administrators and it is impressive window dressing to campus visitors.

The relatively impotent status of student affairs in higher education today, then, in part at least, is the result, on the one hand, of programming growing out of political expediency, staff interest and skills, and responsiveness to student pressure groups, and, on the other hand, of generally ignoring a conceptual/theoretical foundation and systematic research-environmental assessment as the basis for day-to-day decision making and programming. This combination, a theoretical stance and a research/evaluation effort, is the prerequisite to providing an intentional direction for student affairs divisions, in particular, and the entire profession, in general.

A theoretical formulation provides the framework for observing, interpreting, understanding, and communicating about student be-havior. It also provides the framework for developing a program of interventions designed to facilitate student movement toward goal structures which are also derived from the theory. A theoretical formulation provides for hypotheses that, in turn, systematize and give structure to research, and it provides the framework within which surveys and evaluations of student characteristics may be understood and, eventually, even predicted. Finally, the theoreti-cal model is heuristic in sustaining an ever-increasing body of liter-ature and knowledge that provides substance and integrity to the identity of a profession.

Fortunately, a number of available theoretical models lend themselves well to the business of student affairs. Perry, Kohlberg, and Piaget advanced theories in which human characteristics, atti-tudes, beliefs, and behaviors are categorized and then conceptual-ized as stages in human development. In another useful approach, behaviors, attitudes, and beliefs associated with developmental lev-els are identified and conceptualized as tasks that provide meaning and structure to efforts to understand normal progress in the acquisition of those characteristics that are necessary for adequate interactions with the environment. This approach is represented by the work of Ericksen, Havighurst, and Chickering.

Chickering's Education and Identity

Chickering (1969) reviewed the body of research on adolescence and early adulthood available to him in the mid-1960s and concep-tualized seven major vectors of student development which he related to several major components of the typical college environ-ment. His survey included numerous authors' formulations of "developmental stages," "developmental tasks," "needs," and "ty-pologies." Chickering identified what he considered to be the com-mon elements running through all of these formulations, and then he defined these elements as his seven vectors. The first is achiev-ing competence: competence in the areas of the intellect, physical and manual skills, and social and interpersonal interactions. The second vector is managing emotions: becoming aware and then labeling affect. The two major emotions with which students have difficulty are aggression and sex. Becoming autonomous is the third vector; its central theme is emotional, financial, and physical independence and the recognition that interdependence is the capstone of autonomy.

Chickering's fourth vector, establishing identity, was described as being more than the aggregate of all the other vectors. It is an inner consistency of values, emotions, beliefs, and determinants of behavior. The fifth vector, freeing interpersonal relationships, builds on all the other vectors; it is evidenced by greater freedom and the likelihood to be spontaneous, accepting, tolerant of differences from self, intimacy, and individuality. Clarifying purposes is sixth; it includes occupational, marital, socioeconomic, avocational, and general life-style goals. It implies intentionality of direction in life. Finally, there is developing integrity, the last vector. It deals primarily with belief systems that provide at least a tentative guide to behavior. It includes development through three overlapping stages of humanizing values, personalizing values, and congruence of values and behaviors (Chickering 1969).

The utility of Chickering's conceptualization for developing, implementing, and evaluating student affairs functions and programming is not difficult to see. The seven vectors provide a standard against which the comprehensiveness of a student services program can be measured. The standard is useful also for determining the balance of program offerings and assessing possible reasons for existing imbalances. Planning for future developments can be accomplished more efficiently with these seven vectors in mind; and even the specific task of staff selection can become more systematic if the skills necessary for program implementation in each area are considered and efforts made to acquire staff whose interests and skills provide balance across all vectors.

A Schema for Program Planning

The impact of a conceptualization such as Chickering's is greatly enhanced if it is joined with a model for program-intervention strategies. Morrill et al. (1974) developed such a model and it describes three dimensions of intervention. They are target, purpose, and method. Figure 1 depicts the three major dimensions of the "CUBE" along with the components of each.

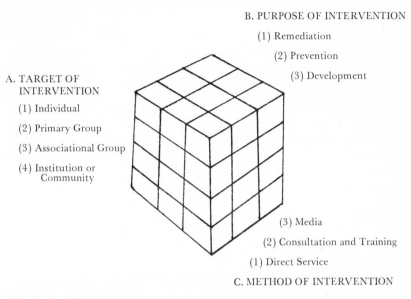

B. PURPOSE OF INTERVENTION

(1) Remediation

(2) Prevention

(3) Development

A. TARGET OF INTERVENTION

(1) Individual

(2) Primary Group

(3) Associational Group

(4) Institution or Community

(3) Media

(2) Consultation and Training

(1) Direct Service

C. METHOD OF INTERVENTION

Figure 1. Dimensions of counselor functioning. (From *Nine Outreach Programs* by W. H. Morrill, E. R. Oetting, & J. C. Hurst, eds. Fort Collins, Colorado: Colorado State University Press, 1974. Copyright 1972 by W. H. Morrill, E. R. Oetting, & J. C. Hurst. Reproduced by permission.)

A student affairs organization (or any of its divisions) that adopted a conceptual framework such as Chickering's and proceeded to build a program of services within that framework would be prepared to take the second step, to use a service delivery model, such as the CUBE, in the interest of both effectiveness and efficiency. For example, attending to the sixth vector, clarifying purposes, well might lead a group of professionals in the direction of establishing more comprehensive career development programming for students. It is at this point that the model for intervention strategies becomes most helpful. It facilitates consideration of whether the target for the career development programming should be individuals, primary groups (e.g., fraternities, sororities, classes, or dorm floors), or even, perhaps, the institution itself, through the elimination of academic major declaration policies, or the instituting of credit-producing classes in career exploration.

The purpose of programming may also be assessed with regard to whether the intervention should be planned for those students who seek assistance because they are bored, discouraged, or failing (remedial); efforts should be made to identify discrepancies between student interest and academic majors and to alert students to that discrepancy with the hope of avoiding difficulty (preventative); or the major efforts should be to assist those students already well along in their career development to find on-the-job experience, in order to facilitate the transition from college to the world of work (developmental).

The method of the intervention is also important to consider for it says much about efficiency as well as effectiveness in the delivery of services. The professional staff of an agency may (and usually does) choose to make direct interventions. In our example, the staff would run workshops, teach classes, write and distribute information, interpret tests, and other such activities, in the interest of assisting students to clarify their purposes through career development planning. It would also be possible, perhaps even desirable, however, for the professional staff to train and/or consult with others to prepare themselves to work in this same way with a much larger population of students. The staff of a career planning and placement center could be trained to help students to understand their interest inventories in selecting and pursuing an employment placement; and the staff could be trained also to use immediate video recall and interviewing skills to intervene with students who need the understanding. Training and consultation in a similar manner could occur with student paraprofessionals, interested faculty and staff, and certain administrators. Finally, a professional staff could choose to intervene to teach career development skills to students through media. Films and videotapes could be produced to do everything from create a readiness in students to actually walk them, in groups, through a step-by-step test interpretation. Other media interventions, such as programmed manuals and audio cassettes, could be designed to accomplish similar purposes.

The power and effectiveness of using a human development conceptualization, like that of Chickering's, in concert with an intervention model, like Morrill, Oetting, and Hurst's three-dimensional "CUBE," was anticipated by Oetting (1967); he proposed that student affairs professionals attend to whether students possess the skills, attitudes, and knowledge prerequisite to the maximum utilization of the college environment. Chickering's seven vectors of development adequately identify and describe the basic characteristics which students need to fully utilize their environment, and the CUBE provides the basis for systematic and comprehensive programming for the purpose of skill, attitude, and knowledge acquisition by those students.

Life-Planning Workshop: Examples of Theory in Action

Chickering (1969) clearly did not see the seven vectors of student development as discrete components. He acknowledged that achieving competence in the social and interpersonal area (vector 1) may well involve learning to manage emotions (vector 2) and the freeing of interpersonal relationships (vector 5). This nondiscreteness also applies to actual intervention programs. An intervention designed to deal primarily with the skills, attitudes, or knowledge associated with one vector may, in fact, overlap with those of another. A good example is the life-planning workshop (Hinkle & Thomas 1972) which was developed at the Colorado State University Counseling Center to deal with Chickering's vector 6, clarifying purposes. Evaluative research completed on the life-planning workshop (LPW) subsequently suggested that the experience also developed a greater internal locus of control in LPW participants. Internal versus external locus of control is a major factor in the developmental task of becoming autonomous (vector 3).

The LPW is a structured group workshop that usually requires about six hours to complete and involves participants in didactic and experiential activities which are designed to teach attitudes and skills associated with taking an active part in planning their futures.

The workshop format consists of sequential activities and exercises, beginning with the participants' involvement in identifying their present circumstance through the many roles they play in life, followed by directed fantasy work in which the participants divest themselves of their principal roles and, in the absence of expectations associated with the roles, proceed through a series of goal-preparation and goal-setting activities. A typical and special day in the future are described in detail according to the participants' wishes, obituaries about themselves are written, as they would like them to appear, and life inventories of positive and negative characteristics are compiled and related to whether these characteristics inhibit or facilitate the probability of the ideal future coming to pass. Finally, the participants complete their fantasy work by re-assuming their actual roles, setting actual long-range and short-range behavioral goals, which are designed to create the future they want, and then evaluating the workshop experience and its impact upon them as of the moment (Birney, Thomas, & Hinkle 1970).

At the conclusion of the workshop 85 percent of the participants stated that the LPW met their expectations which had been created by reading the goals of the workshop prior to the experience. One-third reported a better understanding of themselves in relation to their future plans. One-third indicated that they had established meaningful goals during the workshop and they expressed their intention of using the acquired goal-setting skills to set goals for themselves in the future. Follow-up meetings and questionnaires, from two weeks to seven months post-LPW, revealed that 80 percent of the respondents perceived the experience as "helpful" or "very helpful." Fifty percent of the respondents made decisions and took action toward future goals as a result of the workshop (Thomas 1973).

These evaluation results appear to support the LPW as an effective program for helping students to clarify purposes (vector 6). Additional research indicates an impact on participants' perceptions of self and others and of locus of control. Birney et al. (1970) used a semantic differential to investigate the effect of the LPW on saliency of self and others. A pre-post design revealed differences at the .05 level in the direction of greater saliency. The Concept-

Specific Anxiety Scale (Cole, Oetting, & Sharp 1969) also turned up pre-post differences in anxiety reduction, in connection with both the future and the discreteness of perceptions of self and others. Lynch, Ogg, and Christensen (1974) investigated the impact of the LPW, using Rotter's concept and instrument designed to assess internal versus external locus of control. They reported finding pre-post differences in participants at the .05 level, with greater internal locus of control following the workshop. In Chickering's third vector, becoming autonomous, increasing the internal locus of control and greater self-other differentiation are included as cues of progress. Although the LPW was not initially designed to contribute to this vector, research indicates that it does and that counseling center staff perceive the contribution as a "bonus" for their efforts. Students also are referred now to the LPW not just for future planning skills in particular, but, also, for internal-external locus of control concerns that emerge in therapy.

Originally, the LPW was an intervention that could be categorized in the CUBE as an individual, developmental, direct service activity. Its efficiency has been expanded over the years so that, now, the method is training and consultation (through paraprofessionals), the purpose includes remedial and preventative interventions (by counselors referring students with poorly differentiated self and other concepts and external locus of controls), and the target has been expanded to include associational groups (residence hall floors, fraternities, sororities, etc.). These changes have resulted intentionally from an assessment of service delivery potential as conceptualized in the CUBE.

EDUCATION THROUGH STUDENT INTERACTION

When student populations are assessed in terms of Chickering's seven vectors, deficits in development emerge, for both individual students and large groups of students who have common deficits that impair their ability to use their environment fully. These deficits may be classified into two categories: (a) a straightforward lack of skill or absence of a necessary attitude or value, and (b) a personal characteristic that interdicts and disrupts the expression or use of a skill, knowledge, or attitude.

An example of the first deficit is the inability of most students to work together effectively in small groups to process and learn academic material. Small-group discussion has great potential for enhancing the learning process, but most efforts distintegrate into bull sessions, are dominated by a few more aggressive members, or, at their worst, provide for a pooling of ignorance. The intervention for this type of deficit is usually designed to teach the student(s) the skill, attitude, or knowledge that is missing.

Achieving intellectual, physical, and interpersonal competence are probably listed first by Chickering because they are so basic to human development and the educational process. Indeed, intellectual competence is usually seen as coming within the purview of the academic faculty, so efforts of student affairs professionals in this area often are seen as suspect; and yet, the achievement of intellectual competence cannot be bounded artificially, as often is attempted in our institutions of higher education. In fall 1971, a member of the academic faculty approached a student affairs professional with group-interaction skills, and expressed frustration over the past failures of his students to work together productively to learn course material; he requested assistance in training students in a discussion technique. Over the next two years, various methods and techniques were piloted, modified, discarded, integrated, and tried again. The result of this extended effort was the Education through Student Interaction (ETSI) program, which was designed to teach participants the intellectual competence necessary for productive and systematic group discussion of academic material (Kitchener & Hurst 1974).

The ETSI discussion process consists of an overview, discussion, and evaluation. In the overview process, participants in the group come to a consensus on definitions of terms and a statement of the main theme. Discussion is the heart of the procedure and consists of four steps: (a) an analysis of the content through identification of main themes and subthemes; (b) the critique of authors' ideas from both cognitive and affective viewpoints of logic, evidence, assumptions, and validity; (c) the integration of the material with other information, beliefs, and attitudes; and (d) the application of the material to the participants' own lives on a cognitive and affective level. Evaluation directs the group in self-ratings on comprehension, communication, participation, climate, and presence of affect (Kitchener & Hurst 1975).

Initially, the student affairs staff directly implemented ETSI by going into the classroom to teach students the procedures. Eventually, as the program evolved under the influence of the CUBE, the staff came to consist of a senior staff member, a paraprofessional training faculty, and resource persons who trained the students in the classrooms. It is probably one of the few programs in which a student is involved in training faculty to, in turn, train students. A demonstration film was added to the training package to further enhance the efficiency and automation of the program. The target of the intervention was associational groups; the purpose was developmental in nature, and the method included both the training and consultation of others to actually implement the program with media assistance — the demonstration film.

The ETSI procedure was evaluated under five experimental conditions. A training workshop, the presence of a resource person, and a control group were the independent variables. The five experimental conditions consisted of different combinations of these three independent variables. Student evaluation of the ETSI procedure and self-reports of their experiences were one criterion measure; the Bale's group interaction observation system provided information on group interaction; and student performance on midterm and final exams was the other criterion measure (Bales 1950). The results suggest that the ETSI procedure, when accompanied by a training experience in the use of the procedure and/or the presence of a resource person during the discussion, leads to a significantly more favorable learning experience than no ETSI procedure. The ETSI program alone increased group interaction but it did not necessarily lead to a more favorable learning experience (Arbes & Kitchener 1974).

In sum, the ETSI procedure is an example of an intervention that successfully contributes to students' efforts to achieve intellectual competence, one of Chickering's vectors of development. It is also a good example of a program intervention that provides a critical skill and knowledge prerequisite to achieving intellectual competence and the full use of the learning environment.

THE TEST-ANXIETY PROGRAM

The second category of developmental deficit, a personal characteristic that interdicts and disrupts the expression or utilization of a skill, knowledge, or attitude, is illustrated by the inordinate level of anxiety that interferes with a student's ability to convey information in a test-taking situation. An intervention here might be directed toward the reduction of anxiety in order to free the student from the distractions that interfere with test performance.

High anxiety is recognized to be one of the chief obstacles to students' developmental progress on college and university campuses. Anxiety associated with tests, math, public speaking, and social situations is commonly reported. Usually, the origin of the anxiety was in a conditioning process. When present in inordinate amounts, the anxiety robs a person of the ability to interact productively with all aspects of his environment. Any characteristic that has been conditioned can also be counterconditioned, and the process of test-anxiety desensitization is one of the most extensively used and well-researched counterconditioning procedures. Paul and Eriksen (1964) reported the first success with test-anxiety desensitization and their findings have been supported by, among others, Emery and Krumboltz (1967), Johnson (1966), Spinelli (1972), and Suinn (1968). The test-anxiety program (TAP) at Colorado State University consists of a diagnostic intake to assure the appropriateness of the client and presenting problem, relaxation training, desensitization by counterconditioning through the presentation of a hierarchy of anxiety-invoking situations, and an assessment of treatment outcome.

Initially, the TAP program was rather small and limited to direct individual and remedial interventions by the senior staff. Now, the program heavily uses paraprofessionals in both the interviewing and treatment phases, is highly automated with audiotapes, and perhaps is the most valued offering in the Counseling Center by the faculty who are able to refer students for treatment, both individually and in groups, and for both preventative as well as remedial purposes. The TAP program and the parallel math-anxiety program (MAP) have come to play important roles in the removal of obstacles to achieving intellectual competence.

The social-anxiety and public-speaking-anxiety programs serve the same function in freeing students to achieve social and interpersonal competence.

Reflections

Colorado State University has developed programs in student affairs which are designed to deal with all but one of Chickering's vectors of development, and the one not attended to is significant. It is the seventh vector, developing integrity, which speaks to the development of a personally valid set of values and beliefs that has internal consistency and provides a guide to behavior. As a profession, we just now appear to be on the threshold of learning how to successfully teach personal integrity and the value systems it implies. Perhaps it is time that the fields of psychology and student affairs begin attending more carefully to this, one of the most important vectors of all.

REFERENCES

Arbes, W., & Kitchener, K. G. Faculty consultation: a study in support of Education through Student Interaction. *Journal of Counseling Psychology*, 1974, 21(1), 133-138.

Bales, R. F. *Interaction process analysis.* Cambridge, Mass.: Addison-Wesley, 1950.

Birney, D.; Thomas, L. E.; & Hinkle, J. E. Life planning workshops: discussion and evaluation. *Student Development Report*, vol. 8, no. 2. Fort Collins: Colorado State University, 1970.

Chickering, A. W. *Education and identity.* San Francisco: Jossey-Bass, 1969.

Cole, C.; Oetting, E.; & Sharp, B. Measurement of stimulus-specific anxiety. *Psychological Reports*, 1969, 25, 49-50.

Creager, J. A. Use of research results in matching students and colleges. *Journal of College Student Personnel*, 1968, 9(5), 312-319.

Emery, J. R., & Krumboltz, J. D. Standard versus individualized hierarchies in desensitization to reduce test anxiety. *Journal of Counseling Psychology*, 1967, 14, 204-209.

Hinkle, J. E., & Thomas, L. E. The life planning workshop: a future oriented program. *Journal of College Student Personnel*, 1972, 13(3), condensed on p. 275.

Hurst, J. C., & Hubbell, R. N. Does vociferation = validity? Comprehensive campus opinion on activist issues. *National Association of Student Personnel Administrators Journal*, 1971, 9, 250-257.

Hurst, J. C.; Weigel, R. G.; Morrill, W. H.; & Richardson, F. C. Reorganizing for human development in higher education: obstacles to change. *Journal of College Student Personnel*, 1973, 14, 10-15.

Johnson, S. M. The effects of desensitization and relaxation in the treatment of test anxiety. Master's thesis, Northwestern University, 1966.

Kitchener, K. G., & Hurst, J. C. Faculty consultation: an emerging role for the counseling psychologist. *Journal of Counseling Psychology*, 1974, 21(1), 127-132.

———. *Manual for Education through Student Interaction*. Fort Collins, Col.: Rocky Mountain Behavioral Science Institute, 1975.

Lynch, M. L.; Ogg, W. D.; & Christensen, M. G. The impact of the Life Planning Workshop on perceived locus of control. *Studies in Student Personnel*, no. 37. Manhattan: Center for Student Development, Kansas State University, 1974.

Morrill, W. H.; Oetting, E. R., & Hurst, J. C., eds. *Nine outreach programs*. Fort Collins: Colorado State University Press, 1974.

Oetting, E. R. A developmental definition of counseling psychology. *Journal of Counseling Psychology*, 1967, 14, 382-385.

Paul, G. L., & Eriksen, C. W. Effects of test anxiety on "real life" examinations. *Journal of Personality*, 1964, 32, 480-494.

Spinelli, P. R. Programming for academic anxiety: the use of short-term desensitization procedures within a university counseling center. Paper presented at American Psychological Association, Honolulu, 1972.

Suinn, R. M. The desensitization of test-anxiety by group and individual treatment. *Behavior Research and Therapy*, 1968, 6, 385-387.

Thomas, L. E. *Life planning workshop: evaluation summary*. Fort Collins: University Counseling Center, Colorado State University, 1973.

Comments on Chapter 4

Ursula Delworth

I am delighted to see Chickering's vectors proposed as a framework to develop, implement, and evaluate student affairs programming. Chickering has done us a great service in pulling together much valuable, but previously underutilized, theory and research, and presenting a well-integrated description of seven major vectors of student development. His work, which includes research evidence on student change on the vectors over the college years, provides a solid base for research efforts on our own campuses.

Hurst's call for programming based on a theoretical stance and systematic research-environmental assessment is one that we need to hear and act upon. Only with such a basis can we rationally and appropriately incorporate such factors as staff interest and skills and expressed needs/pressures from students into a programming plan. The use of the dimensions of counselor functioning (the CUBE) is a helpful process for moving from Chickering's framework toward the development of specific programs. It is also a helpful means for staff who want to assess where they are and where they want to go in terms of programming.

The three Colorado State programs, described by Hurst, sound solidly developed and effective. His attention to both absence of skill and factors that inhibit the use or learning of skills is important. It is intriguing to think of evaluating programs on vectors other than the primary one toward which the program was aimed, as done with the life planning workshop. I would like to see the

Colorado State University group incorporate into their evaluation some measure that might speak more directly to expected changes in terms of specific vectors, as Chickering has done using scales from the Omnibus Personality Inventory (OPI).

While I like Hurst's attempt to operationalize the seven vectors in programming, I do not think such an effort can proceed effectively without attention to Chickering's second area of conceptualization: his conditions for impact on campus (see my reactions to Widick and Simpson's paper). Even such well-designed programming efforts as Hurst describes may be doomed to fail in terms of long-range impact unless the college is moving in positive directions that are congruent with the changes induced by the programs. Can such efforts as ETSI succeed in teaching intellectual competence if the teaching and evaluation method (vector 3) used by the instructor is not compatible with the skills and attitudes being taught through ETSI? That is, do students really care about integrating and applying ideas if the instructor's course examination focuses solely on fact? And, do such methods, even if they are used consistently in one class for teaching and evaluation, carry over to other academic experiences, if they are never again discussed and reinforced?

It is more simple, but probably ultimately futile, to think of enhancing growth on the seven vectors through specific programming efforts *without* first assessing the possibility for impact in terms of the six environmental conditions proposed by Chickering. We need, then, to study Chickering's conditions carefully, research them on our own campuses, and aim our strongest intervention efforts toward creating the kind of positive and congruent environments within which our specific programs have the best chance of success.

Roger A. Myers

Hurst began his current paper by citing reasons for the "failure of student affairs programming during the turmoil of the late 1960s and 1970s" with which I do not completely agree. As Hurst saw it, the "failure" resulted from the absence of theory to guide programming, and that absence led to a reactive style which was born of staff responses to student demands. Though this view may be true, my version of the difficulties of that era is that no one ever considered student personnel work, or its goal, student development, sufficiently important to warrant a major investment of resources. I am reminded of my colleague, Adkins (1971), who, while reviewing Ginzberg's (1971) lament of the "failure" of the school guidance profession, uncovered the fact that there were just slightly more guidance counselors in the United States than there were airline stewardesses. Just as the governors of our schools tried to resolve post-Sputnik anxiety with too-little too-late, so have powerful proponents of student development always been stingy with student development resources in our universities, and the greater the university, the more stingy.

It is probably not important to dwell on reasons for impotence (at least, that is what experts in sexual dysfunction tell us) but I want to offer another opinion that was stimulated by Hurst's paper: The student personnel professional's preference for direct methods of intervention (cited by Hurst) coupled with her/his preference for *individual targets* and *remedial purposes* has had a great deal to do with our lack of impact on higher education. The technology of psychotherapy has been our main bow string for most of our existence and that technology is, I submit, incompatible with the other technologies of higher education, despite the occasional similarity of goals.

Hurst's central point is a good one: Working on student development has been hampered by the lack of thinking about student development. Chickering's thinking has obviously served to ameliorate that lack. Hurst and his colleagues have used Chickering's thinking creatively to conceptualize the programming at their service, and though they were not the first to base programming for student development on developmental theory, their results may be the most pervasive and successful. The notion that specific service offerings should be designed with reference to what is suspected about developmental tasks of students is very advanced. Just imagine what our universities would be like if their other functions (e.g., teaching, administration, and certification) were guided by that patently intelligent notion!

The cubist view of intervention (Morrill, Oetting, & Hurst 1974) has been a valuable aid to my thinking about student personnel services since I first learned about it. My students are intrigued by it, though they frequently ask about what goes inside the cubes. In his paper, Hurst has illustrated the content of a few more of the cubes and, given time, I am sure he will illustrate more.

Hurst's description of the life planning workshop (LPW) and its modifications illustrates a meaningful juxtaposition of the cube and Chickering's vectors. How one theory can help decide the what and another can guide the how is clearly portrayed in this example. It is rare indeed that either the what or the how can be enlightened by theorizing; the combination must surely be a first in the student personnel world.

I am also pleased by the way the concept of directed fantasy was used in the LPW to serve the clarifying purposes vector. Though many programs use similar procedures, not many program designers think of life planning in terms of fantasy. It is my estimate that their enterprises would be enhanced if they did. To some extent, Ginzberg, Ginsburg, Axelrad, and Herma (1951) gave fantasy a bad name by tying it to the childhood parts of life planning. My sense is that many of the current life-planning and decision-making schemes specifically devalue fantasy as an appropriate exercise in favor of activity that is viewed as more rigorous. As I see it, fantasy is a major mechanism for trying out various aspects of self in a variety of probable (or improbable) futures, and guiding such fantasy is an intervention that deserves more thoughtful attention.

I find it encouraging that an intervention designed to enhance development on the clarifying purposes vector was followed by beneficial side effects on the becoming autonomous vector. People have frequently expected but not always found the effect (Thompson, Lindeman, Clack, & Bohn 1970; Gurman 1975). It is yet another tribute to the way Hurst and company do things.

In his report on the Education through Student Interaction program, test-anxiety program, and math-anxiety program, Hurst has used Chickering's achieving competence vector to help rationalize some very useful remedial interventions, and the Morrill, Oetting, and Hurst cube to explain some unique methods of service delivery. Fascinating as these reports are, I am interested that our resident cubist has not yet used the insights from these programs to move along the purpose dimension with programming for the prevention of deficits along the achieving competence vector, and for the development of higher level skills in this area. Could the reason be, as Hurst recognized, that "intellectual competence is usually seen as coming within the purview of the academic faculty, so efforts of student affairs professionals in this area often are seen as suspect"?

To recognize that students who do not have group-discussion skills are subjected to pedagogical demands calling for such skills is a valuable beginning. The logical first step is to intervene to make up the deficit. But a true cubist would not stop there. Concern about prevention and higher level development requires a change in target, from the poor deficit-ridden student to the professor who creates the deficit by subjecting students to learning experiences for which they are not equipped.

To be aware that conditioned fear impairs student performance helps to get some students counterconditioned and performing better. But how about the original conditioning and the management of the reward system that brought about the maladaptive response in the first place? Of course students are more accessible targets than faculty and curricula and our prospects for changing them seem remote. However, if only . . . .

REFERENCES

Adkins, W. R. Review of *Career guidance: who needs it, who provides it, who can improve it,* by E. Ginzberg. *Teachers College Record,* 1971, 73(2), 328-332.

Ginzberg, E. *Career guidance: who needs it, who provides it, who can improve it.* New York: McGraw-Hill, 1971.

Ginzberg, E.; Ginsburg, S. W., Axelrad, S.; & Herma, J. L. *Occupational choice: an approach to a general theory.* New York: Columbia University Press, 1951.

Gurman, C. Vocational maturity, self-concept, and locus of control in high school students. Doctoral dissertation, Columbia University, 1975.

Morrill, W. H.; Oetting, E. R.; & Hurst, J. C., eds. *Nine outreach programs.* Fort Collins: Colorado State University Press, 1974.

Thompson, A. S.; Lindeman, R. H.; Clack, S.; & Bohn, M. J., Jr. The educational and career exploration system: field trial and evaluation in Montclair High School. New York: Teachers College, Columbia University, 1970. Mimeographed.

Douglas H. Heath

I would amend Hurst's analysis of why student personnel and counseling programs have not had much impact on faculty and why there is an uneasy truce between student development and faculty types. A persuasive model of maturing that articulates and integrates the typical goals of the student personnel staff *and* of a typical faculty has not been presented. Chickering's model is a first step that maps some goals, but I feel it is incomplete and probably not persuasive in detail to faculty. However, the strength of Hurst's approach is that by using Chickering's model he and others have more self-consciously sought to organize and innovate educational procedures to further growth on such vectors.

My research on the effects of becoming educated suggests a somewhat more complicated model of development. It adequately comprehends all of the effects found from psychological tests and focused interviews as well as the effects cited by most educational philosophers of what should happen when a youth is becoming powerfully educated.[1]

What is of immediate interest are the types of maturing that are and are *not* specified by Chickering's model. Insofar as his model incompletely specifies student development, Hurst's organization of counseling resources based on his model may then tend to ignore key aspects of student development. The correspondence is not always precise, but I suggest that becoming aware of and labeling feelings refers to symbolization of self and values; becoming autonomous as defined by Chickering refers to all personality sectors; establishing identity means integrating and stabilizing one's self-concept; freeing of interpersonal relations refers to allocentric, integrated, and autonomous relations; clarifying purposes refers to symbolizing values; developing integrity may mean integration of self and of one's values. I have argued elsewhere that achieving competence in any complex and demanding situation depends to a considerable extent on the traits associated with maturity (Heath 1977). The following attributes of student development are *not* explicitly comprehended by Chickering's vectors: symbolization, allocentricism, integration and stabilization of cognitive skills, symbolization of one's personal relations, allocentric self and value development, and stabilization of one's values and personal relations.

Chickering's model may not appeal therefore to many faculty who are most concerned with cognitive maturation and only secondarily, if at all, with value maturation. Most faculty ignore completely the maturation of a student's self and personal relationships, which frequently are the focus of counselors and other student development specialists. Because our models of student development have not clearly articulated the fundamental *systemic* nature of healthy development, faculty fail to understand the intrinsic relation of academic learning *and* self, value, and interpersonal maturation. And because counselors tend to underplay the adaptive role of cognitive skill maturation for coping, faculty and counselors too frequently find no common basis for working with and depending upon the other. The effort by Hurst and his colleagues to facilitate maturation of cognitive skills in small-group discussion formats is an excellent illustration of how counselors might be of more direct assistance to faculty, most of whom are quite naive psychologically about how such cognitive skill maturation can be furthered.

If we can accurately map the principal types of students' potential growth in experiencing school, then we can turn more systematically to the issue of what, in principle, are the types of learning experiences that are most conducive to producing what types of effects.

I have tried to sketch for one college the types of environmental factors that contribute differentially to growth in each of the dimensions and personality sectors of my model, but the specific types of factors must surely vary from one institution to the next (Heath 1968). Many of the factors found to have a special potency for producing allocentric maturing (movement from narcissism or egocentrism to other-centeredness), for example, are not readily manipulable by counselors; yet, if counselors were more self-consciously aware of the factors, they might have more of an impact on institutional policymaking. For example, at one male college, allocentric maturing was most facilitated by, in decreasing order, the men's relationships with their female friends, roommates, male friends, type of student perceived to be dominant on the campus, and living arrangements. Sensitivity to such factors might provide, then, a basis for questioning the advisability of building dormitories with single rooms, which eliminate the possibility of students learning how to accommodate to another person over an extended period of time. Such results also suggest that an important focus of a counseling center might be to help young people develop communication skills to create more meaningful interpersonal relationships, skills, I find, that increasingly more students seem to be deficient in. Or one might study the modal student type that is attracted to the college to determine how it might affect the maturing of the student body more generally. While these are more molar types of factors and possible interventions than Hurst tends to propose, my hunch is that, in the long run, they may be more critical institutional-type factors with which counselors should be preoccupied rather than the single one-shot type of interventions or courses whose effects are not likely to be stabilized and unlikely to be transferred to situations other than the counseling program in which they were presumably learned.

NOTE

1. See my chapter in this volume for a discussion of the elements of the model; a brief description is given in my comments on Widick and Simpson's chapter.

REFERENCES

Heath, D. H. *Growing up in college: maturity and liberal education.* San Francisco: Jossey-Bass, 1968.
———. *Maturity and competence: a transcultural view.* New York: Gardner Press (Wiley), 1977.

A Cognitive-Developmental Model of Career Development: An Adaptation of the Perry Scheme

L. Lee Knefelkamp and Ron Slepitza

The development of the career model presented in this paper is best understood within the context of the assumptions that underlie the work. Briefly, these assumptions are as follows.

1. One of the primary identity issues of the college student and young adult is career development—the process of career choice and decision making as it relates to one's concept of self.

2. The field and concepts of career development have continually expanded to encompass new contributions to the views of career development. That expansion has resulted in an increased awareness and appreciation of the complexities of career development as a process and the need to focus on process elements in career counseling.

3. In career development, the individual always has been the primary focus. The career counselor has needed to understand the individual's needs, abilities, interests, personality type, and identity factors so that appropriate career development work could take place.

4. It is now appropriate to expand the definition of process in career development and to add an additional individual difference factor for the counselor to consider, that of the level of cognitive complexity with which the student approaches the career development task.

Career development models have often considered the importance of process, whether process was viewed in relation to decision making (Ginzberg, Ginsburg, Axelrod, & Herma 1951; Tiedeman & O'Hara 1963) or with reference to the developmental process over the life span (Super 1957). These views of process, however, do not specify the *cognitive* processes used by individuals in organizing, integrating, and using career-related information and activities. Jepsen (1974) suggested that a next logical step for the field would be the use of the stage concept from cognitive developmental psychology.

Such cognitive models (Piaget 1951; Kohlberg 1969; Perry 1970) assume that stages or levels of development are sequential and hierarchical in nature and represent qualitative differences in the ways individuals approach the same task or issue (Rest 1973). Thus, level of cognitive processing becomes an important variable for the counselor to consider in presenting career information and decision-making models.

5. A cognitive-developmental career model would be descriptive of the student, but it would have implications for how to promote developmental growth along the continuum of the model (Rest 1973; Widick, Knefelkamp, & Parker 1975).

6. A simple overlay of an existing cognitive model would not be sufficient. A new or adapted model was necessary that was specific to career development as an identity issue.

With the above assumptions as a base, the authors turned to the theoretical work of Perry (1970) for a cognitive model that was relevant to college students and their identity issues. Based upon research conducted with Harvard undergraduates, Perry and his associates derived a cognitive stage framework focusing upon intellectual/ethical development. The Perry model comprises nine positions or stages, each representing a qualitatively different mode of thinking about the nature of knowledge. The stages tend to be reflected in the students' perceptions of the teacher's role and his own role as learner. The nine positions may be grouped into three more abstract categories of dualism, relativism, and commitment within relativism.

Although the Perry scheme was created by design to describe the development of a student's reasoning about knowledge, it is also feasible that such a scheme can be viewed as a general process model. As such, it may provide a descriptive framework for viewing the development of an individual's reasoning about many aspects of the world. Support for this idea has been provided by

Harvey, Hunt, and Schroder (1961) in their cognitive developmental model of "conceptual systems." In this model, an individual has many conceptual systems or cognitive structures for a variety of "content" areas—for example, knowledge, values, significant others—and each conceptual system progresses through a sequence of developmental stages. It is the authors' contention that, since individuals have a conceptual system for career, career counseling, and career decision making, the Perry scheme can be adapted to the development of an individual's thinking about these important subjects.

The New Model

AREAS OF QUALITATIVE CHANGE

In the creation of the career model, we have relied most heavily upon the conceptual contribution of Perry (1970). However, Harvey et al. (1961), Kohlberg (1969), Loevinger and Wessler (1970), and Rest (1973) also have provided empirical support for the idea of the existence of a series of qualitative changes that make up a developmental sequence. The results of our interview data and instrument responses led us to emphasize the following nine areas of qualitative change:

1. *Locus of control*—the source to which the students turn to define themselves and their environment. We found that students progress from a position of control based upon external factors (e.g., parental admonitions, job market pressures, or results of assessment instruments) to a position where information is processed predominantly through their internal reference points.

2. *Analysis*—the ability of the individual to see a subject in its diverse perspectives, to break down the subject into its component parts. As students develop their analytic ability they increasingly become able to see cause and effect relations.

3. *Synthesis*—the ability of the individual to integrate the diverse components of a subject into a complex whole. Because the ability is more complex than analysis, students did not exhibit the factor until they were rather cognitively mature (stages 6 and 7) in their approach to the world.

4. *Semantic structure*—specifically, the nature of the verbs and qualifiers used by students in their written and spoken expressions. In this ability, students progress from a semantic structure characterized by absolutes to a more open semantic structure that allows for greater alternatives and greater use of qualifiers and modifiers.

5. *Self-processing*—the ability to examine oneself and be cognizant of one's defining factors. In its emergence and development, this variable closely parallels that of analysis.

6. *Openness to alternative perspectives*—the extent to which the individual is aware of and recognizes the legitimacy of other points of view and possible explanations, even if the student differs with those perspectives.

7. *Ability to assume responsibility*—the willingness of the student to accept the consequences of his/her actions or decisions regardless of unknown and unforeseen interfering factors.

8. *Ability to take on new roles*—the ability of students to expand their repertoires of abilities and behaviors within the contexts of new roles or activity demands. Students move from a position of not seeking new role or activity opportunities, to a seeking and mastery of them, to an ability to look forward confidently to new opportunities for self within new roles; expansion of old roles and new activities increases as role taking increases.

9. *Ability to take risks with self*—closely related to role-taking ability, this area refers to the individual's increasing ability to risk self-esteem when new and appropriate demands are made. The individual has a fairly confident sense of self that enables him to focus on new learnings and experiences rather than on whether the ego will be damaged.

Figure 1 illustrates the nine variables with respect to the individual and a career.

DESCRIPTIONS OF CATEGORY AND STAGE

These nine variables have been used to create an adapted nine-position career model that describes the movement of a student from a simplistic categorical view, to a more complex pluralistic view of career, career counseling, and career decision making. A student's view of these areas affects the way he/she will approach

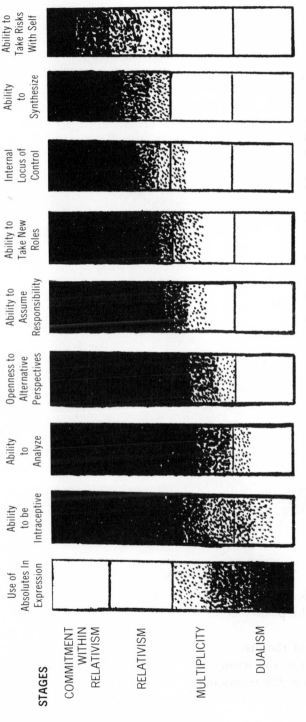

Figure 1. A process model of human development: Areas of qualitative change. Adapted from R. Slepitza & L. L. Knefelkamp. Perry's scheme of intellectual development: An adaptation to career counseling. Paper presented at the American Psychological Association Meeting, Chicago, 1975.

the entire career, life-planning process. It is our contention that as students move upward along the scheme they exhibit a more integrated understanding of the interrelation of personal identity, values, and the entire career life-planning process, and hence they can make more satisfying career commitments.

Dualism. The first stage is characterized by simplistic, dichotomous thinking about the career life-planning area. Lower-stage dualistic-thinking students are almost exclusively controlled by externals in their environment. Adhering to the belief that there is only one right career for them, they tend to turn to parents, teachers, counselors, interest inventories, the job market and economy, as well as to such factors as prestige, power, and financial reward, to define both self and the right career decisions. These students lack the ability both to analyze and to synthesize material and they exhibit only minimal processing of self in relation to the career decision-making process. For them, the career decision-making process exists only to the extent that they can turn to authorities to provide the right answers. These authorities may be the counselor, the interest inventory, or any other external factor that could solve the student's dilemma.

Stage 1. The student has no dissonance in making a career decision because of absolute reliance on the suggestions of external authorities. No self-processing is evident. The student sees only one possible right career. The counselor is viewed as authority.

Stage 2. The possibility of right/wrong career decisions is beginning to be recognized. This possibility causes anxiety and leads to dissonance in the decision-making process. The student has only a minimal understanding of a decision-making process and only to the extent outlined by the counselor.

There should be only one right career. At this stage, processing by the student is only minimal and takes the form of dichotomous thinking. The possibility of right or wrong career decisions creates dissonance.

Because of the dissonance produced by the realization that others have made the wrong career decision, the student views the counselor and the counseling process somewhat more tentatively.

Either the counselor as the authority or the test as the authority should provide the right answer. The process that the counselor outlines for the student must be simple, straightforward, and clear for the student to accept the counselor and the decision-making process.

Multiplicity. As students grow cognitively more complex, they become cognizant of the possibility of making right and wrong choices. This increased complexity creates increased dissonance, and in an attempt to eliminate or reduce the possibility of wrong decisions, students turn to the decision-making process provided by the counselor. The locus of control, however, still rests on those external factors listed earlier. Students are now able to include a variety of factors into their considerations and, consequently, they are able to analyze factors important to career decision making in greater detail. They begin to see cause and effect relations between these multiple factors and right career decisions. As the student matures in multiplicity, the decision-making process expands to include a wider variety of topics that carry different degrees of weight. It is important to note that the student shifts from a faith that one right career exists, which can be discovered somehow, to a reliance on the *right* decision-making process to yield the right career. The student sees the counselor's role as providing that decision-making process.

Stage 3. Students realize a greater possibility of making right/wrong career decisions. This realization leads to increased conflict and anxiety and recognition that the process of making a right decision may be more complex than originally perceived. The student's processing expands to include a greater self vis-à-vis others. The student is ready to begin elements of analysis in the decision-making process.

Students assume the attitude that others seem to have found the right career, and that they will be able to as well. Underlying this affirmation is the converse doubt that others have made the wrong decisions and they may also. The educational/vocational decision-making process takes on a future orientation, a hopefulness that in the end a good decision will be made.

The right decision can be made through the combination of the educational/vocational decision-making process and the assistance of the counselor. The authority is the process. The student views the counselor's role as providing the process and his/her role as participating in the process. Because the process includes such dimensions as values, information, and setting priorities, the student becomes aware of the quantity of components that can influence the decision-making process. Thus the student begins to analyze the career decision in more self-dimensions. The emerging focus becomes how the self and self-values relate to choosing a career.

Stage 4. For the student in stage 4 right/wrong decisions are based on a more complex weighing of the components discovered in stage 3. Multiple possibilities and multiple good choices exist. Students perceive that with all of the quantity that exists they need to set priorities in terms of both internal and external sources. The decision-making process becomes a complex weighing of factors with the hope that, in some cases, the right career exists and it can be found through the process.

In stage 4 the self is still not a prime mover in the decision-making process. Elements of self, however, need to be included with external factors in the decision-making process. The self is subordinated to the influence of test, counselors, friends, parents, economy, and other external influences. The student does not yet accept full responsibility for choosing. At this stage, the counselor is seen as the source for helping the student to set priorities.

Relativism. As individuals enter relativism they experience what can be referred to as the primary flip: the shift of the locus of control from a basically external reference to a predominantly internal point. For the student in dualism and multiplicity, teachers, parents, counselors, and other authority figures have been the prime resources in the decision-making process. When the student moves into relativism, these influences continue to be helpful resources but the student now becomes the prime focus of the decision making process. As students reach these higher levels of processing, they are able to use the skills of analysis in their approach to the career decision-making process. Thus, they establish for themselves, essentially, a self-created decision-making process that is tailored to meet their peculiar needs and interests. Each individual is able to see a wide variety of legitimate possibilities and to detach himself appropriately from the decision-making process in order to proceed in an objective manner. Individuals in this category are capable of understanding and examining a variety of career possibilities, dealing with the positive and negative elements of each, and seeing themselves in a variety of examined roles. As students anticipate making career commitments, they are able to synthesize the many diverse and complex components of the process and to form them into individual resolutions of the process. Thus, they are able to accept responsibility for their career decisions.

Stage 5. Stage 5 is an exploring-doing stage. It begins with a recognition of multiple possibilities and ends with the need to create personal order in and clarification of the decision-making process.

The self is now the prime mover in the decision-making process. Students own the decisions. Although the process differs little from that used in stage 4, students now tailor the process to meet their own needs. They create the process with the assistance of the counselor, who is now viewed as an experienced, knowledgeable souce and not as unquestioned authority. The student has the ability to detach and analyze self and to examine alternatives systematically.

Stage 6. The student begins to tire of all the legitimate alternatives realized in stage 5. Alternatives that were seen once as freeing in their quantity and legitimacy are now experienced as chaotic. The student at stage 6 realizes that the only way to order the chaos is to choose; however, the student is not yet ready to commit the self to a career and, thus, he/she accepts the necessity of making a commitment but is not yet ready to do so. In many respects, stage 6 is a reflective stage enabling the student (1) to establish ties between career and self; (2) to think vicariously about the consequences of commitments to be made; and (3) to confront the reality of the responsibility of commitment as the student's alone. The student sees the counselor's role as one of helping him/her to engage in the reflective process. Although areas of career interest are closely linked to the concept of self, students still lack awareness of the implications of their own styles and, thus, they continue to define career in terms of traditionally defined roles.

Commitment within Relativism. At this point students begin to assume increased responsibility for the career decision-making process; they are not only able to analyze the complexities of the issues in the process, but also to synthesize the various factors to form their own decision-making schemes. They begin to realize and experience that choosing a career is a personal commitment of self. At first, this commitment is experienced as the feared narrowing of their world but, later, commitment is often seen as the beginning of the expansion into a new world. Students experience the joy of watching themselves integrate self with what once was perceived as polarized choices. A second cognitive flip appears to occur when students experience a comprehensive integration of who and what they are with the styles of their interactions with the environment. The theme, "What I am about," flows through the conversations and interviews of these upper-stage individuals. Students begin to see their roles as an integration of who they are as persons and what that stance means in terms of personal values, purposes, and identity. This stance becomes highly individualistic when it is related to career. Career identity and self-identity become more closely intertwined. While forging their career identities, students forge for themselves roles in the world that extend beyond the confines of simple job descriptions. Each student's values, thoughts, and behaviors become more consistent and, at the same time, the student is open to new challenges from and changes in the environment.

Stage 7. Individuals in stage 7 experience the integration of the self and the career role. Initially, the student has a fear of narrowing, of being confined and defined by the role. However, in the latter phase of stage 7, the student experiences the realization that he/she defines the role. This realization leads to an affirmation of self and career and a new focus on individual style of how one acts, how one fulfills the role.

Stage 8. The individual in stage 8 begins to experience all the consequences of the commitments made in stage 7. The consequences are both pleasant and unpleasant, anticipated and unexpected. The consequences present new challenges to the definition of self and to the continuation of the commitments made. Individuals in this stage begin to experience truly the meaning of their commitments; and they are challenged to clarify once again their own values, purposes, and identity. Individuals are challenged to affirm who they are, what it is they believe, and how they will act in the world. Individuals in this stage experience a high degree of integration among all aspects of their lives.

Stage 9. Stage 9 represents a further expansion of one's self-created role. Individuals have a firm knowledge of who they are and how that knowledge affects all aspects of life. Individuals at stage 9 have an acute awareness of the interactive effect they have on other people, places, and things. They are aware of the effects they have on others and the effects that others have on them.

They constantly seek new ways to express what they are about, and what that means for them. They are characterized by an active seeking out and processing of information from the environment, taking on more risks to their self esteem in an effort to fully attain their potentials. They seek new things, new challenges, new ways to interact, but their actions are tempered by an insightful realization of the potential positive and negative effects of their actions on self and others.

Supporting Research

PREDOMINANT STAGES IN THE POPULATION

Work with the model presented in the preceding section has been conducted at both the University of Maryland and The Ohio State University from 1974 to 1976. Data have been collected through written protocols and in-depth interviews. The data reported in the accompanying table collected at both schools reveal the predominant stages of the listed populations in respect to the career model.

Population   Stages

University freshmen and sophomores 2, 3
University seniors 3, 4, 5
First-year M.A. students in educational
    psychology 3, 4, 5
Advanced graduate students in educational
    psychology 6, 7

THE OHIO STATE REPORT

In 1975, research was conducted at The Ohio State University to identify patterns of student behaviors in career decision-making classes and to examine whether those behaviors were characteristic of cognitive stage level.[1] The thirty-five students in the study were all enrolled in career development classes. A written protocol from which career development stage classifications could be attained was administered to the students. One aspect of the study required the class facilitators, all graduate students in counseling psychology, to complete rating forms on which they characterized each student according to six dimensions (student expectations of the class, student motivation, student attitude toward class structure, student view of career choice, self-awareness, and expectations about the role of the facilitators).

The results of the facilitators' evaluations of the students support the existence of the areas of qualitative change, which were the basis for the career model. The evaluations also support the developmental movement within each area, such as from dualism to relativism. In the following data ($N = 35$), dualists (D) are stage 2 and below and transition (T) people are stage 3(4).

Area: Student Motivation

A. Student motivated to deal with career planning by external pressures — parents, peers, college rules, or grade in the course (D = 68%, T = 33%).

B. Student motivated to deal with career planning from an "internal need" (D = 32%, T = 67%).

Area. Class Structure

A. Student learned most when class was fairly well structured; student liked clear rules and guidelines (D = 68%, T = 50%).

B. Student learned most when class was fairly unstructured and students were allowed by self-direction to explore; student enjoyed activities that required initiative and self-defined learning goals (D = 26%, T = 50%).

C. Student did not get involved (D = 5%, T = 0%).

Area: Self-Awareness

A. Student is relatively unaware of self and career alternatives (D = 21%, T = 0%).

B. Somewhat aware (D = 57%, T = 67%).

C. Highly aware (D = 21%, T = 33%).

Area: Student View of Career Choice

A. Student tended to believe in "right" career for self; student tended to depend on the "right" sources to identify the "right" career (D = 47%, T = 0%).

B. Student tended to believe that many careers could meet their abilities; student felt that the actual career choice was an awesome task and that he/she needed much more explanations and experience so the wrong choice would not be made (D = 15%, T = 13%).

C. Student tended to believe that many careers could meet their abilities; student perceived the need to choose among alternatives and to make initial commitments so he/she could more actively control his future (D = 36%, T = 87%).

Issues to Consider

Our involvement with the creation of this model and our attempt to answer the questions it raises have given us a greater appreciation of the complexities of the career development dilemma in students' lives. It is our conclusion that Perry's cognitive developmental scheme was an excellent springboard for our work. However, a simple overlay of Perry on the career development issue is not sufficient for the task. What is needed is an adapted model—one that encompasses the concepts of cognitive developmental theory and the unique and fascinating complexities of career development. Our work has led us to focus on the following issues.

Difference between Choice and Commitment. It is appropriate for the theorist and practitioner to ask what happens to individuals who make career decisions at various points along the continuum of development presented in the model. What are the essential differences between a career choice made in dualism and a commitment made within relativism? How are those differences operationalized in terms of the individual's interaction with the environment and the satisfaction derived from such interactions? According to Bodden (1970) and Bodden and Klein (1972), increased cognitive complexity yield higher levels of congruence between occupation choice and personality choice. According to Holland (1966) this congruence yields greater satisfaction.

Movement from External to Internal Locus of Control. The results of our first two years' research tend to indicate that the prime factor separating the dualists from the relativists is locus of control. Individuals at each end of the continuum are confronted with the uncertainty and confusion of making career decisions in a complex society. The primary difference among the individuals is found in the source to which the individual turns to deal with this uncertainty. Individuals at the dualist end of the continuum need to reduce the anxiety and confusion of choice by the discovery of the "truth." In seeking such a discovery, the individual turns to external reference points to define the "right" choice. The students at the middle and upper ends of the continuum consider external factors but also depend on self when meeting this same crisis. Such individuals are able to make decisions within the framework of doubt and risks and to assume responsibility for the consequences of such decisions. The dualistic-thinking student is unable to assume such responsibility or to take such risks.

The Fear of Narrowing and the Sense of Loss. In investigating how individuals approached the task of making commitments, we discovered a rather interesting paradox. In coming to commitment, students experienced the narrowing and associated fear and regret in choosing one alternative from among many. Indeed, a true sense of loss was frequently expressed. It is true that commitment to one course of action is not to choose other courses of action. Yet, in the ramifications of those commitments, we found that students experienced that what was once perceived as a narrowing became an opening that encompassed many aspects of the self. What was once regret became affirmation.

New Catechism Phenomenon. As we examined more and more

of our data we became aware of a phenomenon we had not anticipated, that of the students parroting frequently heard career development maxims—the new catechism—when responding to the
career protocols. It is a difficult task to distinguish between a
statement that is truly relativistic and one that is written by a
strict dualist who has memorized the current "truth" (e.g., "there
is no right career for anyone," or "many factors must be considered when choosing a career"). The phenomenon raises challenging
questions: What method of data collection is most appropriate for
guarding against this problem? How can one design career development interventions that foster student development and not simply the learning of a new catechism?

Description to Prescription. The movement from a descriptive
model of student career development to prescriptive interventions
designed to foster movement along the model is a step to be taken
with deliberate care and caution. We see the need for continued
work in the following areas. (1) The model should be tested on
various populations and with studies of a longitudinal nature.
(2) The variables of qualitative change need further specification
and validation. (3) A reliable, valid, and efficient instrument should
be developed that will enable practitioners to place students along
the developmental continuum. (4) Staff development and counselor education programs are necessary to enable the counselor to
work within the concepts of the model to promote developmental
growth.

Conclusion

The model and the data presented in this article represent only our
initial efforts at confronting the task of developing an accurate
and useful career decision-making model. It is important to us that
our work be viewed in the context of previous work in career development and as a logical next step that builds on that development. And it is always useful to remember that students manage
to remain larger than our categories; it is the practitioner who is
most helped by descriptive models. We remain encouraged by the

results of the first two years and their potential usefulness to students of student development and practitioners of career development.

NOTE

1. The authors acknowledge the contributions of C. Widick and S. Stulck of The Ohio State University for the data presented in this section.

REFERENCES

Bodden, J. L. Cognitive complexity as a factor in appropriate vocational choice. *Journal of Counseling Psychology*, 1970, 17, 364-368.

Bodden, J. L., & Klein, A. J. Cognitive complexity and appropriate vocational choice: another look. *Journal of Counseling Psychology*, 1971, 19(3), 257-258.

Ginzberg, E.; Ginsburg, S. W.; Axelrod, S.; & Herma, J. L. *Occupational choice: an approach to a general theory.* New York: Columbia University Press, 1951.

Harvey, O. J.; Hunt, D. E.; & Schroder, H. M. *Conceptual systems and personality organization.* New York: Wiley, 1961.

Holland, J. L. *The psychology of vocational choice.* Waltham, Mass.: Blaisdell, 1966.

Jepsen, D. A. The stage construct in career development. *Counseling and Values*, 1974, 18(2), 124-131.

Kohlberg, L. Stage and sequence: the cognitive-developmental approach to socialization. In D. Goslin, ed., *Handbook of socialization theory and research.* New York: Rand-McNally, 1969.

Leovinger, J., & Wessler, R. *Measuring ego development.* San Francisco: Jossey-Bass, 1970.

Perry, W., Jr. *Intellectual and ethical development in the college years.* New York: Holt, Rinehart, & Winston, 1970.

Piaget, J. *The language and thought of the child.* London: Routledge & Kegan Paul, 1951.

Rest, J. Developmental psychology as a guide to value education: a review of "Kohlbergian" programs. *Review of Educational Research*, 1973, 44(2), 241-259.

Slepitza, R., & Knefelkamp, L. L. Perry's scheme of intellectual development: an adaptation to career counseling. Paper presented at the American Psychological Association meeting, Chicago, 1975.

Super, D. *The psychology of careers.* New York: Harper & Row, 1957.

Tiedeman, D. V., & O'Hara, R. P. *Career development: choice and adjustment.* New York: College Entrance Examination Board, 1963.

Widick, C.; Knefelkamp, L. L.; & Parker, C. The counselor as a developmental instructor. *Counselor Education and Supervision*, 1975, 14(4), 286-296.

Career Planning and Decision Making: A Developmental Approach to the Classroom

Judith G. Touchton, Loretta C. Wertheimer,
Janet L. Cornfeld, and Karen H. Harrison

A new career-planning course for undergraduates was introduced on the College Park campus of the University of Maryland (UMCP) in the fall of 1975. The course represented a unique form of theory-based career development intervention that grew out of the common experiences of the University of Maryland and other colleges. This paper gives a brief history of the course, an overview of critical issues in student development, and a discussion of the design, development, and results of course evaluations.

History

The decision to offer a theory-based career development course at UMCP resulted from the interaction of three influences: (*a*) the particular history of a similar course which had been offered for several years on the campus, (*b*) changes in university environments nationwide, and (*c*) the creation of a student development team at UMCP.

A career-planning course had been offered to UMCP students since the early 1970s. Like many courses dealing with the personal concerns of students, the course initially was not given academic credit but was part of the Free University system. As the course evolved, it was awarded academic credit, in part because of its association with an academic department and in part because of an increasing awareness of the legitimacy of its content. Inclusion of the course within the academic curriculum came, then, as a result of two factors: (*a*) recognition that the substance constituted le-

Note: The authors gratefully acknowledge the invaluable contributions of Dr. L. Lee Knefelkamp during all phases of this project.

gitimate content learning for students; and (*b*) recognition that the personal development of students is a legitimate focus of education and that courses in "deliberate psychological education" warrant support.

While the course was being developed, conditions at universities were changing dramatically. College students displayed a heightened awareness of career concerns, mirroring intense pressures from society to prepare for jobs upon graduation. However, at many schools, including the University of Maryland, what formerly had been a Placement Office became a Career Development Center. The shift from placement to career development reflected a move away from an emphasis on job seeking and job placement in the senior year to an emphasis on the developmental aspects of career planning that spans all the college years. Currently, the job outlook for graduates is critical, and there is a growing awareness that waiting until the last year in college to think about and plan for a career is, all too often, to delay too long.

During the period that the course and the university environment were changing, a third force was operating at UMCP. A high degree of cooperation was forged between the established student personnel agency—the Career Development Center—and the academic department of Counseling and Personnel Services; the result was a mutually beneficial relation. Through the joint effort of these two agencies, a student development team was created. The team played a crucial role in the design of the career development course and the subsequent evolution of broader based career development programming.

As is appropriate on any team, members had different roles and functions which, overall, were shared. The primary theory came from faculty in the Department of Counseling and Personnel Services. The Career Development Center provided pragmatic observations, practical considerations, and implementation of concepts. The model to which the team adhered closely resembled the one described by Parker (1971) in which persons whose primary interests are theoretical interact with persons whose emphasis is in practice.

Reasons for a Developmental Design in Career Instruction

As the team began its work in developmental instruction, it recognized the need to focus on the following questions: (1) What is development? (2) What do we need to know about the development of college students in general? (3) What do we know about University of Maryland students in particular with respect to issues of development and career? (4) Given our information about our students, how can we intervene appropriately to reach our goals? (5) How can we evaluate our efforts to determine if defined goals have been reached? Each question is answered below.

1. *What is development?* The word "development" and the phrase "student development" have almost as many meanings as there are people using them. The terms have been used so haphazardly that they have become imprecise. What does "development" really mean? Many people have applied the term to sequential change, hierarchical change, and increases in complexity; but no one has defined it as well as Sanford (1966) who stated that development is the process of the individual's growing in a way that allows him to become increasingly complex. Development differs from change, which describes any condition that is altered from a previous condition, and also from growth, which implies a non-directional expansion of the personality. Development refers to qualitative changes that take place and contribute to the individual's increasingly complex interpretation of his world, allowing him to integrate and act on a wide variety of differentiated experiences and influences. Sanford argued that a delicate balance of challenge and support must be achieved before development can occur. He also raised the issue of individual differences in development, recognizing that individuals grow and develop at rates that are unique to their personality and experience.

According to Harvey, Hunt, and Schroder (1961), cognitive development takes place within various areas of concern or conceptual systems, such as family, religion, or career. The existence of these systems suggests that it is possible, indeed necessary, to investigate an individual's approach to knowledge according to a specific content area—in this case, career concerns.

2. *What do we need to know about college students in general?* There is an increasing body of literature on the college student, especially that subsumed under ego identity theory, person/environment theory, and cognitive developmental theory. The central questions asked by the theorists are: (*a*) What are the identity issues and the developmental tasks of college students? (*b*) What is the effect of the environment on these issues and tasks? (*c*) How do students grow and increase in complexity? The answers to these questions provide considerable information and knowledge about students in general and the impact of the university environment on students.

An important ingredient in the process of increasing complexity is the engagement of the individual in the task of exploring new ways of thinking. Salient issues are more likely to facilitate this type of involvement. Recent studies of college students have indicated that career is a major concern to members of this population (Cross 1971; Yankelovich 1974). Thus, the career issue is of sufficient importance to college students to be expected to engage them in a developmental experience.

3. *What can we find out about UMCP students with respect to the issues of development and career?* Having identified the central issues for college students in general, we turned to an application of these issues to UMCP students. In addition to the theoretical information on college students in general, we sought direct information on UMCP students through the data collected by the Career Development Center and the general observations of the center's staff. These preliminary data provided a picture of the Maryland student which was later confirmed by the data collected through the formal assessment of the research design.

The Career Development Center's shift from a placement to a developmental emphasis made it increasingly important to help students to know themselves as an integral part of their career development. A critical question became, To what extent were students involving themselves in the process and becoming "active agents" in directing their own lives? In adopting this approach, members of the team were functioning in a new role for student personnel workers—one that "involves understanding students' developmental stages, knowing how students deliberately might be changed, and knowing what the university and student personnel workers might do to bring about change" (Parker 1971).

4. *How can we intervene appropriately given this information and our goals?* The decision was made to effect a career development intervention in the classroom. Such an approach allowed the team to address identity issues directly, to design the environment to meet student needs, and, within this context, to affect the complexity with which students view careers.

Developmental instruction provided the methodology for the ● design of the classroom intervention. The developmental instruction model was chosen because of the methodology and because it is theoretical and data based. Developmental instruction is a process model of instructional methodology based on Perry's cognitive developmental theory and organized around Sanford's concepts of support and challenge. (For a fuller description of the concepts of developmental instruction, see Widick and Simpson's chapter in this volume.) A description of the application of developmental instruction to the course is given later in this paper.

The career developmental model, adapted by Knefelkamp and Slepitza from the Perry scheme of cognitive development, was used as both a guide to designing instructional modes and a measure of student growth. In adapting the original Perry model to career development, Knefelkamp and Slepitza asserted that, just as students view the classroom, authorities, and subject matter in widely different but measurable ways (Perry 1970), so may they view careers, career counselors, and career decision making in widely different but measurable ways. Basically, their model describes the movement of a student from a simplistic, categorical view of careers, career counseling, and career decision making to a more complex, pluralistic view. The model describes three phases through which students progress in their thinking about careers: dualism, multiplicity, and relativism. The questions raised by the model are: (1) Can the counselor classify the student's developmental stage with respect to career? (2) Can the counselor work with the student more effectively because of that knowledge?

The career model suggests that developmental changes that take place as the student progresses from dualism to relativism can be discussed with reference to nine "variables of qualitative change": (a) locus of control, (b) analysis, (c) synthesis, (d) semantic structure, (e) self processing, (f) openness to alternative perspectives, (g) ability to assume responsibility, (h) ability to take on new roles, and (i) ability to take risks with self. The variables that are most helpful in conceptualizing and working with the needs of dualistic-thinking students are the following: locus of control—the source to which the student turns to define himself and his environment; analysis—the ability of the individual to see a subject in its diverse perspectives, breaking down the subject into its component parts; semantic structure—specifically, the nature of verbs and qualifiers used by students in their written and spoken expressions; dualistic-thinking students are characterized by extensive use of absolutes (e.g., always, never, every); self-processing—the ability to examine oneself and be cognizant of one's defining factors; and openness to alternative perspectives—the extent to which the individual is aware of and recognizes the legitimacy of other points of view and possible explanations, even if the individual differs with the perspective. (A full description of the adapted model is contained in this volume in the paper by Knefelkamp and Slepitza.)

5. *How can we evaluate our efforts to determine if defined goals have been reached?* The evaluation procedure is described below.

Research Design

A primary assumption of the Knefelkamp-Slepitza model is that a student's level of cognitive complexity affects the way he approaches the career development process. Theoretically, an increase in the complexity of thinking leads to a more sophisticated approach to career and life-style issues. Further, new levels of cognitive skills obtained as a result of increasing complexity of thinking about careers are expected to generalize to other issues also.

In designing the new course, it was hypothesized that a developmentally taught course would lead to a greater growth in cognitive complexity with respect to career than would a course taught as it had been previously. In order to test this hypothesis, a research model was used in which six sections of the career-planning course were offered, and students registered for these sections without awareness of the differences among them. Instructors were assigned to particular sections according to scheduling convenience. The accompanying diagram depicts the research design.

Experimental	*Traditional*	*Mixed*
3 classes $(N = 42)$	2 classes $(N = 17)$	1 class $(N = 17)$
Taught developmentally by instructors specifically trained in developmental instruction	Taught in traditional method by instructors having no knowledge of developmental instruction	Taught in traditional method by instructors knowledgeable about developmental theory and developmental design
Curriculum content same	Curriculum content same	Curriculum content same

As the model suggests, the content of the course material remained essentially the same across all sections. Students spent the same amount of time in class (two hours per week). Only instructional method differed among the three modes. Three sections were designed in accordance with the developmental instruction methodology, two sections were taught as they had been in recent years, and one section was taught by an individual who possessed some knowledge of developmental theory and developmental instruction but who did not formally teach in the developmental design. Students were given pre- and posttests with reference to developmental stage as it related to career decision making. All classes were given course-satisfaction surveys at the end of the semester. The results of the course evaluations are discussed below.

STEPS IN DEVELOPMENTAL CURRICULUM DESIGN

The objectives of the student development team were to affect student development deliberately, use a theoretical base, and design specific classroom interventions. The design involved work in two primary areas: (*a*) the process area, or instructional methodology, and (*b*) the content area, or curriculum.

Process. The early steps in design involved (*a*) specifying a target population, (*b*) hypothesizing the needs of that population, and (*c*) selecting and designing elements of the course to foster growth and acquisition of knowledge by students.

The target population for the course comprised freshmen and sophomores at the University of Maryland. It was hypothesized that these students would be in dualism or early multiplicity according to the Knefelkamp-Slepitza model. Although the students who actually registered for the course included juniors and seniors as well as the target population, students in all four classes were later assessed at the same cognitive stage level, that is, in dualism and early multiplicity. The section instructors also found that their students, males and females, represented many races and varied considerably in age.

Needs of the population of the classes were hypothesized theoretically and from ongoing observations. Research in developmental instruction continues to show that people in dualism have different instructional needs from those at the higher levels. Students in dualism, multiplicity, and relativism approach the classroom differently; that is, they differ on what is supportive and what is challenging for them. Because it was hypothesized that dualist-thinking students would predominate in the career development class, the curriculum was designed with them in mind.

The selection and design of elements to be included in the new course was guided by the three goals for developmental instruction: to teach content, to help students to relate ideas from the course to other areas of their lives, and to expand the complexity of their thinking about career issues (Knefelkamp 1974; Widick 1975; Widick, Knefelkamp, & Parker 1975). A developmentally taught course is one in which all three goals are deliberately sought in all phases of the presentation.

Designing the course developmentally involved so presenting the content that dualistic students were given the appropriate levels of support and challenge. Theoretically, such a balance would provide an environment in which cognitive growth and development could be encouraged. Recent research has suggested that this balance can be achieved through variation in four aspects of instruction, the four variables of developmental instruction: structure, personalism, experience, and diversity (Knefelkamp 1974; Widick 1975; Widick et al. 1975). The accompanying diagram indicates the appropriate balance for dualistic students.

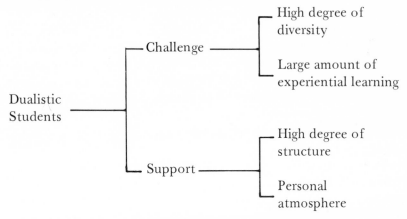

The application of this model began with the identification of the four variables as they applied to each method of presentation. Figure 1 indicates how each instructional method used in the course fit into the model. The four variables of developmental instruction were identified for each class exercise. An evaluation was then made of the appropriate balance between support and challenge for dualists, and this balance was built into each exercise. The judgments were based on a theoretical description of the needs of dualists as well as the instructor's past experiences with students in previous career classes.

Curriculum Content. The developmentally designed course included and expanded upon the content of the traditional course — exploration of self and exploration of the world of work — in three units, as follows: (a) Careers and who people are: Topics include why people work, what we need to know about people to think about them in careers, analysis of literary works dealing with people in careers. (b) Knowing who you are: Topics include interests, needs, values, integrative skills, and self assessment. (c) Putting it all together: Unit includes occupational exploration through visits to the Career Library and Experiential Learning Office, conducting career biographical interviews, and decision-making skills. Emphasis was placed on the integration of information about the self

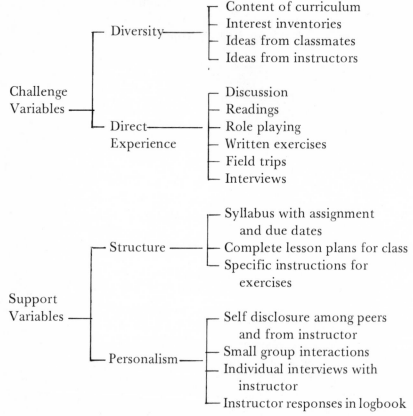

Figure 1. Sources of challenge and support for students at dualism level.

and the world of work, and on acquiring a sense of being an "active agent" in control of one's life.

Interaction of Process and Content. Both process and content issues clearly form an integral unit. The integration is reflected in the design of individual classes in the various assignments and exercises and, it is hoped, in all aspects of the course. One of the best illustrations of this integration is found in the use of log books by the students.

The log book, which contains a student's written assignments and instructor's responses, has two purposes: to extend the goals of the class beyond the classroom; and to provide an avenue of personal communication between instructor and student, thereby adding another dimension to class experience. Each student keeps his own log book and turns it in three times during the semester. Due dates are given in the syllabus and coincide with the end of class units. In addition, logs are turned in at the midpoint of unit 1 to allow instructors to ascertain whether students are using them as intended.

The log book has a definite structure. It is divided into four sections:

Reactions to class: The student writes at least one paragraph in response to one or more aspects of each class period. The purpose of this assignment is to allow the instructor to monitor the extent to which the class is meeting the student's needs and to provide the instructor with information that will be useful for redesigning the class at the end of the semester.

Study questions: During the semester, the student responds to three study questions that relate to and demand integration of respective major units of the course. The purpose is to encourage students to grapple with ideas presented in class and to relate them to their own experiences, and to expand upon the ideas and perspectives presented.

Dialogue with instructor: The student responds to the instructor's comments in the "reactions to class" and "study question" sections of the log. In effect, the instructor and student carry on a written dialogue. Thus students are encouraged to expand on selected points, which the instructor views as needing further clarification or analysis, and the instructor is able to offer appropriate support and challenge on an individual basis.

Class notes and handouts: The student keeps class notes and printed handouts in this section of the log. Thus, all course materials are kept in one place.

Instructors respond personally to student comments in the first three log book sections. It is in these highly individualized responses that the instructor is able to consider carefully the developmental needs of each student and to affect the student in deliberate ways. Instructors attempt to follow a three-step procedure in responding to logs: (1) Select the issue to which to respond on the basis of variables of qualitative change needing attention. (As indicated earlier, the variables of particular relevance for dualistic students are semantic structure, openness to alternative perspectives, analysis, self-processing, and locus of control.) (2) Determine if student comment merits a supportive response, a challenging response to stimulate thinking, or a response suggesting further exploration in the dialogue section. (3) Design the response in accordance with the above determination, basing it on the instructor goals presented in Table 1. Frequently, the instructor will include more than one type of response (e.g., support and challenge) to insure that the student's emotional perspective as well as content is afforded adequate attention. Although this procedure may sound mechanistic, instructors consider it deliberate and highly personal. Great care is taken to achieve the desired balance of support and challenge and to model types of thinking and response which students can emulate. Students typically respond positively to the instructors' comments, often they write much more and try harder for quality when they discover how carefully their logs are being attended to. Instructors often feel that they spend as much time responding to the logs as students spend writing in them.

The log books are the major vehicle for personalizing the course,

Table 1. Primary Instructor Goals for Students in Dualism/Multiplicity

Variable	Instructor Encourages Student To:
1. Locus of control	Move from primarily external definition to more internal ones
2. Analysis	Use supportive evidence, expand thinking, increase awareness of cause/effect
3. Synthesis	Recognize and integrate pluralistic perspectives
4. Self-processing	Increase personal insight and awareness of self
5. Semantic structure	Use fewer absolutes in thinking and communication
6. Openness to alternative perspectives	Increase exposure to, generation and legitimizing of alternative perspectives on issues
7. Ability to assume responsibility	Begin to accept consequences of decisions and actions
8. Ability to take new roles	Understand and empathize with others
9. Ability to take risks with self	Place self in new situations

but students also receive individual responses in class and in curriculum development. Taken together, these factors contribute to maximizing student development in the classroom.

Results

Data for the evaluation of all sections of the course were obtained from three sources: a pre-post instrument especially designed to assess students' complexity of thinking about careers as described in the Knefelkamp-Slepitza model; and surveys of student satisfaction designed for students by the Career Development Center and the Department of Counseling and Personnel Services, respectively.

COMPLEXITY OF THINKING ABOUT CAREERS

A primary source of evaluation data was the amount of cognitive stage movement achieved by students in each instructional model. This movement was measured according to the full Knefelkamp-Slepitza cognitive developmental model for career development which describes nine stages through which people progress as they move from a more dualistic to a more complex view of career. In the developmentally taught experimental sections, 76 percent of the students showed some increase in complexity of thinking about careers, as measured by the instrument; in the traditional sections, 41 percent of the students showed similar growth; and in the mixed section, the comparable figure was 65 percent.

The data in Table 2 show the percentage of cognitive stage gain between pre- and postassessment for students in the three instructional modes. Note that in the experimental section 71 percent of the students began the semester as dualists but only 21 percent were still at that stage at the end of the semester. In the experimental section, 29 percent began in multiplicity; by the end of the semester, 79 percent of this class were assessed at that stage. Although there was stage movement by individual students in the traditional sections, the summary table reflects no movement in the class as a whole because some students moved forward and others backward, thus canceling out average movement. The data for the mixed section reflect substantial movement by students from dualism to multiplicity, but not as much as in the experimental sections.

The data in Table 3 provide the clearest summary of the effects of the course in stimulating gains in cognitive complexity with respect to careers. The average stage movement for students in the developmentally taught experimental sections was 0.59, as compared to 0.17 in the traditional sections and 0.39 in the mixed section.

Table 2. Pre- and Postassessment of Cognitive Stage Categories for Students in Experimental, Traditional, and Mixed Instructional Modes

	Experimental (N = 42)				Traditional (N = 17)				Mixed (N = 17)			
	Pre		Post		Pre		Post		Pre		Post	
Category	N	%	N	%	N	%	N	%	N	%	N	%
Dualists	30	71	9	21	8	47	8	47	11	65	4	24
Multiplicity	12	29	33	79	9	53	9	53	6	35	13	76
Total	42	100	42	100	17	100	17	100	17	100	17	100

Table 3. Average Stage Movement within Each Class Section

Section	Experimental	Traditional	Mixed
1	.69 (N = 14)	.25 (N = 8)	.39 (N = 17)
2	.56 (N = 16)	.10 (N = 9)	. . .
3	.53 (N = 12)	. . .	. . .
Average stage movement . . .	.59	.17	.39

SURVEYS OF STUDENT SATISFACTION

Overall evaluations for the course, including instructor variables and content, were given very positive ratings in all sections. However, the developmentally taught sections consistently showed higher satisfaction levels by students in the following areas: (a) instructor preparation, mastery of subject, and responsiveness to student needs; (b) contributions of course structure and procedures to learning; (c) feelings of competence in subject matter; and (d) ranking of course as valuable and one they would recommend to others.

Summary

This paper has described the design and implementation of a theory-based course in career planning and decision making by a student development team. The theoretical contributions from two areas—the concepts and methodology of developmental instruction and the Knefelkamp-Slepitza cognitive developmental model of career development—facilitated the design of a course that more closely met the needs of the students and provided a fuller understanding of how these students were conceptualizing career issues.

The increased sensitivity to client needs and to how these needs can be met which is suggested by the two models would be helpful in designing and implementing other career-oriented programs and services. Some examples are training career counselors, staff development, the organization of career libraries, methods of designing and conducting workshops, consultation with faculty, and liaison with other other student personnel professionals.

REFERENCES

Cross, K. P. *Beyond the open door.* San Francisco: Jossey-Bass, 1971.

Harvey, O. J.; Hunt, D. E., & Schroder, H. M. *Conceptual systems and personality organization.* New York: Wiley, 1961.

Knefelkamp, L. L. Developmental instruction: fostering intellectual and personal growth of college students. Doctoral dissertation, University of Minnesota, 1974.

Parker, C. A. Institutional self-renewal in higher education. *Journal of College Student Personnel,* 1971, 12, 6.

Perry, W., Jr. *Intellectual and ethical development in the college years.* New York: Holt, Rinehart, & Winston, 1970.

Sanford, N. *Self and society: social change and individual development.* New York: Atherton, 1966.

———. *Where colleges fail.* San Francisco: Jossey-Bass, 1967.

Widick, C. An evaluation of developmental instruction. Doctoral dissertation, University of Minnesota, 1975.

Widick, C.; Knefelkamp, L. L.; & Parker, C. A. The counselor as developmental instructor. *Counselor Education and Supervision,* 1975, 14(4), 286-296.

Yankelovich, D. *The new morality: a profile of American youth in the seventies.* New York: McGraw-Hill, 1974.

Comments on Chapter 5 and 6

William G. Perry, Jr.

Knefelkamp, Slepitza, and their colleagues were the first to give me hope that my demon specter's power could be neutralized. We can see immediately the model they provide, in that you always see more than a given pair of theory-spectacles allow into vision. For me, their revelation of qualitative changes in locus of control, analysis, synthesis, and semantic structure has illumined salient aspects of all those students' protocols I looked at all those years.

I find especially helpful their distinction between choice and commitment based on the person's sense of the locus of control. It enlivens the sense of personal investment—the act of faith—which the person brings to the act of commitment.

I am eager to know what they think, also, of some person, like Reisman's inner-directed man of the nineteenth century, who seem to have felt a strong sense of agency, but perhaps of a different kind.

Their use of role-play feels highly productive, and I observe that they usually imply a plurality—of roles, that is. I find the word "role" a tricky business, especially in areas of career development. Students look ahead and see a set of "roles" and assume that they must choose one and try to "fill" it, that is, fit "into" it. Once again they smell death. Have Knefelkamp and others found ways of assisting students to perceive that roles are smaller than people, that people have several roles, and that identity is derived less from roles than from the style of balancing the expectations pertaining to many? This prospect is frightening, too, of course, but at least it is more lively.

I should gently beg the Touchton et al. team to consider carefully the implications of certain choices in language. Modern psychological talk offers us all-purpose words and phrases that sound in-group and macho: "intervention," "impact," "target" (and even "impacted target" and "impacting intervention" which, thankfully, are not used.) These words carry implications of influence and causality that, aside from their condescension toward "targets," may seriously mislead one's thought about the causal sequences involved and even the sources of the energy. Indeed, the authors say "the objectives of the team were to affect student development deliberately . . . and design a specific classroom intervention." Somehow, to me, an intervention designed to affect development deliberately is presumed to act directly, to *cause* development. My nightmare specter rises before me. What would the difference be if you were to use words like "foster" or "provide for" instead of "affect"; or to speak of "opportunities" or "provisions" or "interactions" instead of "interventions"? Would you feel that they were somehow weak? I would feel them much stronger for they refer to the only *real* powers we possess.

I know I am fighting a losing battle against the use of the word "intervention" for *everything* we do. But I am trying to recruit people who actually "intervene" in others' lives very rarely. Mostly, I take it, one *engages* with them, and so on. We must find words for what we really do and use them; our inventions will be the more expressive and our students will respond all the more. Who wants to be intervened or impacted? What is being done is great.

Ursula Delworth

The proposed model is a much-needed step between Perry's conceptualizations and the actual planning and offering of developmental career programs to students. The authors have obviously used it well in designing their intervention. The career class is a fine example of planning from a conceptual base, and of using a systematic process that includes careful evaluation. It illustrates the way program development should happen but, still too often, does not!

The authors point to the creation of the student development team as an effective and rewarding vehicle for dealing with issues and developing programs. My experience in using the team approach with a variety of concerns on campuses in the West, during the past three years, has been equally effective and rewarding. Clearly, we are past the point of claiming that either academic units or student affairs have all the answers. It is encouraging to see more and more teams with members from both areas, all committed to dealing with issues and strategies aimed at the enhancement of students' lives in the college environment. Our WICHE planning team model includes students (those who live in the environment and are targets of interventions) as full team members. Their contributions have had a very positive effect on team process and the outcome of programs developed by the team.

The team appears to have incorporated in their design one of Chickering's conditions for impact—positive relations with faculty. It will be interesting to see the programs and re-designs they develop to deal with his other conditions for impact. For example, could some of this work be done with intact groups of residence hall students, in order to link the potential of the class with the potential for development inherent in the residence hall setting?

I would like to know more about the data on students collected by the Career Development Center and used in the development of the course. How will these data be useful in planning future interventions? Are more or a different kind of data needed? There appears to be a potential for gathering information on student personality types and types of environments that exist on the Maryland campus, using Holland's typology, in order to enhance student understanding and choice. It may also be that only certain types of students are using the course at present. It may also be that certain types of students appear to be able to use the course more effectively. If so, future efforts might focus on how best to structure programs to accomplish the same developmental goals with students who vary in personality orientation. The team also may find it helpful to know the major environment types present on campus as a guide to students and, possibly, as data which would be used to develop types of environments that are not strongly represented on campus.

Ultimately, it also will be of great importance for the team to design ways in which student development through all nine stages can be facilitated. This development may be accomplished through specific programs but, I suspect, it will also depend heavily on team members' knowledge of the total campus environment and on their ability to guide students in "routing" their way through that environment.

David E. Hunt

The Knefelkamp-Slepitza and Touchton et al. papers illustrate the relation between a theory and its application in the classroom, and I will present my reactions to each paper separately.

"THE PERRY SCHEME: A COGNITIVE-DEVELOPMENTAL ADAPTATION TO CAREER COUNSELING — A PROPOSED MODEL"

Knefelkamp and Slepitza describe a theory of development specific to careers and career counseling which is based on Perry's nine-stage model. They articulate this career-specific version of development by proposing nine areas or defining variables, which are expressed at a "middle level" of abstraction that is more specific than a developmental stage but less specific than behavioral description (e.g., "ability to assume responsibility"). Their middle-level analysis might be compared to the seven vectors proposed by Chickering (as described by Hurst). It was flattering to note that they refer to Harvey, Hunt, and Shroder (1961) as one basis for justifying their specification of the domain of development (especially since the book has been out of print for almost ten years). Nonetheless, the issue of generality—specificity remains the most troublesome one confronting a theory of development. Developmental theories expressed at a general level, such as Erikson, Ausubel, Piaget, Loevinger, Perry, and the initial version of conceptual systems theory proposed by Harvey, Schroder, and myself, can neither lead to specific predictions nor serve to develop practice unless the domain (school, work, home, church, etc.) is specified and understood. I see such general "theories" as high-level abstractions that serve mainly as metaphors for practitioners who work in the world of specific persons, times, and places. I will elaborate my reasons for this idea at other points; for now, let me stress that such general theories of development are almost never modified or corrected in light of empirical evidence or personal experience (imagine what would happen if Erikson tried to reverse stages 5 and 6).

The unresponsiveness of developmental theory to empirical evidence also partly accounts for my difficulty in reacting to the middle-level, career-specific theory proposed by Knefelkamp and Slepitza. I understand that they have formulated these nine areas and their career-specific referents partly through experience, and I commend such a practice-to-theory approach. However, it is difficult to comment on their adapted model except very generally. One can wonder about the nine areas: Are they all needed? (e.g., What is the distinction between "locus of control" and "ability to assume responsibility"?) Are there other areas which should be included? (e.g., What about interpersonal skills, etc.?) I realize that these examples may seem like nit-picking but, without empirical data consisting of factor analytic evidence in longitudinal form, there is really no way to answer such questions. The central feature of the developmental model seemed to be the two "primary flips," and, as the authors suggest, it will be very interesting to note whether these two transitions are observed in their longitudinal studies.

The question, "One might then ask what happens to individuals who make a career decision at various points on the continuum" is perhaps the most critical issue in the paper because (a) it makes clear what has been only implied earlier: that all students do not develop to the highest stage (or, more generally, the necessity for distinguishing between contemporaneous and developmental analysis); (b) it raises the related problem of how a counselor can react to a student at stage 1 who insists on making a firm career decision and, through his acting on that decision, moves himself into an irreversible position; and (c) related to the first two questions is the issue of life-span career choice, or the "one life—one job" idea, in which the question arises about how midcareer changes are viewed in this model.

Finally, a word on the "new catechism," a problem created by our dualistic thinking about thought and action. We encounter this same problem in our work on indexing conceptual level by scoring the conceptual complexity of written fragments when we encounter what we call a "cliche" response which, like the new catechism response, is difficult to distinguish from what we think are more valid referents. There are two parts to the problem: (a) assessing how a person thinks from a sample of what he writes when we know that there is not a one-to-one correspondence between thought and action (i.e., written behavior), and (b) understanding how it is that what a person thinks (when accurately assessed) is related to how the person acts in a particular situation. These are very large problems, indeed, and I think that sensitivity to the new catechism and observing students who use it in other settings, as these authors propose, may help us to understand this complex issue.

"CAREER PLANNING AND DECISION MAKING: A DEVELOPMENTAL APPROACH TO THE CLASSROOM

Touchton, Wertheimer, Cornfeld, and Harrison describe their team efforts in implementing the Knefelkamp-Slepitza model into classroom practice in a careers course. They developed classroom procedures by extending Sanford's conception of the educational environment as a blend of challenge and support, through assuming that most of their students would be characterized by dualistic thinking. Their Figure 1 summarizes their "middle-level" specifications for instructional approaches matched to dualistic thinkers, and as such are very similar to the matching model presented by Widick and Simpson. Another similarity is that the "delicate balance of challenge and support" requires the "parallel artistry" described by Widick and Simpson.

The team that conducted this study addressed the issue, What is development? early, and, in agreement with Sanford, concluded that its central feature is increased complexity which, if one must settle for only a single definition, is probably reasonable. However, the implicit issue in this section is to distinguish development from change (the new catechism?) and from growth, distinctions that require a lot of methodological effort and sophistication. In attempting to distinguish development from trivial nondevelopmental change, I make the assumption that development is more likely to generalize over space and time, that is, that developmental change will pervade more situations and endure longer than trivial nondevelopmental change.

The authors also extended the Knefelkamp-Slepitza model to an interactive developmental theory by explicating the general environmental prescriptions required for development in each of the nine areas (Table 1). The five areas that were the specific focus of the instructors' effort were treated through "written dialogue."

Written dialogue is both a valuable instructional device and in this particular case, a potential source of difficulty. If I were to play devil's advocate, I might interpret the changes summarized for the experimental group in Tables 2 and 3 to indicate only situation-specific alterations in student's writing, essentially, a continuation of the student's (altered or corrected) messages to the instructor. Particularly because much of the experimental intervention was behaviorally and situationally similar to the method of evaluation, it would be helpful in future work to attempt to include other (nonwritten) criteria of program effects. One other query on evaluation: I wonder if the team considered analyzing satisfaction scores differentially for "dualistic" and "multiplicity" students, as was done for stage change in Table 2? Differential effects in satisfaction may have occurred but gone undetected.

Finally, a few reflections on the process of "implementing" a theory. It seems clear to me from the enthusiasm that pervades this report that much of the beneficial student effects occurred because Touchton, Wertheimer, Cornfeld, and Harrison were committed to these ideas, and acted on their commitment. Some people say that such results are only "Hawthorne effect" (were the mixed groups "half-a-Hawthorne"?), and dismiss the results. When I work with teachers, I take all the Hawthorne effect I can get. Therefore, I prefer to view the enthusiasm and belief of the team as representing the highest stage in Perry's hierarchy and that they conveyed it to their students. One could hardly ask for more.

REFERENCE

Harvey, O. J.; Hunt, D. E.; & Schroder, H. M. *Conceptual systems and personality organization.* New York: Wiley, 1961.

Roy Heath

Most of the career-counseling experience I have had was at the University of Pittsburgh where I was the head of the Counseling Center between 1956 and 1963. Therefore, much of what the authors are saying took me back to that period. As I recall, we did our career counseling without the benefit of the careful delineation of where our students were in the developmental process which the authors describe. I am assuming from their research they have perfected the means of identifying just where a given student places in their developmental scheme.

All in all, the thrust of the paper is encouraging. It is a far cry from the two-step mode of operation in which, after an initial interview, the student returns for one more conference, primarily to hear the results of the Strong Vocational. What is attractive about the new approach is not only the identification of developmental stage but the effort by the counselor to foster movement upward. It all makes good sense, provided that the counselor is sufficiently sophisticated to know what he is up to.

There are two reflections I offer here in response to this paper.

I wonder about locus of control and how generally students move from external to internal. There would seem to be many students who, for many years prior to college, have been basing their career expectations on internal control. For example, I am thinking of the student who arrives at college already convinced that he will go into engineering, based on his experience that he is gifted in understanding and working with things mechanical. He may or may not have the benefit of significant others in support of this notion. But in the cases I am thinking about it would have been difficult to argue that the notion was not well internalized, based on the authority of his own experience. In such cases the counseling center may never see this fellow unless he finds that he cannot do calculus. Another example would be the pre-med student who has learned well before college that he enjoys administering to others' physical needs, whether they be pets or younger members of the family. Here, too, the counseling center may never see this student unless he finds to his great dismay that he cannot do better than a C in biology.

I wonder about the impact of our current social order on career decision making. In the 1950s, a student could have more reasonable expectations about what might be in store for him or her "out there." Nowadays, a great fluidity must be complicating the decision process. The student today, sometimes well before he enters college, knows from the experiences of older brothers and sisters, uncles, and cousins that one can not count on the opportunity to do something vocationally simply because he likes to do it. Also he or she hears of protean man who envisions three or four careers sequentially. And what about the impact of TV listening as limiting the process of self-discovery? When children were left on their own resources for what to do when they were bored, a greater opportunity for establishing competence and interest of an intrinsic nature presumably was afforded.

Douglas H. Heath

The application of the Perry model of cognitive development to the career decision process is remarkably similar, though much more differentiated in specification, to the Ginzberg model of decision making published in 1951. I have reinterpreted the Ginzberg model in terms of my model of maturing that seems to capture more globally the same types of processes that Knefelkamp and Slepitza hypothesize (Heath 1965, 1968). By reformulating the career decision process in terms of an adaptation model of maturing, it is possible to make personality predictions about who will and who will not make more vocational decisions or, in terms of the authors, move from a dualistic to a relativistic position.

The problem of developmental theorists is to propose a model that is general throughout the life span and not just applicable to specific age-limited periods of development. By confining a model to only the college-age period, one encounters the theoretical dilemma that a student can reach a "relativist" stage with no implications that he can cognitively mature further. Hence, in the research reported by the authors, they find movement in their dualists and, embarrassingly I would say, generally not in their relativists, which raises the question, Why should relativists go to college if no further growth is possible for them? I do not deny the value of a model specific to a certain age period, but its theoretical linkages to not only childhood but also adult periods in development need to be specified if it is to be a truly developmental model. Unless, of course, one assumes that development ceases in early adulthood, an assumption for which I now have considerable data that refutes it.

One approach to a life-span model is to conceive of maturing, a word I prefer, in adaptational terms. That is, I assume that throughout life a person is faced by crises, demands for new adaptations, and that the dimensions that define the process of adaptation can be specified. Persons who have developed the personality traits associated with maturing on each adaptive dimension, therefore, are better able to adapt more effectively in subsequent situations demanding new adaptations. In other words, more mature persons should be able to adapt more effectively to subsequent events in their lives than less mature persons.

An adaptive dimensional model of the maturing process has been extensively validated now on numerous transcultural samples and found to be highly useful in several longitudinal studies, one of which is relevant to the Knefelkamp and Slepitza concern with career prediction. I hypothesize that when faced by a demand, like a career choice, a person begins, in Ginzberg's terms, to become "increasingly aware of what [he] likes, of what [he] does well, what are [his] important values . . . [he] becomes aware not only of the forces within himself but also of the external environment" (Ginzberg, Ginsburg, Axelrod, & Herma 1951, p. 29). In my terms, he becomes more mature in his capacity to represent his experience accurately, whether for himself, values, personal relationships, or his environment. This increased symbolization capacity includes the authors' self-processing dimension. As one tries to represent the factors in one's life, one searches for other information or, in Ginzberg's terms, "he develops new ways of looking at

and appraising those aspects which have a direct bearing on him"
(p. 29); he begins to take different perspectives, discovers what
counselors, parents, and friends think of him, and so on. That is, he
becomes increasingly more allocentric, capable of taking a multiplicity of perspectives toward himself or a problem; his values become less self-centered and he becomes more understanding of
other persons. The authors talk of a similar process, that of analysis, the cognitive aspect of allocentric thinking, or of openness to
alternative perspectives, and ability to take on new roles. In the
next phase of the adaptation process, a person begins to put his
ideas together; he begins to see and formulate relationships, tentative hypotheses. That is, his thinking becomes more complexly
differentiated, as Perry suggests, or more integrative, as do his self-
concept, values, and personal relationships, also. The authors' concept of synthesis applies here. Then a youth begins to test out his
ideas, like getting a summer job in the area he is contemplating
as a career. Does this tentative integrative fit really hold up when
matched against the reality demands of the tentative career choice?
The problem is identity stabilization. I call this dimension of adaptation stability. Finally, in Ginzberg's terms again, "he begins to
exercise increasing control over it" (p. 29), a dimension of the
adaptive process that I call autonomy. His thinking becomes freed
of childish modes, like dualistic forms of thought, as well as more
independent of parental or other influences. His self-concept and
values become more autonomous and he can begin to act more independently in his decision making. The authors talk of locus of
control, assumption of responsibility, and ability to take risks—
all aspects of increasing autonomy.

Now, there are several values to such an adaptational model of
maturing. (a) It is theoretically systematic and comprehensive, so
it has a tidiness that may be appealing to some. (b) It provides a
set of hypotheses by which to predict the personality traits of persons who are more adaptively mature and who, presumably, should
make more mature vocational decisions. (c) It locates the decision-
making process in a more contextual comprehensive model of personality development than only a cognitive model does.

One can ask, Just how predictive is such a model of maturing?
In a longitudinal study of young men (Heath 1976) on whom I

have more than 100 measures of high school and college personality, academic, and other competencies, and more than 400 measures of competence as adults in their midthirties, I have been able to demonstrate that the psychological maturity of such men when they were in college is most powerfully predictive of their subsequent vocational adaptation. Of the numerous measures of adolescent maturity that were predictive, I found, for example, that the integration and stability of their self-concept were consistently predictive of their subsequent vocational adaptation. (Vocational adaptation was measured by a twenty-eight-item Vocational Adaptation Scale completed by a professional colleague who knew their work most intimately, the closest friend, the wife, and themselves). The evidence was even more compelling with respect to the adult predictors of vocational adaptation. Maturity, as I have defined it, very consistently and significantly predicted vocational adaptation. The study has clearly demonstrated that at the core of what is adult competence (including other types of adult competencies like marital relationship) are a core set of personality traits that define psychological maturity, and those traits can be conceptualized in terms of a dimensional model of maturing.

REFERENCES

Ginzberg, E.; Ginsburg, S. W.; Axelrod, S.; & Herma, J. L. Occupational choice: an approach to a general theory. New York: Columbia University Press, 1951.
Heath, D. H. Explorations of maturity. New York: Appleton-Century-Crofts, 1965.
———. Growing up in college: liberal education and maturity. San Francisco: Jossey-Bass, 1968.
———. Adolescent and adult predictors of vocational adaptation. Journal of Vocational Behavior, 1976, 9, 1-19.

Roger A. Myers

If I were William Perry, I think that I would be very pleased to see the efforts of Knefelkamp, Slepitza, Touchton, Wertheimer, Cornfeld, and Harrison. To have one's theoretical scheme give rise to other productive theorizing and hypothesizing is one thing; to see one's scheme lead directly to action is quite another. There is also something special, I imagine, about emerging as a dominant theorist in a highly valued, widely dispersed, socially useful, but hereto-

fore atheoretical social agency. I have seen other career development and placement functionaries grope for a legitimizing theoretical base; those who follow Perry's piping, however, have been
more successful and confident in their search. There is a better-
than-fair chance that we are witnessing a new departure in student
personnel work, unlike many departures that have been proclaimed
in the last three decades. (Let me share with you an admission
against self from a respected senior colleague who once said to me
in confidence [which I am now breaching], "I am not very good
at identifying what the frontiers of our field will be, but I am very
good at knowing when I'm on one."

Like Widick and Simpson, Touchton et al. have given us a
glimpse at a masterpiece of curriculum design. They deserve robust
credit for following Perry (through Knefelkamp and Slepitza) and
Rank (through Sanford) to a set of specifications for instruction
that not only dare to tailor learning experiences to developmental
needs but, also, audaciously collect data toward the end of finding
out if learning experiences so conceived and so dedicated do what
they were intended to do.

Two things intrigue me about the Maryland group's question,
What is development? and their answer. Somewhere – was it
Freud? – I seem to have acquired the belief that an essential aspect
of development was described by the recurring cycles of integration and disintegration. As one achieved the tasks of a given developmental phase, one consolidated those gains into an integrated
style of functioning. In order to move to the next phase, however,
one inevitably encountered a breakdown of the organizing concepts and coping behaviors that kept one whole in the earlier
phase but precluded successful attack on the tasks of the phase
that followed. One thing that is intriguing about the Maryland
group approach is their sensitivity to this integration-disintegration
phenomenon. This sensitivity is expressed in the balancing of challenge and support in their curriculum design.

The second thing that intrigues me is the reverence for ol' Frank
Parsons. Touchton and her associates almost write him off as "traditional," but very quickly pay homage in their developmentally
designed course that includes the following units: (1) Careers and
who people are (Parsons would have said something like "require-

ments for a condition of success and satisfaction."); (2) Knowing who you are (Parson's self-knowledge); and (3) Putting it all together (Parsons rather naively called it "true reasoning" about the relation of the other two elements.). As Calia pointed out a few years ago, Parsons's turn-of-the-century notions are still very much with us, and their simplicity has a kind of endearing aesthetic quality.

As a counterweight to my cloying admiration of the work stimulated by Knefelkamp and Slepitza, I must now proceed to exaggerate some quibbles with the Touchton et al. rendition.

Quibble No. 1. I think that the students who, through no fault of their own, begin in the multiplicity category are rather shamefully treated. They are subjected to the unguents and balms concocted for the dualists, and such remedies do them little good, as I read Table 2. Most of them do not develop at all, and those who do show only slight progress. One might suspect a ceiling phenomenon, except that multiplicity is clearly not the end goal. Should not an instructional technology so intent upon tailoring instruction to the learner's needs recognize that multiplicity types have rights too? In fact, I suspect that they were not damaged by what they endured, but their apparent victimization suggests that some criterion external to the Perry-Knefelkamp-Slepitza developmental scheme should have been employed to see if anything else were happening. I also suspect that our theorist-practitioners are really more interested in stamping out dualists than in promoting development for all comers. Good enough; it is a lot better than not caring.

Quibble No. 2. Ever since Greenspoon, Ver Plank, Krasner, Krumboltz, and others started increasing the frequency of plural nouns and information-seeking behaviors by surreptitiously reinforcing random emissions of desired behavior, I have wondered if it would not have been easier to tell the subject flat out that you wanted her/him to pluralize her/his nouns or thumb through the Occupational Outlook Handbook. Similarly, I wonder if, knowing the elegantly specified Knefelkamp and Slepitza path to career success and satisfaction, one could not just grab the kid by the lapels and say, "Look here, this is the way to go—get your head on straight!"

What I am suggesting in my outrageous way is the inclusion of a prestige-suggestion condition in the empirical tests of the new developmental instruction. Such a suggestion, it seems to me, goes right to the heart of the Knefelkamp and Slepitza fears about "the new catechism." Raters' problems be damned; what if parroting the right notions leads to incorporating the desired beliefs and modifying the self-concept in the desired direction? Perry would not feel violated, I will bet. Do not tell me that it would not work as well as the same message wrapped in TLC; show me data. Do not waffle about being manipulative; the entire scheme is patently, candidly, and admirably prescriptive. If individual freedom is your hang-up, console yourself that individuals are freer to ignore prestige suggestions than they are to resist psychologically designed instruction.

Theoretical Perspectives

On the Relevance of
Architects and Stonemasons

Roger A. Myers

In his oral presentation, Hurst spoke about the difference between cathedral architects and stonemasons (and of his preference for architects) in a metaphor designed to urge student personnel practitioners toward consciousness of larger goals, more and better theorizing, and more courageous rhetoric about the purposes of student development.

I pondered his remarks with some discomfort because he raised to my consciousness the fact that I am a stonemason. The people who taught me most of what I know and believe were intellectual descendents of Paterson, Williamson, Darley, Wrenn, and others who worked at Minnesota. My mentors and their mentors were not so much inspired by Robert White and Henry Murray as by Hugo Münsterberg (Williamson 1965). Although they were as interested in theory as any psychologist, their traditions have been mislabeled as atheoretical because they were not obviously holistic. They were preoccupied with human development, but no developmental psychologist took them as seriously relevant. They were layers of brick and stone who taught the craft of the mason, yet they knew an inspiring cathedral when they were engaged in the building of one.

I am bothering you with the facts of the early (foreclosed?) resolution of my identity crisis because it has colored my reactions to this conference in a number of ways. Perhaps some of them will become apparent in the rest of this paper.

Disquiet No. 1

My stonemason's head got me into some trouble with parts of the conference and I would like to share with you my reactions to those troubles. The first arose from the vocal skepticism about the use of theory. I experienced this skepticism—widely shared but by no means universal—as an unfair and inconsistent application of standards for what a good theory is and what good a theory is not. We were all taught that a good theory is comprehensive, explicit, internally consistent, parsimonious, and generative (i.e., useful). We have all learned that no theory about human behavior meets these standards, and many of us have managed to live in comfort with that fact.

The cases presented demonstrate that the theories that guided them have been, at least, useful. If they do not meet all the other criteria for good theory but are demonstrably useful, that seems to me to be acceptable for the student personnel practitioner.

Douglas Heath has provided us with an excellent view of what it takes to build a completely adequate theory. The theorist devotes large portions of his or her life to studying, investigating, thinking, and writing. Student personnel practitioners rarely have the time or temperament for this kind of work. Their patent social roles demand that they act. One harbors the hope that they will inquire and reflect about their actions, but whether they do or not, they must act. When people must act, they use whatever implicit or explicit theory is available.

The cases have used theories that were technically inadequate but, by demonstration, useful in certain settings, which suggests to me that the theories deserve to be held in a condition of tentative worth. That is, two things are now known about these theories: (a) they are available for reuse and for further trial; and (b) there is a favorable probability that they are not, under all circumstances, worthless (Myers 1971). The quest for totally adequate theories is a noble one, but to delay action and inquiry until such theories are constructed seems wasteful and foolish. There are walls to be built.

Disquiet No. 2

Another center of trouble was characterized by a serious reluctance to use theories of student development because of their prescriptive nature. Suspicion and anxiety seemed to result from the notion that to structure student personnel programs or instructional experiences in order to bring about specified changes in students might jeopardize one's eligibility for membership in the Association of Humanistic Psychologists.

*Along with Douglas Heath, I am aghast at such reluctance. Again the cases at the center of this conference are persuasive. The conscious intent to provoke the development of students toward specified goals must surely be superior to the wish to permit student development in whatever directions it takes. To accept the role as an agent of student development demands a prescriptive commitment, there is no alternative.

Career Development

Viewing the development of students through the lens that focuses on careers has been a viable enterprise for more than three decades (e.g., Osipow 1973). My familiarity with career development theories persuades me that, although they include many useful elements, the conversion of the theoretical insights to implications for practice is not a simple matter. Nor am I greatly impressed with the scope of such insights. I believe that it is important to think about careers in developmental terms and to think about development in career terms. I also believe that focusing on students who are making choices about their futures is highly productive for the long run. I am sometimes depressed that developmental psychologists and personality theorists ignore the career development literature.

I am convinced that work roles are a critical concern in human development. Knowledge of how one anticipates, prepares for, engages in, departs from, and avoids work roles can lead to explicit sets of prescriptive means for promoting the development of an-

other. A few useful insights about the nature of career development follow.

Evidence persuades me that, for any individual, it is better to be
actively engaged in the processes of anticipation, preparation, engagement, departure, and avoidance than to be passive. That is, developmental goals can be achieved better by promoting such activity than by permitting passivity (Jordaan 1974; Jordaan &
Super 1974).

Exploring one's future during adolescence, either in instrumen-
tal behavior or fantasy, leads to greater success and satisfaction in
adult work roles than does the absence of such exploration (Jordaan & Super 1974; Walvoord 1978).

All exploration is helpful to career development, and exploration which is premeditated, planned, and evaluated is the most
helpful. The highest level of such activity, exploring to test hypotheses about oneself, is the most facilitative of development
(Walvoord 1978).

Despite our wariness about what the future will bring, knowing
what the world of work is like at any given time is predictive of future success and satisfaction (Jordaan 1974).

Being concerned with the choices one needs to make during a
career—including when the choice points will come, what the
choice options are, and how to be prepared to choose—is associated with success and satisfaction in adult work life (Jordaan 1974;
Jordaan & Super 1974).

There may be other insights that are useful for the practice of
promoting the career development of students, but these are the
only ones I am willing to champion at the moment. Not only do I
believe in their efficacy, but I also firmly believe that student personnel practitioners can promote activity, exploratory behavior,
knowledge of the world of work, and concern with choice in the
students whose development they seek to influence. Most important of all, despite the reluctance of some, I am also convinced
that doing so (1) enhances the development of everyone, (2) inhibits the development of no one, and (3) violates no one's human
dignity or integrity.

Disquiet No. 3

Most troublesome to me are those attempts to persuade others that inquiry about student development is somehow antithetical to real human concern. It has been asserted that having students complete questionnaires and take psychological inventories is dehumanizing and frequently communicates that we regard them as subjects rather than human beings. Lament was heard because our armamentarium of well-crafted psychological instruments is less than one might hope for. Even statistical treatments of data about student growth have come under attack.

Although I have a bricklayer's empathy with these concerns, I am driven by a question that must be put to those opponents of inquiry: How do practitioners decide what needs doing, what to do, what needs changing, and what should be discontinued in their practices? In a region of the country with which I am very familiar, practitioners answer such questions by carefully evaluating how they feel about what they have done and checking those feelings out with their analysts. In all parts of the country, these questions are answered by administrative decisions which can be neither justified nor countered. Among these high-powered decision-making strategies, systematic inquiry deserves at least equal status, regardless of its shortcomings.

For me, each of the cases illustrated the value of careful research, no matter how flawed. Despite assertions to the contrary, I believe that bad data are better than no data. Bad conclusions may be worse than no conclusions, but such evil does not extend to the data on which the conclusions are based.

Salute

Finally, I want to congratulate the participants who shared their cases with us.

Each presenter began with barely adequate but *very useful* theory, engaged in creative design of practice under very difficult natural conditions, and conducted conscientious research to assess the efficacy of that practice and its future. Each case represents student personnel practice in its highest form. One gets glimpses of cathedrals abuilding.

We stonemasons salute you.

REFERENCES

Jordaan, J. P. Life stages as organizing modes of career development. In Herr, E. L., ed., *Vocational guidance and human development*. Boston: Houghton Mifflin, 1974.

Jordaan, J. P., & Super, D. E. The prediction of early adult vocational behavior. In D. F. Ricks, A. Thomas, & M. Roff, eds., *Life history research in psychopathology*. Minneapolis: University of Minnesota Press, 1974.

Myers, R. A. Research on educational and vocational counseling. In A. E. Bergin & S. L. Garfield, eds., *Handbook of psychotherapy and behavior change: an empirical analysis*. New York: Wiley, 1971.

Osipow, S. H. *Theories of career development*, 2d ed. Englewood Cliffs, N.J.: Prentice-Hall, 1973.

Walvoord, J. E. Correlates and outcomes of exploration in the high school and post-high school years. Doctoral dissertation, Teachers College, Columbia University, 1978.

Williamson, E. G. *Vocational counseling*. New York: McGraw-Hill, 1965.

A Model of Becoming
a Liberally Educated
and Mature Student

Douglas H. Heath

When we educate or counsel, we must inevitably ask, Educate or counsel for what purposes? Few academicians or counselors whom I know seldom make explicit to themselves or their students the values and psychological assumptions that underlie their choice of goals, curricula, or teaching or counseling methods. A wide chasm seemingly separates the purposes and methods of most traditional academicians and counselors. Some faculty members emphasize the acquisition of information; a few self-consciously and systematically seek to nurture specific intellectual skill maturation. Academic faculty typically assume the role of didactic dispensers of information to achieve their goals. Counselors emphasize the development of the "whole person," particularly, interpersonal relations, self-concept, and, occasionally, study and reading skills. They typically use a variety of nondidactic one-to-one verbal, self-reflective, nondirective, behavior modifying, or other nonexhortative methods. The typical faculty member views the "whole person" notion as vacuous, if not irrelevant to his purposes. The typical counselor views the academician as psychologically naive, and, occasionally, destructive to student development because of his narrow commitment to only cognitive excellence.

There is no persuasive model of the process of becoming a liberally educated person that provides academic faculty members and counselors with a commonly shared set of purposes, or with in-

Note: The research was supported by the National Institute of Mental Health, grant 11227, the W. Clement and Jessie Stone Foundation, and the Spencer Foundation.

sights about the most effective ways to achieve such purposes. Most educational philosophers would make their stand with the counselor rather than today's academician. A content analysis of the ideas of twenty-five of the principal educational theorists since Socrates revealed widespread agreement that a liberally educated person should become more reflective, and aware of himself, his values, and other people; more social and humane in his interests, values, and identifications with other people and their traditions; more integrative in his thought as well as in his values, ideas about himself, and relations with other persons; more centered in his values; more independent of other viewpoints; and in greater control of his own powers (see Appendix A, Heath 1968). None of the educational theorists surveyed claimed that education should nurture only the mastery of cognitive information and a limited set of academic skills.

But the academicians's charge that the concept of the whole person is insufferably vague and meaningless to the practicing teacher is correct. Just what does Whitehead's (1929) emphasis on the development of the "self," Dewey's (1928) on "growth," and Raushenbush's (1965) on "to make maturity the more it might become" tell us specifically? Nothing. We do not have methods for measuring most of the alleged outcomes of the liberal education of which educational philsophers talk. Our insecure infatuation with precise and objective measures has restricted our efforts almost solely to the measurement of bits of acquired, and rapidly lost, information.

Psychosexual theory has nothing to say about adolescence and adulthood; Eriksonian psychosocial theory (Erikson 1950) is too programmatic, vague, and tends to ignore cognitive growth; Perry's (1970) approach is cognitively restricted in emphasis, although perhaps not in implication, and in age span; Chickering's theory (1969) tends to ignore the specification of cognitive development, humanization, and stabilization of a person's values, awareness of personal relationships and allocentric self-development. Because we have amassed bits and pieces of ideas but not *systematically* organized them, we cannot comprehend yet the richness of the alleged effects of a liberal education.

Proposed Criteria of an Adequate Model
of Healthy Development

What criteria might both academician and counselor expect an adequate psychological model of healthy growth to meet?

ENCOMPASSES LIFE SPAN

A model of healthy growth should apply to the life span and not be limited to some specific chronological age period. The process of becoming liberally educated starts in early childhood and, not infrequently, blossoms in adulthood. Any model that confines itself to the period of age seventeen to twenty-one years is suspect to me: it lacks generality and, inevitably, provokes a host of spurious psychological issues, such as, if entering freshmen are primarily dualists in their thinking, what were they when they were six or fifteen? If relativistic thinking is the "high point" of cognitive maturing and such a stage can be reached during college, then is further cognitive maturation impossible, other than the application of relativistic modes of thought to more and more diverse types of problems? Furthermore, the failure to extend our insights of development in one limited age period to the larger life span may distort our understanding of the specific age period itself and its needs.

Too narrow an age perspective of student development may run afoul of a basic principle of maturing which I have found in study after study: growth is deeply systemic. Excessive development in one sector of the person begins to induce resistance to further development in that sector until compensatory development occurs in the neglected sectors of the personality. Although this principle intuitively is "known" by most counselors, its effects frequently are not manifest until after college, in many students. For example, I have extensive data about the maturation of a group of men at ages sixteen to seventeen (SAT scores), nineteen to twenty (college grades, faculty evaluations, and extensive personality data), and thirty-one to thirty-two (several hundred measures of competence and maturity). High scholastic aptitude during adolescence for this group was inversely related, fifteen years later, to many of the components that define a mature and competent adult. A heavy emphasis on cognitive maturation had made them egocentric and interfered with the maturation of their interpersonal skills, which were more critical to their adult competence than the information and limited verbal, abstract skills they had learned in college (Heath 1977a). A model of development for college years only, not leavened by an understanding of preceding and subsequent events, distorts our understanding of the principal types of growth that *should* occur at different ages.

COMPREHENSIVENESS

An adequate model of development includes all of the principal types of maturing and immaturing effects that may occur during the process of becoming educated. Hundreds of studies suggest that becoming liberally educated produces a meager handful of effects: increased cognitive flexibility, more aesthetic appreciation, more socially liberal values, humanization of one's conscience (Newcomb & Feldman 1969). In fact, the effects of our colleges and classrooms may be found to be much more extensive and enduring than these four if, when we research the effects, we cast a wider net than our too-focused studies frequently use. What is blocking a more comprehensive understanding of the process of healthy growth? (a) Few researchers have comprehensively mapped what actually takes place when a person is becoming liberally educated or is maturing. (b) Measures do not exist for many of the effects of healthy growth hypothesized by both educational philosophers and psychological and social theorists (Heath 1968). (c) The preference for cross-sectional rather than longitudinal studies severely restricts our understanding of change over time (Wohlwill 1973). (d) The reductionistic mind set of most researchers has led to the ignoring of the systemic complexity of the growth process and the focus on one or two effects only — frequently, cognition and the effects of a specific classroom or school intervention. (e) Ninety-nine percent of researchers and teachers have failed to examine which effects of schooling *endure* when a student leaves the classroom or school. For example, studies of alumni of my college suggest that the pattern of effects that endures into adulthood is quite different from that which was assessed during college (Heath 1968, 1976c).

GENERALITY

An adequate life-span model should be general. It should apply to persons of both sexes and different ethnic, social class, and socio-cultural backgrounds. A scientific model of healthy development should be universal, not a model applicable only to blacks or Spanish-Americans or the Nuer tribe in Africa. This is not to deny that each person uniquely differs in some ways from every other of the several billion persons on our planet, or that groups of people differ from other groups in other ways. But all of us are alike in many ways, including, I propose, how we mature when we are free to become, healthy, growing persons. Our genes, nutrition, gender, social class, and cultural values direct and block different facets of our growth in diverse ways; thus, they provide a rich (though not infinite) variety of patterns through which our growth is manifested. For example, American societal biases for centuries set a pattern for women to be dependent, unconfident, timid, fearful, interpersonally conforming, and emotionally labile (Block 1976), traits that the women themselves judge to be immature. Are we to develop a separate model of healthy development for women in which such modal feminine traits are our referent for maturing? Do we create a model of healthy development for the Sicilian culture that defines its mature males to be aggressively autonomous, interpersonally suppressive of women, and tenderly barren? In other words, the criterion of universality eschews culturally manifest typicality as an appropriate scientific criterion. The issue of whether a universal model of healthy development can be created will be decided by more careful empirical studies in the future and not by the relativistic ideology that has dominated American social science these past decades.

To obtain such a universal, scientifically valid model of maturing, we must generate more abstract psychologically genotypic rather than highly specific phenotypic criteria to define healthy growth. I propose as a hypothesis that we can discover such criteria by examining the psychological dimensions that describe the development of people as a system. I first looked for clues to what those genotypic dimensions of healthy growth might be by examining the clinical, theoretical, and empirical literature for the traits describing mentally healthy, psychologically sound, optimally functioning, self-actualizing, fulfilled, emotionally mature, "ideal" persons. Although the biologists, clinicians, social and developmental psychologists, and researchers differed in their emphases and the number of traits used to distinguish mature from less mature persons, they tended to repeat certain underlying dimensions (Heath 1965). Most agreed, for example, that a more mature system was more complexly differentiated and integrated than a less mature system. Most agreed that people who matured, whether through development or psychotherapy, became more other-centered, and more capable of empathically understanding other points of view. Most also agreed that a human system tends to become more stable as well as more autonomous of its immediate impulses or of environmental influences, with maturity. And almost all agreed that a more mature *human* system is more aware, reflective of its own functioning. Such fundamental developmental dimensions provide hypotheses to explore students' growth in college environments known to have especially powerful maturing effects.

VALUE FREE

An adequate model of healthy development should have value-free criteria. As long as our models are open to the charge that they just reflect our idiosyncratic or cultural values about maturing, we fail to approach the generality a scientific model should have. We do not arrive at such a relatively value-free type of model by one large bootstrap operation. Rather, we gradually purify our conceptions of healthy development by empirically testing, revising, retesting, and revising again in one situation after another, seeking to identify recurring patterns. (For the theoretical and methodological strategies to identify such value-free universals, see Heath [1977c].) But I suggest that as we test the generality of the *patterning* of differences, say, between more mature and less mature persons in different cultures, we will discover that the process of adapting effectively to our complex sociocultural environments tends to depend on the presence of certain traits, and those traits are the ones we can identify from a model of maturing. This is not to deny that our personal and societal values are the principal determinants of the primary goals for which we educate or counsel. To educate for academic excellence, technical competence, or creativity, or to counsel for adjustment or personal growth, is to make a judgment about which goal is more valued. But, *if* we elect to educate or counsel for the value which most educational philosophers opt for, namely, the personal growth or maturing of our students, then I would make the powerful—what some have called audacious and others foolish—claim that we can begin now to specify in more general, systemic, and value-free terms just what dimensions define that personal growth or maturing. The degrees of freedom for individual bias determining what traits define such growth are becoming fewer as we learn more about the nature of such growth in many different educational or other sociocultural environments.

Other criteria also should mark an adequate model of healthy development. It should be one that can be operationalized and validated; it should generate new hypotheses and insights; it should, in connection with other studies about the conditions of maturing, provide useful guidelines, for example, to educators or counselors about how to further the growth of students more effectively.

Such criteria are too ambitious for any current model to meet, certainly the one I describe below. Yet, they reflect an attitude, a value orientation, if you wish, about the kind of model we ought to work toward: one that spans the lifetime and is comprehensive, general, systemic and dimensional, value free, testable, valid, generative of new insights, and useful.

A Proposed Model of Healthy Development

To construct and test a model of healthy development requires some decisions about assessment strategy. Obviously, to begin the study of healthily functioning, competent, and maturing persons requires the use of human judgment to identify such persons. If adequate psychological tests measuring maturing and its dimensions had been available, the twenty years of research to develop methods for and validate the model I present could have been greatly foreshortened. I had to begin where most personality research begins: with human judges whose judgments were likely to be affected by idiosyncratic values and biases about what a competent, well-functioning, mature student was like. To control for individual biases, I have always used large numbers of diverse judges (including students, faculty, administrators, counselors, coaches, and even *portiers* in Italy) who knew well many of the students of the population being sampled and who, in objective ways, systematically considered everyone in the population for his degree of competence and maturity. The judges had no knowledge of the study, its hypotheses, or procedures. Judges in five different cultural areas—Istanbul, Ankara, Sicily, Pisa, and Philadelphia—agreed remarkably well on the mature and immature exemplars in small populations of students who were known intimately in their many different roles. Once the persons had been selected by consensual judgments, other judges, typically close friends, then completed detailed and different types of ratings about the students, as double checks on the original selection judgments. Very high agreement typically has been found among the different types and sets of judges, even when the specific method of evaluating a person was radically different.

When the focus of the studies has been on the determinants and effects of becoming educated, rather than on verifying predicted differences between mature and immature persons, groups of students (and alumni) have been selected randomly for study at different points during their college careers (Heath 1968).

The actual assessment of the persons in all the studies I report has relied on a holistic multilevel, multiform, in-depth procedure that typically has yielded several hundred different measures of the students' personalities. To respect the systemic complexity of personality functioning while measuring a presumed comprehensive model of maturing demands that the students be assessed with respect to both conscious and less-conscious levels of behavior and cognitive, self-conceptual, motivational, and interpersonal development. Accordingly, I have routinely used (a) self-ratings, such as adjective check lists, personality inventories like the MMPI, Study of Values, and the Perceived Self Questionnaire; (b) projective tests like the Rorschach; (c) measures of the actual behavior being assessed, such as the Phrase Association Test, Self-Image Questionnaire dimensional procedures, and tests of cognitive efficiency;

and (d) extensive ratings by judges. To test for convergent validity, a variety of different types of tests measuring the same hypothesized dimension of maturing have been used.

The data base, which now confirms many hypotheses of the model of maturing as well as its generality, consists of the following: (1) intensive exploratory study of selected mature and immature college men to determine how they differed (Heath 1965); (2) exact replication of the preceding study to test the generality of the model's predictions of the patterning of differences between mature and immature exemplars in several of the principal cultural-religious areas of the world (Heath 1977c); (3) longitudinal study of the development, and its determinants, of college men from freshman through senior year, and of the enduring effects on alumni of their higher education (Heath 1968, 1976c); (4) longitudinal study of men studied as freshmen and upperclassmen and in their early thirties to test the adequacy of the model for describing maturing during adulthood, to assess the principal adolescent and college predictors of such maturing (Heath 1976a, 1976b, 1976c, 1977a, 1977b), and to identify the adult determinants of such development (Heath 1977d); (5) other researchers have used the model and some of its methods with children, women, and other college populations to test a variety of more specific hypotheses about maturing (e.g., Lowry 1967; Tippett & Silber 1966).

I now briefly describe the dimensions of the model and its relation to education, some of the methods used to measure maturing on the dimension, and a few sample findings about the validity of the model's hypotheses.

Figure 1 portrays the five principal interdependent dimensions and the sectors of the personality on which dimensional maturing has been studied. When we study the "whole person," we must analyze attributes of his "person." Psychologists typically have categorized the person according to cognitive or intellective skills, self-concept, values (or motives), and personal relationships. My model of maturing suggests twenty basic hypotheses about the maturing of the whole person. Let us briefly examine each.

The first dimension defining maturing is the increased potential for symbolizing one's experience. A principal effect of edu-

DIMENSIONS

Personality Sector	Symboli-zation	Allocen-tricism	Integra-tion	Stability	Autonomy
Cognitive skills					
Self-concept					
Values					
Interpersonal relations					

Figure 1. Heath model of maturing.

cation is to provide a student with the tools, such as words, numbers, and musical forms, by which to represent his experience with the external and internal worlds. Increasingly, as he matures, he is able to turn his thought processes back on themselves to monitor, check, and alter them reflectively. Such capacity for symbolization enhances imagination (one goal of a liberal education for Hook [1946]), the ability to foresee consequences (another goal of a liberal education for Dewey [1964c]). A more mature, in contrast to a less mature person, is more able to symbolize his understanding of himself accurately (an educational goal for most educators since Socrates), as well as to articulate his values and motives (an enduring goal of counselors). Finally, maturing is hypothesized to be directly related to improving the understanding of one's relationships with others.

Important as is reflective intelligence (Dewey identified it as a critical attribute of the educated person), psychologists have not developed adequate measures of the ability for such reflection. Numerous types of methods have been developed, however, to assess accuracy of self-insight. The method I have found consistently to be the most powerful is very simple: compare the degree of disagreement between how an individual rates himself on thirty different scaled traits (Self-Image Questionnaire, SIQ) with comparable ratings by different judges who know him well, like close friends, teachers, spouse, or business colleagues. The results are remarkably consistent for every study of maturing. Increased self-insight is a major effect of becoming educated (Heath 1968). It distinguishes the mature from the less mature student in five different cultures (Heath 1977c). It is related to many measures of adult competence in my current studies.

The second dimension that describes the maturing process is what I call growth from auto- to allocentricism. The movement of growth for most theorists is away from narcissism to other-centeredness, from egocentric or primary to socialized or secondary forms of thought, from a narrowly circumscribed self-concept to an expanding one, from prejudice and bias to tolerant understanding of others. Dewey talked ceaselessly about education nurturing a person's empathic ability to take a "multiplicity of perspectives" (1964a); Van Doren (1943) talked of the educated person as one who will "endeavor to rear within himself that third man who is present when two men speak, and who is happy when they understand each other" (p. 68). And most educators believe that education should encourage more allocentric values, like "social consciousness and a social conscience" (Hutchins 1943) or "respect for the rights and views of others" (McGrath 1959). Finally, a variety of educators say that education should "humanize," should confirm to a person his social identity and create in him a deep sense of identification with all persons.

Again, when the research began, few measures were available with which to assess, for example, allocentric relativistic thinking, including increased analytic and logical skills. When the original studies had confirmed that maturing might be described validly by the dimensions listed in Figure 1, a summary general self-report type of test, the Perceived Self Questionnaire (PSQ), was created to rapidly secure measures of maturing on each dimension for each sector of the personality. The scaled fifty items provide a total score of dimensional maturity. The PSQ has been used now in a variety of studies and the results are highly consistent. It is more powerfully predictive of a wider range of measures of psychological maturing than are the MMPI, Rorschach, and other conventional tests of psychological adjustment and health (Appendix B in Heath 1968; 1977c). The test is not psychometrically impeccable, fit for individual assessment, but, I believe, it secures its predictive efficacy because of the theoretical rationale on which it is based.

To measure allocentric cognitive maturing (also measured by Holt's Rorschach scores for primary and secondary process thinking), one scaled PSQ example is, "My thoughts and judgments about intellectual problems are usually realistic and practical." An allocentric self-concept refers to the ability of a person to predict accurately how others who know him well will rate him on the Self-Image Questionnaire. Again, the evidence is unequivocal. In all five cultural areas studied, the more mature person is more able than the less mature person to predict accurately what others think of him. More allocentric or tolerant and understanding personal relationships were found to rank, in one college, as its fifth most important effect on students, but to rank tenth and eleventh in two other colleges, indicating a very important fact about higher education. Different types of institutions not only vary in the magnitude of their maturing and immaturing effects but, also, they may vary greatly in the patterning of their effects (Fieselmann 1973; Heath 1968).

The third related dimension on which maturing occurs is integration. Growth, as Sanford (1962) has told us, is toward increasingly more differentiated and integrated structures. Our cognitive processes become more relational, deductive, and complexly flexible. Our self-concepts become not only more like our ideal selves, the traditional definition of self-image congruence by counselors like Rogers, but also more like our social selves, those selves we believe that other persons think of us as having. The consequence is that we no longer need to play roles in our relationships with each other as we become more mature; we can become more emotionally spontaneous. Our values, as Allport (1937) long ago suggested, become more coherent and consistent with each other and with our actions. And we increase in our ability to create reciprocally mutual cooperative relationships with other persons (Piaget & Inhelder 1969).

Educators have much to say about the progressive integration of a person as he or she becomes liberally educated. To refer to more flexible integrative thought they use phrases like "understanding human endeavors in their relations to one another" (Meiklejohn 1920, p. 38), "discovering combinations of ideas before their worth is known" (Bruner 1963, p. 6), and developing generalizing skills (Newman 1891). But becoming educated is more than just developing relational skills, the principal maturing effect that I found of my own college (Heath 1968). Educators also talked of developing a more "coherent and integrated self" (Dewey 1964b, p. 177) or becoming more connected to other men (Hutchins 1936).

A persistent methodological failing of my studies of maturing has been the unavailability of adequate measures for *directly* assessing the maturity of a person's interpersonal relationships. Self-report measures of integrative personal relationships, direct and indirect report indices of the mutuality of husbands' relationships with their wives, and judge ratings consistently combine to suggest that a more mature person has more close friendships and is more open to closer mutuality relationships. But I have not found a way to test behaviorally such qualities of mature relationships. Hence, the hypotheses about interpersonal maturing are some of the least well-documented in my studies.

The fourth genotypic dimension defining maturing is increasing stabilization. I mentioned earlier that development on a dimension or in a sector of the personality can become exaggerated, distort the system's equilibrium, and lead to resistance to further development until the system has resumed its growth in the lagging areas of the personality. Too great stability relative to maturing on the other dimensions may lead to rigidity and inhibit the openness to increasing differentiation that describes the progressive integration of the personality. Such a principle provides counselors with a guideline for assessing psychological health or "maturity." It is the person and not his specific behavior that is mentally healthy or unhealthy. For example, homosexual or other tabooed sexual behavior, I would claim, is not in and of itself unhealthy or immature. A man who was maturely aware of his relationships with others and who was tolerant and understanding and capable of forming mutually reciprocal relationships could well participate in homosexual relationships and, according to all my criteria, be very healthy. In fact, one of my students, in a study of young adult male self-identified homosexuals and heterosexuals, found no differences in their psychological health or maturity, as measured by the methods developed for assessing the dimensional model of maturing (Feinman 1973). This is not to say that some homosexual or heterosexual behavior does not reflect unconscious acting out in self-centered exploitative, and mercurial ways. The point is that it is the maturity or psychological health of the system itself that is the standard for evaluating the healthiness of specific acts.

More mature persons have more stably organized cognitive processes. When psychoanalysts talk of ego strength, I believe they are referring primarily to a person's ability to maintain secondary process thinking even while thinking about personally disturbing thoughts. This key insight of Freud, that the thinking of the more mature person "must concern itself with the connecting paths between ideas, without being led astray by the *intensities* of those ideas" (1956, p. 602), is critical for counselors and teachers to understand. Students frequently are unable to maintain the objective, logical, and conceptual integrity of their thoughts when they must think about philosophical, political, and other types of troubling personal issues. Their thoughts easily become disorganized under the stress of examinations or issues that are "too close" to them. A variety of experimental procedures have been designed to measure the degree to which persons are able to maintain their conceptual, analytic, and judgmental efficiency when they are solving problems composed of threatening information, such as aggressive and sexual themes (Heath 1965). Again, the evidence is very compelling. It has been strongly confirmed for the five cultural areas that the more mature person is able to maintain the stability of his cognitive functions or to bounce back more rapidly if he becomes disorganized than the less mature person (Heath 1977c).

The educational philosophers that I surveyed did not have much to say about the dimension of stability, but they used phrases like "steadiness of intellect" (Newman 1891) and developing an intellect with "its own principles of order and continuity" (Dewey 1964b).

A more mature person also has a more stable self-concept or identity, a proposition for which Erikson is known. This hypothesis has been amply confirmed in my various studies and by other researchers. The more mature person's values, as well as his relationships with others, are also more stable than those of less mature persons. Chickering (1969) identified the establishing of such an identity as a main effect of becoming educated. Perhaps because of differences in our methods, such identity stabilization ranked much less important in three diverse colleges — sixth, twelfth, and thirteenth. The stabilization of the students' values and personal relationships actually tended to be more important effects of the three colleges than confirming the students in their identity. My studies of the maturing of young adults during their twenties informally suggest that many did not really "clinch" their subjective sense of identity until they had tested their evolving ideas about themselves in their occupations (Heath 1977d).

The fifth and last dimension that defines maturing is autonomy. Maturing is associated with the increasing ability to respond selectively and deliberately to the press of the environment as well as to control one's impulses and childish wishes. One becomes more "freed" of unconscious impulse determination or environmental control. An important measure of whether a person has stabilized and then become more autonomous in what he has learned is whether he can transfer or generalize his learning to another situation. It is a testimony to our ignorance of the learning process that we teachers believe that if a person "passes" our examinations he has "learned" what he temporarily recalled. According to the model of maturing, the true test of whether he has "made his own" that which he has learned is whether he can use that skill in some other course or situation for some other purpose. Similarly, a more mature person has a more autonomous self-concept; he knows who he is and can resist altering his view of himself under pressure. Some evidence suggests that the more mature person is more selectively discriminating in what he allows to affect his concept of himself than the less mature person (Tippett & Silber 1966). That a more mature person not only has more stable but also more autonomous values has been confirmed now for several different cultures (Heath 1977c). Finally, he can be more independent in his relationships with others, although, according to the equilibrating principle, not so independent that he becomes a self-sufficient narcissist incapable of allocentrically understanding and responding to the needs of others.

Many educators identify the increasing autonomy of a person's intellectual skills as a primary effect of education, for example, "free to use the intellect" (Van Doren 1943); "capacity to weigh evidence dispassionately" (Gardner 1956, p. 6); or "freed intelligence," "intellectual courage," or "freedom of thought." Similarly, Van Doren discussed being prepared to "meet resistance" to one's values, Newman (1891) talked of securing "command over [one's] own powers," and Hook (1946) of being able to "stand alone."

I have had continuing difficulty securing reliable measures of the different aspects of autonomy, possibly because of an inadequate theoretical definition of the dimension or of its developmental complexity. For example, on various self-report measures of maturing, freshmen have proved to be more "autonomous" than seniors. My post hoc explanation, supported by other evidence, is that the freshmen had reached a stable level of equilibrium in high school; within that context, they saw themselves as self-sufficient, independent persons, and they so described themselves during their first week at college. Shortly after, however, many found that if they were to continue to grow, they had to become more allocentrically open, even emotionally dependent upon, the influence of other people. The consequence was a seeming regression in autonomy as they matured on other dimensions. By the time they became seniors, they were more autonomous in many ways, such as in cognitive ability; but because they had not yet tested their growth in situations outside the college, they remained uncertain of just how maturely independent they could function. Consequently, they tended to test as less autonomous on self-report types of measures than when they entered college. Changes in their reference groups, increased lack of self-confidence temporarily induced by college, and inadequate measures of autonomy combine to leave the hypotheses about autonomy not well confirmed.

Adequacy of Model of Student Maturing

Let us now apply the criteria of an adequate model of healthy development to the model of maturing, which was sketched briefly above.

LIFE SPAN

Because the model is a dimensional rather than "stage" or "developmental task" type, it theoretically should be applicable to personality change from birth to death. A dimensional model, at one level of abstraction, avoids the messy methodological and theoretical problems associated with verifying a sequential universalistic "stage" model for different ages. When appropriately translated, the model of maturing has been useful for studies of five and six year olds. It has distinguished mature and immature adolescents and young adults. It has not been applied to the study of older persons, so that we do not know yet how validly it describes the dynamics of "successful" aging.

COMPREHENSIVENESS

The model has consistently proved to order comprehensively the major cited effects of college as well as the effects of growing up through one's twenties and early thirties. Independent judges, coding detailed interview reports about changes experienced during these years, have not discovered recurrent major effects that could not be categorized by the model. Although judge reliability in such coding is very good, I believe that the abstractness of the model may very well obscure more differentiated changes that, if made more explicit, might alter the model. The model has been empirically derived and can easily be altered to include other dimensions. For example, an effect of achieving a new level of equilibrium in adaptation is the release of affective energy formerly used to monitor one's self self-consciously, to maintain nonintegrative defenses, and the like. The sense of released energy, subjective sense of power, and excitement and joy, even, is not captured by the model, except as a consequence of the adaptive sequence.

The model is more programmatic than it is a detailed specification of the course of symbolization and allocentric maturation during the life span. Perry's (1970) detailed analysis of the cognitive changes during college provide the specification for one time period, although his model cuts across the dimensions in its focus on cognitive skill development. As we learn more about the development of empathy and role taking, we may be able to bring a more detailed understanding to different "levels" or "stages" of allocentric growth, for example.

GENERALITY

Most personality theorists, as well as researchers, seldom test the generality of their findings across different samples in different types of situations. The generality of the model has now been tested in five different cultural areas. Ninety percent of its hypotheses were confirmed. The remaining 10 percent were neither confirmed nor disconfirmed (Heath 1977c). The generality of the model across different social classes has not been systematically studied; quite unintentionally, however, the Sicilian sample in the cultural study included mainly the sons of uneducated peasants. Most of the hypotheses held for this sample as well. Partial studies have demonstrated that the internal pattern of relations among the dimensions holds for college-educated women, but the absence of comparable in-depth studies of women is a major empirical failing. I hold, however, to the hypothesis that the model is perfectly general, but it will have to be empirically tested by others on more diverse groups to obtain the necessary evidence to confirm or disconfirm the hypothesis.

VALUE FREE

The issues about the roles of value judgments in creating a model of healthy development have been discussed in detail elsewhere (Heath 1977c). We can say, at least at this time, that judges in Protestant-Jewish, Catholic, and Moslem countries agree on the traits that distinguish mature and immature male students. It is our first evidence that what defines psychological maturity *may* be relatively free of cultural bias. If we analyze what other religio-cultural groups assume to be and identify as more mature, in contrast to less mature persons, I believe that we would find considerable agreement as well (Heath 1977c; Soddy 1961). (Martha Lutman [personal communication, 1977] has pointed out the similarity of the dimensional model of maturing to the assumptions of Zen Buddhism about the goals of living as described by Owens [Tart 1975].)

OTHER CRITERIA

A very extensive data base, greater than for most other student developmental models, now confirms and clarifies the model of maturing reported here. Intriguingly, the measures used to assess the model are emerging as very powerful predictors of subsequent adult competence and maturity. That is, the best predictors of subsequent adult vocational adaptation are measures of adolescent psychological maturity (Heath 1976a). Also, the dimensions of psychological maturity, as measured in college students, predict a variety of adult competencies, such as creating satisfying marital or interpersonal relationships.

The model of maturing has led to the theoretically based development of various measures and suggested new hypothesized relationships among different attributes of cognitive skill development and other aspects of the personality. For example, I would predict that a relativist, as measured by Perry's cognitive scoring system, would be dimensionally more mature in his self-concept and interpersonal relationships than a dualist.

I have found that the model of maturing is useful in raising questions about our educational goals and instructional procedures. I have shown elsewhere how the model can be used to suggest more rationally planned change in our schools and colleges (Heath 1971, 1973, 1974a, 1974b).

One other criterion of an adequate model is the ability to use it to make theoretical contact with other ways of ordering the same phenomena. I have not found a satisfactory way to deal with the various stage concepts of development. As a system matures it goes through a series of successive cycles of disorganization, efforts to adapt, and equilibration at, typically, more advanced levels of systemic organization. That is, psychological maturing is not a continuous or linear process, most clearly after puberty. Many persons may show little personal maturing for long stretches of time. I have found some seniors who are almost identical in their values, concepts of themselves, and cognitive skills when they graduate as when they were freshmen. But I also know from my studies of adult men that maturing continues into the adult years (Heath 1977d).

What induces continued growth? Several types of motivational sources confuse, disrupt, and trigger renewed efforts to create a more adaptive self-organization. Obviously, neurophysiological alterations, such as the emergence of the semiotic function for Piaget, the arrival of puberty, or the advent of menopause help to define a universal regularity in the life span that may justify the concept of stage. A second impetus to new growth is any marked change in the environment that requires new adaptations. The ceaseless changes that are typical of our current society require even greater maturity for persons to be open to continued adaptability in the future—one reason, I believe, for the emerging consensus among educators that the principal goal of education in the future will be to further a youth's educability or ability to adapt continually. A third source may be, for a more mature person, a personal goal of self-actualization that leads one to disrupt one's life self-consciously and willfully in order to induce new challenges and, hence, the possibility of new growth. Only now are researchers beginning to identify the characteristics that predict the type of person who will continue to mature through his adult years (Block 1971; Lowenthal, Thurnher, & Chiriboga 1976).

However, as disorganization and confusion are initiated (and every good college has self-consciously considered how to disorganize its freshmen *constructively* those first few weeks), the typical adaptive response is to try to symbolize, understand, and think out the reasons for the confusion and pain. In the process, a person seeks out other points of view, from a roommate, parents, teacher, or book, for example. This allocentric phase of the adaptive process leads to more differentiated thinking, to a variety of possible steps to take, and to the framing of more integrative ways of proceeding. The repetition or testing of that proposed solution may lead to its stabilization, if it is rewarding, like the consolidation of one's sexual patterns or more efficient ways of studying. Eventually, one's new responses, values, and interpersonal skills become stabilized and autonomous, less self-consciously manipulated, and more harmoniously and gracefully transferred to other

persons or other courses. With that automatization comes the release of energy that was formerly bound up in self-consciously
learning how to adapt, a feeling of power, and a more stable, pre-
dictable level of functioning.

Now, what the stage theorists do, I think, is to identify the principal developmental tasks or potentialities that seem to occur at
roughly similar periods of time for most persons in a society. The
determinants of that sequential ordering are complex and varied,
but each "stage" represents a new possibility for disorganization,
which can lead to either regression or more mature adaptation.
The model of maturing identifies the personality traits that are
likely to lead at each stage to its successful resolution. It is for this
reason that the model of maturing has turned out to be a good
predictor of subsequent adaptation to later stages, such as vocational, marital intimacy, and parenting demands.

I remain uncomfortable, however, with the assumptions of stage
theorists, particularly when they move away from early cognitive
development, or clearly physiologically based demands, to social-
emotional-interpersonal development. For Erikson, identity precedes intimacy, but Douvan and Adelson (1966) found that, for
American girls, intimacy precedes identity. I find that the adult
men I studied created stable intimacy patterns before they felt
centered in their vocational identities. Levinson (personal communication, 1974) deduced from a study of men in their forties
that there is in males a crisis stage during the early thirties. I have
studied thirty year olds directly, and only a minority seemed to be
experiencing some "crisis" in their vocational or marital lives at
the time, and I would be hard pressed to identify the "crisis" by
any simple label. Loevinger (1966) discussed autonomy as a late
adult stage; but Erikson (1950) identified autonomy in early childhood. If we could agree on how terms such as autonomy are defined, and if a sequential order were found for different life experiences, my hunch is that the order would be culturally determined,
or it would be only a manifestation of the psychological logic of
the aging process, for example, generativity defined as becoming a
parent, ordinarily, after the intimacy of marriage. Sociocultural
determination of the "crises" in one's life—for example, retire-
ment—makes stage concepts too arbitrary for a universal, general

model of healthy development. I have never found such conceptualizations to be very provocative or to generate specific relational hypotheses about maturing. In contrast to colleagues who have only done cross-sectional research or who have not studied the course of a person's life over any considerable portion of time, researchers who have studied personality development longitudinally apparently have not found the stage concept to be very useful as a theoretical organization for their data (Block 1971; Honzik 1971; Kagan & Moss 1962; Murphy 1962; Neugarten 1968; Vaillant & McArthur 1972; White 1966).

In closing, I return to the theme with which I began. I suggest that there is emerging a theoretical model of maturing that comprehends and orders the goals of educational philosophers, and that it may provide a common basis on which academicians and counselors can meet. If we accept that a liberal education should promote the healthy growth of an individual, then the model of maturing may offer an initial direction. The power of the liberal education we could offer to our students is not the ever-changing informational content we too frequently try to stuff into their heads, but the control it gives our students of their continued maturing and adapting to meet the demands of an ever-changing world.

REFERENCES

Allport, G. W. *Personality: a psychological interpretation.* New York: Henry Holt, 1937.

Block, J. *Lives through time.* Berkeley, Calif.: Bancroft, 1971.

Block, J. H. Assessing sex differences: issues, problems, and pitfalls. *Merrill-Palmer Quarterly*, 1976, 22, 283-308.

Bruner, J. S. *The process of education.* Cambridge, Mass.: Harvard University Press, 1963.

Chickering, A. W. *Education and identity.* San Francisco: Jossey-Bass, 1969.

Dewey, J. The process and product of reflective activity. In R. D. Archambault, ed., *John Dewey on education.* New York: Modern Library, Random House, 1964. (a) (Originally pub. 1933.)

Dewey, J. Progressive education and the science of education. In R. D. Archambault, ed., *John Dewey on education.* New York: Modern Library, Random House, 1964. (b) (Originally pub. 1928.)

Dewey, J. School conditions and the training of thought. In R. D. Archambault, ed., *John Dewey on education.* New York: Modern Library, Random House, 1964. (c) (Originally pub. 1933.)

Douvan, E., & Adelson, J. *The adolescent experience.* New York: Wiley, 1966.

Erikson, E. *Childhood and society.* New York: Norton, 1950.

Feinman, S. Psychological maturity and homosexuality. Senior thesis, Haverford College, 1973.

Fieselmann, A. The college environment as an affector of maturity. Senior thesis, Hanover College, 1973.

Freud, S. *The interpretation of dreams.* New York: Basic Books, 1956. (Originally pub. 1900.)

Gardner, J. W. Fifty-first annual report, 1955-56, Carnegie Corporation of New York. New York: Carnegie Corporation, 1956.

Heath, D. H. *Explorations of maturity.* New York: Appleton-Century-Crofts, 1965.

————. *Growing up in college.* San Francisco: Jossey-Bass, 1968.

————. *Humanizing schools.* New York: Hayden, 1971.

————. What is a powerfully liberally educating college? *College and University Journal,* 1973, 12(4), 12-16.

————. Educating for maturity. *College and University Journal,* March 1974, 15-22. (a)

————. Maturing in college. *Newsletter* (Council for the Advancement of Small Colleges), 1974, 17(5), 4-8. (b)

————. Adolescent and adult predictors of vocational adaptation. *Journal of Vocational Behavior,* 1976, 9, 1-19. (a)

————. Competent fathers: their personalities and marriages. *Human Development,* 1976, 19, 26-39. (b)

————. What the enduring effects of higher education tell us about a liberal education. *Journal of Higher Education,* 1976, 47, 173-190. (c)

————. Academic predictors of adult maturity and competence. *Journal of Higher Education,* 1977, 48, 613-632. (a)

————. Maternal competence, expectation, and involvement. *Journal Genetic Psychology,* 1977, 131, 169-182. (b)

————. *Maturity and competence: a transcultural view.* New York: Gardner Press, 1977. (c)

————. Some possible effects of occupation on the maturing of professional men. *Journal of Vocational Behavior,* 1977, 11, 163-281. (d)

Honzik, M. P. Perspectives on the longitudinal studies. In M. C. Jones, N. Bayley, J. W. Macfarlane, & M. P. Honzik, eds., *The course of human development.* Waltham, Mass.: Xerox, 1971.

Hook, S. *Education for the modern man.* Toronto: Longmans, 1946.

Hutchins, R. M. *The higher learning in America.* New Haven: Yale University Press, 1936.

————. *Education for freedom.* Baton Rouge: Louisiana State University Press, 1943.

Kagan, J., & Moss, H. A. *Birth to maturity.* New York: Wiley, 1962.

Leovinger, J. The meaning and measurement of ego development. *American Psychologist,* 1966, 21, 195-206.

Lowenthal, M. F.; Thurnher, M.; and Chiriboga, D. *Four stages of life.* San Francisco: Jossey-Bass, 19

Lowry, D. Frustration reactions in twenty-two six-year-old boys. Senior thesis, Haverford College, 1967.

McGrath, E. J. *The graduate school and the decline of liberal education.* New York: Bureau of Publications, Teachers College, Columbia University, 1959.

Meiklejohn, A. *The liberal college.* Boston: Marshall Jones, 1920.

Murphy, L. B. *The widening world of childhood.* New York: Basic Books, 1962.

Neugarten, B. L. *Middle age and aging.* Chicago: University of Chicago Press, 1968.

Newcomb, T. M., & Feldman, K. A. *The impacts of college on students.* San Francisco: Jossey-Bass, 1969.

Newman, J. H. *The idea of a university, defined and illustrated.* New York: Longmans, Green, 1891. (Originally pub. 1852.)

Perry, W. G., Jr. *Forms of intellectual and ethical development during the college years.* New York: Holt, Rinehart, & Winston, 1970.

Piaget, J., & Inhelder, B. *The psychology of the child.* New York: Basic Books, 1969. (Originally pub. 1966.)

Raushenbush, E. Talk to Quaker educators. Philadelphia, 1965.

Sanford, N. What is a normal personality? In J. Katz, et al., eds., *Writers on ethics: classical and contemporary.* Princeton, N.J.: Van Nostrand, 1962.

Soddy, K., ed. *Cross-cultural studies in mental health: mental health value systems.* London: Tavistock, 1961.

Tart, C. T. *Transpersonal psychologies.* New York: Harper & Row, 1975.

Tippett, J. S., & Silber, E. Autonomy of self-esteem. *Archives of General Psychiatry,* 1966, 14, 372-385.

Vaillant, G. E., & McArthur, C. C. Natural history of male psychological health. I. The adult life cycle from 18 to 50. *Seminars in Psychiatry,* 1972, 4, 415-427.

Van Doren, M. *Liberal education.* New York: Holt, 1943.

White, R. W. *Lives in progress,* 2d ed. New York: Holt, Rinehart, & Winston, 1966.

Whitehead, A. N. The aims of education. In *The aims of education and other essays.* New York: Macmillan, 1929. (Essay written in 1916.)

Wohlwill, J. F. *The study of behavioral development.* New York: Academic Press, 1973.

Personality
and the Development
of Students in Higher Education

Roy Heath

All students are not alike. They come to college in varying degrees of readiness for what could be one of the greatest adventures of their lives. They differ, too, in what catches their fancy, what dampens their enthusiasms. A particular college experience or certain mode of instruction may challenge one student and move him toward further development as a person. But for another student, that same challenge may be utterly regressive in its outcome. Psychologists interested in the development of students increasingly are in the position to illuminate individual differences and their implications for education. In this paper, my comments are restricted to the arena of higher education in the United States. One of the problems confronting those engaged in psychological research in higher education is the need to sort out, midst the great array of individual differences, the differences to attribute to varying levels of maturity and the differences to attribute to variations in temperament. To fail to attend to both of these dimensions can result only in confusion. Where a student stands in regard to temperament and level of development is reflected in characteristic patterns of behavior, that is, in his or her personality. Our research must begin with the observation of these patterns of behavior with due attention and consideration, of course, for the context in which the patterns are exhibited.

Emergence of a Model of Ego Functioning

In the early 1950s, I had the opportunity to observe systematically the development of thirty-six Princeton undergraduates from

213

the month they entered college until their graduation in June 1954. These men were selected from a stratified random sample of their class. I was their academic advisor during their freshman and sophomore years and continued to see them regularly in interviews and small groups during their final two years. All agreed to participate as subjects in this longitudinal project, part of a broader study to evaluate a Princeton education, which was financed by a grant from the Carnegie Corporation of New York.

The subjects were not paid for their services. None asked to drop out of the project and twenty-eight of the thirty-six continued through to graduation in 1954. Of the eight who did not graduate, two died, one of leukemia at the close of his first year, and the other from a rock-climbing accident in the spring of his junior year, three were dropped from the university for academic failure: two for disciplinary reasons and one left voluntarily at the end of his sophomore year. All were white males, as were all of the 725 members of the class of 1954. It happened that all of the eight cases of attrition were of the same type of temperament (X). (The discussion of the types follows this paragraph.) All of the eight Ys and the nine Zs and the remaining eleven Xs were graduated on schedule. (For a full report of this study, see Heath [1964].)

My principal observational access to these students was in the one-to-one interview. Over 700 interviews were recorded, coded for identity, and converted to typed transcripts which were used for further analysis. Early on, during the study, four patterns of interview behavior emerged. Eventually, I came to label the behaviors as type X, type Y, and type Z, and a variant discovered later of each of these types which I called type A. A thesis began to emerge: These interview patterns were characteristic of the ways Xs, Ys, Zs, and As interacted with their respective worlds. A description of the four patterns of interview behavior is in order. The students come to the interviews, for instance, primarily for different motives. Let us begin with those I identified as pattern X.

The X often came primarily because he felt obligated. Once there his principal motive was to remain unscathed. A successful interview for him was one in which he left as well off as he came in. The X is a constricted personality who moves to minimize his losses rather than to maximize his gains. For the X, the frame of the interview is all important because it structures what is expected of him. If he is clear on this point there is less anxiety. He sees himself as a practical person and is relieved if he departs feeling that he has met the interviewer's expectations. Once clear on the purpose of the interview, he probably sits back to fend off questions the best he can. The X likes to reside in a steady, clear frame and he is quite content to leave the creation of the frame to someone else.

The low Y, in contrast to the low X, is an ambivalent personality. In an attempt to resolve the ambivalences, he typically uses both his intellect and action to offset any negative feelings within. He does so in true reaction-formation fashion. He comes to the interview anticipating that he might be judged as "good" or "bad." Therefore, he plans ahead for the encounter. Success for him in the interviews means scoring points. The making of a favorable impression is imperative, should he value the judgment of the interviewer, as it enables him to live more comfortably with himself. Thus, the Y uses the frame (the ball park, so to speak) set up by the interviewer as an opportunity to score. Typically, he is on time for the interview and hates to leave until he has furthered his cause, to wit, himself.

The behavior of the low Z in the interview contrasts with both X and Y. The Z is a dilated personality. If he is in a good mood, he begins right off with an account of why he is in such good spirits. If he is in a poor mood, he may slump into a chair, glance around the room, and then look up at the interviewer as if to say, "At least I am here." Perhaps he attends to the agenda initially but, sooner or later (probably sooner), he introduces what is bothering him. And what troubles a Z is very much in the foreground of his thoughts. For the Z, the interview is an opportunity for catharsis. In other words, it is the Z, not the interviewer, who ultimately structures the frame of the interview. The ball park becomes irrelevant.

The fourth group, the As, tended to view the frame of the interview more distinctly as a necessary ingredient in the research project. The other types seemed to place more importance, especially in the early years, on my role as their faculty advisor. As a group, the As, in contrast, were far less dependent upon me for advice for both curricular matters and personal problems. In fact, I tentatively labeled the A group as the "independent type." The As saw themselves as colleagues, collaborators in the research. Typically, they asked from time to time, "How is the project going?" and made suggestions. The content of the interview, then, contained less personal reference; they were acting for me as observers of the Princeton scene in general, of how it was affecting others as well as themselves. I found myself enjoying this group immensely. Time passed almost unnoticed during the interview. Before we knew it, we were good friends.

Primarily from what I was seeing as differences in interview behavior, by the end of the first semester I was already placing each man in one of the four clusters—A, X, Y, or Z. For the remainder of their freshman year I found myself self attempting to divine the relation of the four clusters to each other. Three of the four clusters, the Xs, Ys, and Zs, seemed to portray a common theme. The day-to-day lives of these men were tilted toward a defensive stance, toward coping with what Maslow (1962) later referred to as deficit needs. One did not have to peer very deeply below the surface to surmise that the men were caught up in a struggle to remain afloat in a sea of choppy waters. But the particular mode of defensive stance varied with each cluster. The Xs characteristically used a form of denial that suggested the repression of unwanted thoughts and feelings. Some of the Xs were amazingly complacent under circumstances that threatened to overwhelm them and sometimes did. The Ys used a more aggressive stance to suppress rather than repress alien thoughts and feelings, a form of denial that was suggestive of reaction formation. The Zs' defensive stance was characterized by periods of exaggerated preoccupation with personal difficulties and fantasies of impending disaster, most of which, of course, never actualized.[1]

The men of the A cluster, in contrast to those in the other three clusters, appeared to be reasonably on top of things. Difficulties came their way but, if conflicts developed, they were more readily resolved, for the most part. There was more evidence of an underlying confidence that most matters could be met. Thus, they were free to invest their energies and more of themselves in ongoing interests and in the development of friendships on campus. In short, those of the *A* cluster were characterized by a superior mode of ego functioning. They were embarked on a more steady course toward self-actualization.

By the middle of the subjects' sophomore year, a two-dimensional model of ego functioning took form. This later conceptualization was sparked by two developments in the way I viewed the men in the project. Due, perhaps, to the lapse of interactions over the summer vacation, I found myself taking a fresh look at each man. Some were obviously changing. And the change I first noticed was toward a superior mode of ego functioning.[2] In other words, they were growing. Also, my neat classification of each man into one of four personality clusters became, on closer inspection, somewhat raveled. Some men were obviously intermediate types, some were more correctly classified as *XY*s and *YZ*s. Thus, the three clusters of *X*, *Y*, and *Z* dissolved into a continuum of temperament, point *X* through *Y* to point *Z*. Orthogonal to the dimension of temperament was the dimension of level of development or maturity. The status of a given student's personality came to be described by his position in the model, the intersect of his rating on two dimensions. Figure 1 illustrates this model of ego

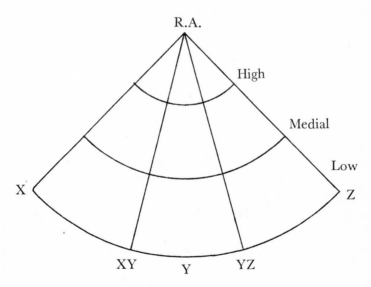

Figure 1. A model of ego functioning.

functioning in its final form. The fact that the model became tri-angular rather than rectangular in shape was an acknowledgment that as members of the project developed toward maturity they assumed greater similarity in a mode of ego functioning. (For a fuller treatment of the characteristics of the men with superior ego functioning, see Heath [1973].)

At the apex of the model stands the reasonable adventurer whose versatility in the use of both primary and secondary pro-cesses is beyond dispute. Low Xs may be reasonable but they are not noted for being adventurous. On the other hand, the low Z may have moments of adventurousness but unreasonably so, too often. The reasonable adventurer, then, represents a dialectic, an idealized form of superior ego functioning. The hallmark of the reasonable adventurer is his playfulness. He enjoys playing with ideas and with others. His capacity for not taking himself too seriously is remarkable.

Individual Differences in Temperament: The XYZ Continuum

One of the more interesting outcomes of the Princeton study was that practically all of the changes noted in personality during the four years could be attributed to change in level of development. In contrast, a student's position on the XYZ continuum remained remarkably stable. This finding gave support to the notion that the temperamental aspects of personality are relatively immune to change, at least by the time a person reaches late adolescence. It may be that the determinants of temperament are primarily genet-ic. Sheldon's study (Sheldon & Stevens 1942) of physique and temperament suggests this possibility. All of the Ys in the project were predominantly mesomorphic in body build. Neither the Xs nor Zs were exclusively of one type of physique. The Zs, however, were overrepresented by ectomorphs and the Xs by endomorphs (Heath 1964, p. 23). This finding, although theoretically relevant, is outside our concern with the psychological aspects of the XYZ continuum, as derived from the Princeton study. Before introduc-ing some further results of the investigation, relevant formulations of other theorists and investigators should be noted. Jung's distinction between extraverted and introverted personalities is particularly relevant.

Jung (1959) proposed a dimension of extraversion and introversion that cuts across his four function types of thinking, feeling, sensation, and intuition. For Jung, extraversion and introversion were general attitude types, a distinction based upon a person's basic attitude toward an object. "The introvert's attitude to the object is an abstracting one; . . . The extravert, on the contrary, maintains a positive relation to the object, . . . his subjective attitude is continually being oriented by and related to the object" (p. 414).

Jung saw the behavior of the extravert as typically accommodating to the objective situation. "The extravert owes his normality to his ability to fit into existing conditions with relative ease. He naturally pretends to nothing more than the satisfaction of existing objective possibilities. . . . He tries to do or make just what his milieu momentarily needs and expects from him and abstains from every innovation that is not entirely obvious, or that in any way exceeds the expectation of those around him" (p. 419). Further on, Jung pointed out the potential danger to the stability of the extraverted personality. "I have emphasized a tendency toward a certain onesidedness in the extraverted attitude, due to this controlling power of the objective factor in the course of psychic events. . . . Adjustment and assimilation to objective data prevent subjective impulses from reaching consciousness. These tendencies (thoughts, wishes, affects, needs, feelings, etc.) take on a regressive character corresponding with the degree of repression, i.e., the less they are recognized, the more infantile and archaic they become" (p. 423).

Jung's psychodynamics of the extravert fit well with those of the students placed in the lower X section of the model, especially with the extravert's propensity to conform to the expectations of his environmental frame or milieu. I am reminded also how recklessly impulsive the low X can become under the influence of alcohol or during the excitement of a student riot.

The introverted attitude was characterized by Jung as follows: "The introvert interposes a subjective view between the perception of the object and his own action, which prevents the action from assuming a character that corresponds with the objective situation" (p. 471). Another way of putting it, I assume, is that the introvert brings much of his inner reality into play with each objective situation. In extreme cases the inner life determinants outplay the outer world determinants of action; with the extreme extravert, the objective situation heavily prevails at the expense of subjective expression. Jung's description of the introvert sounds very much like the Zs I have known, especially those at the lower level of maturity who operated at an inferior mode of ego functioning. But we are left with the question of how to relate Jung's extraversion-introversion dimension to the men falling in other sections of the model. Jung (1959) seemed to take the position that a person is either an extravert or introvert, and apparently he left no place for intermediate types. Much as I view dichotomous distinctions with reservation, the essence of Jung's thought cannot be dismissed easily. Obviously, there are persons whose natural dispositions incline them to be empiricists and some who find the idealist position attractive. There are the practical men and the visionaries, as Anderson (1976) recently observed. One could argue that we need both approaches in the search for truth. Yet, one is persuaded that even in Jung's terms we cannot expect much of a contribution in either science or the arts from persons who are *extremely* extraverted or introverted. Do major insights come about through a state of mind, however momentary, in which unity of subject and object appropriately occurs? Psychologists who are experienced with the Rorschach Test, for instance, have come to expect mature and creative subjects to respond with an abundance of both human movement and appropriate use of color, connoting a large measure of both the introversive and extratensive.

Interestingly, a clue to resolving our difficulties with Jung comes from a closer reading of Jung himself. Recall that when he wrote of extraversion and introversion he referred to them as a general attitude of *consciousness*. In his writings, he also referred to a general attitude of the *unconscious*. "I regard the relation of the unconscious to the conscious as compensatory" (Jung 1959, p. 422). The unconscious of the extravert, he wrote, has a definitely introverted character, for example. If we view the maturing process or individuation (to use Jung's term)[3] as involving a resolution of contradictory tendencies in the superior forms of ego functioning, we would assume that many of the heretofore unconscious tendencies play a more positive and direct role, rather than regressive role, in the actions of mature persons. We assume that when the low extraverted X matures, in time, to become a high X in our model, a capacity to resolve contradictory tendencies in himself has been acquired. And, of course, we say the same for those of the Z temperament. The next question, logically, as we attempt to relate Jung's notions to the model, is, What about the Ys?

Since the completion of the Princeton study in 1954, a series of studies have indicated in their findings an affinity with the XYZ continuum of temperament and disposition: George Klein's distinction between "levelers" and "sharpeners" in his work on cognition and perception (Klein 1970); Donn Byrne's (1961) personality scale of repression versus sensitization; Getzels and Jackson's (1962) use of Guilford's distinction between convergent and divergent thinkers;[4] and finally, Asenath Petrie's (1967) studies of individual differences in experiencing pain, in which she distinguished between "reducers" and "augmenters" under conditions of repeated tactile stimulation. Each of these personality distinctions speaks readily to the poles of the XYZ continuum, but each has little to say about those in the middle range, the Ys. Yet the Y, at least in his behavior patterns, is clearly distinct from either the X or the Z and not merely a fusion of the two extremes, in my experience. So the search was on for an underlying construct that would make sensible the temperament variable as a dimension and not a typology.

Several years ago, while rereading Huxley's *The Doors of Perception* (1954), I came across a passage with an idea, a resplendent idea, that struck home.

Reflecting on my experience, I find myself agreeing with the eminent Cambridge philosopher, Dr. C. D. Broad, "that we should do well to consider much more seriously than we have been hitherto inclined to do the type of theory which Bergson put forward in connection with memory and sense perception. The suggestion is that the function of the brain and nervous system and sense organs is in the main eliminative, and not productive. Each person is at each moment capable of remembering all that has ever happened to him and of perceiving everything that is happening everywhere in the universe. The function of the brain and nervous system is to protect us from being overwhelmed and confused by this mass of largely useless and irrelevant knowledge, by shutting out most of what we should otherwise perceive or remember at any moment, and leaving only that very small and special selection which is likely to be practically useful." According to such a theory, each one of us is potentially Mind at Large. But in so far as we are animals, our business is at all costs to survive. To make biological survival possible, Mind at Large has to be funneled through the reducing valve of the brain and nervous system. What comes out at the other end is a measly trickle of the kind of consciousness which will help us to stay alive on this particular planet. [Huxley, pp. 22-23.]

Although the exact mechanism for reducing inputs into consciousness may not yet be clear, the fact that each of us must make use of such biological process seems unarguable. Is it not possible to assume that the same reduction valve or consciousness filter reduces inputs from subjective sources, such as thoughts and images, as well as inputs from outside the organism? Consider also two further propositions: (1) That each of us experiences variations in the effect of the consciousness filter. At eight o'clock in the morning the filter may be more constricted, and in the evening, for some of us, it may be more dilated. (2) That individuals differ consistently in the density of the filter, the amount of flow, so to speak. Suppose, for example, that Person 1's filter, even under its most dilated state, permits less input into consciousness than Person 2's filter, even in its most constricted state.

If both of these propositions are true, it is possible that the intervention of a biological variable explains some of the differences in mode of ego functioning. Such a variable would permit the consideration of differences in temperament in terms of differences in the porosity of the consciousness filter and could be related to the XYZ dimension. Some of the differences in Xs, Ys, and Zs could be explained by differences in flow, in the number of items in our conscious awareness at any given time. One could see the X type as possessing a relatively dense filter, the Z as having a relatively dilated filter, and the Y as possessing an intermediate degree of infiltration.

Presumably, those persons with the greatest influx of material into consciousness suffer from a greater degree of intrusion of subjective influences upon their perceptions; those with low flow, presumably, endow their perception of the outer world with less subjective coloring and, thus, are able to attend, under most conditions, to the objective situation more fully. The X, having the least amount of flow, can opt for the simplest form of defense, repression. He casts unwanted thoughts to the peripheries of consciousness or out of awareness entirely. This behavior accounts for his sometimes reckless complacency when the objective situation actually threatens is survival. Also, the condition of low flow would account for X's tendency to react only to the more salient features of his immediate environment and to be content with oversimplification. In other words, he is a leveler rather than a sharpener in his perceptions.

For the Y, an intermediate amount of flow can be postulated; but too much to permit repression. So he opts for the next best possible form of defense: suppression by overintellectualization. He typically manages the greater complexity in his conscious life by being *analytical*, in contrast with the X who is content with responding to what is "out there" in terms of the most obvious.

The Z, having the most porous filter, is characteristically flooded with input. That is probably why he is an overreactor (evidenced mostly in his gestures and facial movements), in contrast with the X who comes across to us as an underreactor, with a more bland responsiveness to the objective situation. One can also conjecture that the Z, under conditions of high flow, finds analytic thinking difficult, which probably accounts for his tendency to be more *synthetic* in his thinking and to rely more on *intuition* in making value judgments. When it comes to the problem of dealing with unwanted thoughts, the Z apparently has no choice but to "live with them." He is, thus, a sensitizer. He exorcises these items in the center of consciousness until they gradually come to appear less threatening. Thus we see the Zs tendency to "worry a worry to death." With a wide repertoire of items in consciousness, his range of associations permits him—almost impels him—to be a more divergent thinker. The Z has great capacity to attend to detail. This capacity, of course, presents difficulties in the orderly management of a given situation. On the other hand, experiencing life the way he does, a greater tolerance for complexity is established. I would not want to imply, however, that the Z prefers complexity or that he uses it compulsively as a Y often does.

Finally, the relation of Jung's typology of extraversion and introversion to the concept of the consciousness filter must be explored. In Jung's terms, the Z is characteristically introverted, primarily because, for him, subjective material (thoughts, feelings, images, etc.) is more intrusive and, therefore, mediates his response to objects. He perceives an object clearly but his *interpretation* of its meaning is defined as much by what he brings to the objective situation as by the object itself. Therefore, the actions that ensue for a low Z are based upon a context (frame) largely of his own making. But as the Z matures he internalizes more of the outer world with his psychic life. When internalization occurs, he responds to objective situations more appropriately.

The X is more extraverted because, primarily, his subjective life is less salient, less demanding, in the competition with his objective situation. Thus his response to an object is more completely defined by the objective frame. Subjective elements often enter into his consideration but usually *after* the event has transpired and is less relevant to what might happen next. The personal desires of a low X are often compromised by the passing stream of events. As the X matures, his sphere of consciousness is greatly expanded and he becomes less repressed. Hence, he is more capable of responding with actions that do greater justice to his inner strivings and desires.

The Y is potentially as introverted as extraverted. Since he is characteristically more ambivalent about his subjective self, his responses are more fully defined by the objective situation. He looks to the environment in which he moves for opportunities to better his place in the objective situation as a way of assuaging his reservations about his inner life.[5] What intervenes in the transaction between the object and himself is not a myriad of subjective associations, as in the case of the Z, but a quick intellectual judgment of whether the demands of the objective situation hold promise for something good or bad. Movement toward maturity for the Y usually awaits an event. Either matters become so difficult that he gives up the fight and surrenders to an encounter with his alien thoughts and feelings on a more constructive basis, or he encounters someone who convinces him that he is lovable in his own right. Either event holds greater promise of the resolution of contradictory elements in his psychic life. So, with maturity, the Y becomes as much at home within himself as in the world outside. He is, thus, in the upper reaches of the model, a personage who is quite ambiverted, perhaps more completely so than either the high X or high Z. In that sense, the Y emerges as a strong character, a person one can count upon for warmth and perseverance, even under the most difficult conditions.

Three Test Results

DRAW A HOUSE, TREE, AND PERSON

The H-T-P Test, originated by John Buck, is a projective test. Each of the three objects—a house, tree, and person—are drawn on separate pieces of white paper with no more specific instructions than "draw in succession a house, a tree, and a person." No time limit is imposed. In the Princeton group, the most striking differences among the Xs, Ys, and Zs were in the drawing of the tree. Although there were exceptions, the Xs tended to draw a rough outline of a tree, and to do so rather quickly. The Ys tended to use heavier strokes with particular emphasis on the trunk and base. The Zs tended to draw a more fully articulated tree with greater attention to detail, including such embellishments as a bird perched on a limb. As a group, the Zs seemed to be more absorbed in the production. There are sketched in Figure 2 drawings that are typical of the Xs, Ys, and Zs, respectively.

The X productions appear to be in keeping with their global, undifferentiated perceptions. The Y drawings seem to reflect a concern for displaying strength. The Z drawings reflect their customary attention to detail and shading. Also, as might be expected of dilated personalities, these Zs were less conventional in their drawings, exhibiting a flare for the individualistic.

THE INHIBITED MOTION TEST

On this task,[6] the subject is asked to write the phrase "United States of America" on a sheet of lined paper, and to do so as *slowly* as possible, without both stopping the movement of the pencil and lifting the pencil from the pad. Essentially, it is a test of endurance, of perseverance. The average time taken by the three

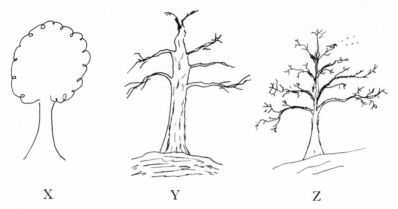

X   Y   Z

Figure 2. Typical drawings of trees by X-, Y-, and Z-type students.

groups was as follows: $Xs-3.1$ minutes, $Ys-6.5$ minutes, and $Zs-9.3$ minutes. (There was some overlap among the groups but I doubt that the difference among the means is statistically significant.) One X took 7 minutes; two Ys took 10 and 12 minutes, respectively; one Z, who could not seem to have cared less, spent only 2 minutes on the task; but one Z kept me waiting for 21 minutes. What can we make of these findings?

In talking with the men separately afterwards in a debriefing session, it became apparent that the Xs tended to perform the task within the framework of reasonableness. They cooperated in terms of what they thought any sensible person would do. In other words, the key point of reference for them was what they imagined *others* might do under a similar demand. Having no specific guideline, they fell back on an old standby for them, that is, do what is normal.

The Ys, too, had other people in mind. They made subjective judgments of how others in the project might do and then set out to best them. They were competing with the others.

The Zs approached the task very differently. They tended to view the test as a challenge to their endurance. It was a game against themselves, a test of their limits.

The results clearly support the notion that both the Xs and Ys use the social context as their frame of reference. The two groups, however, use the social context differently. The Xs try to stay within the limits of what their subculture would accept, would consider reasonable. They conform to the values of the group in keeping with their efforts to maintain their identity with the group. The Ys, on the other hand, use the subculture and their interaction with it as a source of prestige and self-esteem. Each must excel, but he does so in terms of what he imagines the group standard to be.

But the Zs' grounding is inner and outside the social context. On this test, they seemed to be indifferent to how others might perform; they cared most about finding out something about themselves. To them, this was a test of their own capabilities. Each plunged into the task to discover his limits. What others might have done was largely irrelevant. For instance, when the series was over, I told the student who had taken the longest time that his score was the best in the project. He smiled and said, "I'd like to try it again sometime. I bet I can do better than 21 minutes."

THE STEREOSCOPE TEST

In this test, devised by John Engel, a stereoscope is the equipment. During 1953, while Engel was a graduate student in psychology at Princeton, he was in the process of designing an experiment to test certain aspects of psychoanalytic theory. At his request I administered the stereoscope test to as many of the participants in my study as cared to take it. The insert card contains two pictures, each one-inch square, of sections of a photograph of Michelangelo's "The Dying Slave." Picture 1 shows the head and portions of the left shoulder and upper left arm. Picture 2 shows the pelvic area, penis, and upper thighs. Engel wondered if the "repressors" in my project would fail to perceive picture 2, even though it was superimposed upon 1 by means of the stereoscope lenses. A pretrial card was used so the subjects could adjust the scope to accommodate for differences in interpupillary distance. Then the subject was directed to close his eyes while the test card was being inserted. Then he was told to open his eyes and to keep them open for a period of sixty seconds, and to blink with *both* eyes should he feel the need to blink. Also, he was asked to maintain a running oral account of what he was perceiving for the full exposure time of sixty seconds, and this account was recorded. The results for the Princeton project are shown in Figure 3.

Picture #2

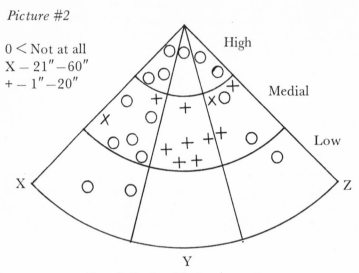

0 < Not at all
X − 21″ − 60″
+ − 1″ − 20″

Figure 3. Results of the Stereoscope Test.

I divided the subjects into three groups according to their responses to the test: those who perceived picture 2 within twenty seconds, those who perceived 2 between twenty and sixty seconds; and those who saw only picture 1 during the entire exposure time. All of the subjects saw the head, initially. Some alternately saw picture 2. At times, some of the subjects were seeing the two pictures superimposed and commented that "something" was interfering with the clarity of the head. Each subject was asked not to discuss the test until all of the subjects had been tested.

Frankly, I was surprised at the results although I should not have been. After some pondering, I concluded that the results made sense in terms of differences in ego functioning among the subjects. I was not prepared, apparently, to recognize how readily the ambivalence of the Ys—my "yes, but" people—was reflected in their visual perceptions. Practically all of the other subjects maintained the perception of picture 1 throughout the entire sixty-second exposure period. The fact that picture 1 was more readily seen is understandable for it contains greater salience, with its details of facial features and hair. My hunch is that the sexual content—the penis—in picture 2 well may have been irrelevant, and the difference in salience between the two pictures was the reason picture 1 usually won out in the competition with 2. It would be interesting to test this hypothesis by using more neutral material.

As a postscript, I should mention the experience of one of the students, a medial X. A month after the testing he asked me about the results. "I was wondering if there was something sexual in the test," he said. I asked why he suspected it. "It was strange," he replied, "after leaving your office in the psychology building I was walking back to my room and thinking about the tests I had just taken. Suddenly, a picture of the midregion of the statue, with a penis there, came into my mind." So I showed the student picture 2. "That's it! It's funny, but at the time I am sure all I saw was the picture with the guy's head." I reported this finding of delayed recognition to John Engel. What conclusion he drew, I can only imagine.

At any rate, we obviously record more inputs than manage to get through the consciousness filter. One is reminded of a comment of Freud's about one of his cases: "He knew but he knew not what he knew."

Implications for Higher Education

I have tried to illuminate personality differences in ego functioning from my observations of the development of thirty-six students during their four years of college. For those of us interested in fostering the development of students in higher education, I believe that my observations and conceptual formulations hold implications for both curricular and student affairs programs. Let us start with our low Xs.

The X is highly dependent on external surroundings as moorings for his security. He even composes his self-concept largely on his perception of others' perceptions of him.[7] He needs a residential atmosphere that is steady, coherent, and free of confusion. We cannot expect progress in the development of interpersonal intimacy and academic interest unless we are first successful in making X feel at home. In other words, his most crucial need in his first year of college is incorporation, the true feeling that he is a member of the whole body. (See first interview with "Bob" at Princeton for a reflection of this dominant need [Heath 1964, p. 100].)

Once his social moorings are secure, the X should be ready for challenge. The challenges should come in small increments to insure the probability of success. He needs the experience of success to loosen his defensive infrastructure. Marked failure is particularly debilitating for the low X and tends to foreclose further venturing on his part. Challenges may come, of course, in various forms. There follow several we might consider:

1. The small discussion group is especially profitable for the lower X provided that he is not permitted just to sit and listen. A seasoned instructor looks out for X's participation and watches his body language. I used to scout for a slight tilt forward or a flicker of the eyes as a signal that our X had something to contribute and then I quickly called on him before doubt set in.

2. Requiring the X to compose short poems and essays and encouraging his originality and free run of the imagination is another helpful challenge. The low X has ideas but he is often stalled from expressing them because of his number one fear—exposure. Nothing inhibits the low X more than the possibility of appearing ridiculous.

3. Early in his college career, the lower X should be encouraged to get help in good study practices. The bugaboo of the low X is one that he rarely recognizes in himself: complacency. He possesses a mode of ego functioning that tends to allow unwanted thoughts to recede to the peripheries of consciousness. In studying for an examination, for example, he concludes too readily that he has studied enough. Assigning another student (hopefully a high X or Y) to study with him can be helpful. The X needs the watchful eye of a resident dorm advisor.

4. Finally, the X especially needs exposure to what I call "inner life activators." He needs courses.in the humanities, such as art, literature, and music. Such exposures seem to bypass his defenses and stimulate the inner self to press for expression. They

seem to unite his inner and outer selves so that his heretofore isolated fantasy life can move out into the world of others.

The Y personality does not need special attentions, at least not the kind that is fitting for the X. The Y thrives on challenges and he actively seeks them out. If he experiences a series of failures in his interpersonal relations and academic courses, he is forced to confront himself. The earlier this confrontation happens in college, the better. It is not a very happy sight to see someone go through four years of college caught up in a personal civil war. How can a Y's personality reorganization be brought about as early as possible in the college community? Several ideas come to mind:

1. The Y needs direct feedback on the effect of his behavior on other persons which can be provided in a small residential hall. The selection of his roommates is very important. For reasons not discussed here, a coed dorm would be preferred in most cases that I can think of; unfortunately some Ys may have to live at home and commute to college.

2. Once the Y senses that he needs help in interpersonal relations, participation in some form of group therapy is in order. From my experience, group encounters are preferable to individual therapy sessions for the Y. He is too adept at manipulating the therapist, the present author, at least. If individual therapy is indicated after some group encounter, Gestalt rather than Rogerian methods are more effective for the Y. In my opinion, nondirective therapy is tailor-made for the X but relatively ineffective for the Y, and for the Z, too, as a matter of fact.

3. Courses in psychology that center on the analysis of individuals or the complexity of personality, like the one Peter Madison teaches at Arizona, can be the most valuable experience of the Y's college career. The courses can provide both the self-confrontation and the theoretical understanding he needs to foster his personality reorganization, and the earlier the better.

However it comes about, the Y needs to discover that he can be lovable without adornments. Paradoxically, it is often his precollege achievement, such as having been an outstanding athlete, a student council president, or a high honor student, that interferes with the Y's later development. An effective college program may be his last chance to get over the watershed. There are plenty of challenges to come after college, too. How fortunate it would have been for all of us if our best-known Y had brought to resolution the no-win battle against himself while he was in college and before he became president!

The Z's personality is internally directed. To a large extent, he creates his own scene. He contrasts with the X, who takes his cues from his surroundings, and with the Y, whose behavior is derived from both external and internal considerations. (The lower Y is highly dependent upon a stable environment, in terms of cultural values, in which he can act to counterbalance whatever alien impulses leak into consciousness.)

In the context of higher education, the primary need of the Z is not direction but access. He needs the freedom to roam about the campus culture. What he is looking for are niches that are congenial to his strivings. It is stifling to the development of the lower Z to find himself locked into a subculture that is apathetic or hostile to his desires. What he would face in such circumstances would be a choice between withdrawing socially or creating a role, such as the clown in the fraternity, in which to satisfy at least some of his needs.

The Z is often a loner. His ties to groups are tenuous, at best. It is not so much that he sees himself above the crowd but that his sights and potential identification are beyond the crowd. What the Z is looking for is drama. He is immensely attracted to stirring movements, whether political, religious, or literary, that may speak to his fantasies, in fact he may become the leader of a movement. If so, his leadership position may become precarious because he is apt to be a purist, an absolutist, with little inclination or competence to make accommodations with the other participants.

The Z needs a faculty in which there are intellectual leaders in their fields. When there are, the Z can be counted on to search out and find a mentor, one with whom he can identify and have long conversations, and one who has time for a budding disciple.

Finally, the Z's growth is highly dependent upon a curriculum that is flexible enough to satisfy his special needs and manner of operation. If such opportunities are provided, we can count on the Z to invest a great deal of vigor and sustained interest. It is no accident that the Zs in the Princeton study demonstrated their greatest growth toward becoming reasonable adventurers in the last two years of college. In other words, growth spurted once they had found their niches.

In sum, if we are to press for the full development of our students in higher education we must not only tune our programs to differing levels of development but also to variations in temperament, as illustrated by the description of Xs, Ys, and Zs. I have tried to indicate that the growth process among various types of personality may differ, and these differences can make a difference in what we should offer them to further their development toward maturity.

NOTES

1. At examination time, for instance, the Zs typically were beset with fears that they had done worse on the exams than eventually proved to be the case. They were in marked contrast with the Xs, who remained moderately confident that they had done well up to the point when the posted grades indicated otherwise. The Ys were the best predictors of their grades on exams. After completing an exam they were in the habit of referring back to the study material as well as discussing the exam questions at length with others who had taken the exam with them. The Xs were so sure that they had done well and the Zs so sure that they had done poorly that neither did much back checking.

2. The basic value judgment here, of course, is implied in the concept of self-actualization. I justify labeling some persons "superior" in ego functioning because these men by and large were experiencing greater satisfaction in their daily lives and managing their affairs with ordinary prudence, without undue dependence upon others.

3. Individuation "signifies an extension of the sphere of consciousness, an enriching of the conscious psychological life" (Jung 1959, p. 563).

4. One of the tests Getzels and Jackson administered to their high school students was the Uses Test. The subject is asked to list all the uses of a common object, such as a pencil, brick, and paper clip, which he can imagine within a given length of time. One of the highest scores I have personal knowledge of was obtained from a medial Z student of mine at the University of Pittsburgh in 1963. For instance, one of the uses he gave for a paper clip was as "a crutch for a wounded grasshopper."

5. Just why the lower Y tends to take an adversary position toward his inner life and toward others is a question I have not completely thought through to my satisfaction. It is true that he tends to be naturally aggressive in disposition, but does this fact explain the characteristically adversary role that he assumes?

6. This test was used by June Downey as part of her battery in the Will Temperament Test.

7. The author has designed a test of self-concept as related to different segments of the reasonable adventurer model. It is called the Modes of Existence Test. Copies for research purposes are available by writing to the author at the following address: 1193 South East Street, Amherst, Massachusetts 01002.

REFERENCES

Anderson, Q. Practical and visionary Americans. *American Scholar*, 1976, 45(3), 405-418.

Byrne, D. The repression-sensitization scale. *Journal of Personality*, 1961, 29, 334-349.

Getzels, J. W., & Jackson, P. W. *Creativity and intelligence.* New York: Wiley, 1962.

Heath, R. *The reasonable adventurer.* Pittsburgh: University of Pittsburgh Press, 1964.

————. Form, flow, and full-being. *Counseling Psychologist*, 1973, 2(4), 56-63.

Huxley, A. *The doors of perception.* New York: Harper & Row, 1954.

Jung, C. G. *Psychological types.* New York: Pantheon, 1959.

Klein, G. *Perception, motives, and personality.* New York: Knopf, 1970.

Maslow, A. *Toward a psychology of being.* Princeton, N.J.: Van Nostrand, 1962.

Petrie, A. *Individuality in pain and suffering.* Chicago: University of Chicago Press, 1967.

Sheldon, W. H., & Stevens, S. S. *The varieties of temperament.* New York: Harper & Row, 1942.

Students and Their Institutions:
An Interactive Perspective

Ursula Delworth and Ellen Piel

Ours is hardly an age of optimism about the value and future of higher education. Legislators, citizens, students, and scholars alike are taking our colleges to task on a variety of issues. Student-services staffs particularly are being challenged to articulate and validate their worth on campuses.

Our current dilemma arises, at least partly, from our failure to define adequately and perform a role that is uniquely ours. In earlier periods of institutional growth and plenty, student-services personnel allowed the academic faculty to decree that their role was central, and student-services personnel were content to play peripheral and supportive roles to facilitate the faculty's agendas. Our basic position has been reactive. We have acted to preserve the status quo of the educational system by carrying out many time-consuming and relatively unrewarding tasks that, nonetheless, kept the colleges running and the students in line. When college was considered to be the proper place for only academically gifted persons, student services allowed itself the role of "easing" students off campus and into settings that would prove to be more productive for them, or so it was hoped. When the academic faculty adopted a broader and more humanistic approach, we allowed ourselves to be defined as "adjusters" and we aided students who were not making it in the college environment to fit in better. The students alone were considered responsible for "not making it" as the environment was implicitly viewed as suitable. More recently, we have been moving away from the first two rather static positions toward a developmental perspective (Banning & Kaiser 1974).

This approach defines a student-services role that recognizes the necessary growth tasks of late adolescence and early adulthood and provides opportunities to facilitate such growth.

Development for Persons

All three roles have some merit. Certainly, each may have to be played at various times with various students. To date, the third, the developmental stance, has the most to recommend it as a fruitful basis for our identity and interactions. Professionally, it is the most clearly our own and less reactive to the positions of others. In addition, it can broaden the scope of our activities on campus by including within its purview the entire student group, not just those who have failed to fit into the academic community. The emphasis of our interventions shifts from favoring the few to enhancing the many. So far, however, few attempts to operationalize this view have rested upon solid models of development, and there has been a noticeable lack of evaluation of whether "development" did indeed occur as a result of such programs. A more sophisticated approach to conceptualization and implementation is essential.

The work of the theorists represented in this book, plus that of a few other theorists (e.g., Kohlberg 1969; Loevinger & Wessler 1970) hold great promise for realizing the potential of the developmental role for student services. Here we have schemes, models, and some mediating processes upon which we can build solid developmental programs. The models allow us to assess the current developmental level in students and to evaluate our interventions in terms of changes in developmental level. Finally, as suggested by several authors, faculty members can become our co-designers and implementors to build these programs. The cooperation will erase the conception of us as subordinates, we hope, and establish the system of joint responsibility for facilitating student growth and achieving institutional goals which has so long been missing in higher education.

Development for Institutions

The models of developmental programs for students are one-sided, however, and they need to be placed in a wider framework. Development may be conceived of as a task for not only students but institutions as well. Indeed, we are suggesting that valid, enduring growth and development in students will occur best when institutional growth and development are as much a matter for our attention as are growth and development of individual students.

Cross (1975) encapsulates this position well in the title of her article: "Lesson in Ecology: You Can't Change the Student Body without Changing the System." She stated that "when [higher] education moved from an emphasis on selection to an emphasis on teaching and learning, it moved to changing the educational process itself with responsibility for the quality of the graduating class" (p. 3). We believe that the quality of the graduating class no longer can be validly insured by the careful weeding out or shaping of students. Instead, we need to broaden our view of the educational process in the two senses presented by Cross (1976).

1. We must attend to the unique learning competencies and weaknesses of the individual student by developing educational curricula that recognize personal qualities and capitalize upon them to maximize the person's learning. We in student personnel work have the knowledge of student characteristics and development that is invaluable for designing such personalized educational curricula.

2. We must recognize the need for students to develop expertise in areas other than those traditionally covered in higher education. Cross pointed to the importance, to every student, of developing competencies in dealing with things (e.g., machines, home repair) and other persons. Interpersonal skills cannot be assumed to grow automatically as the student matures. We in student personnel can focus our knowledge of this area into programs that are specifically designed to enhance a student's relationship skills.

If we adhere to the two points in educational planning, then significantly positive growth in each student will result.

Formal recognition of each student's needs and skills is only half the task in changing the focus in student development, however. Institutions differ from each other, have a differential impact on students, and can change. Ignoring their extremely important role in the student development and educational process dooms us to overly simplistic formulations and relatively poor predictive power concerning the potential impact of our interventions.

We now have evidence to indicate that (a) the type of institution affects student persistence, and (b) college attendance has some enduring effects in the personal lives of students. The factor of institutional type can encompass characteristics from geographical location to religious affiliation. Astin's (1975) massive study of persistence in college shows that students maximize their chances of graduating if they attend private universities in any region or public four-year colleges located in the northeastern or southern states (independent of student characteristics, such as ability or grades). Astin also pointed out that, in general, persistence is enhanced if the student attends an institution in which the social backgrounds of other students resemble his or her own background, independent of academic ability, and that living in a residence hall during the freshman year increases the student's chances of finishing college.

Second, the impact of college on the lives of students extends far beyond increasing their store of information. Feldman and Newcomb (1973), after compiling and analyzing studies on the impact of college, stated a number of general findings regarding this impact. Among them are the following: (1) Freshman-to-senior changes in several (personal) characteristics have been occurring with considerable uniformity in most American colleges and universities, in recent decades. Although each piece of data on these changes represents only an average trend in one particular setting, nearly all studies show the same direction of change. (2) The degree and nature of different colleges' impacts vary with their student inputs, that is, entering students' characteristics, which differ among types of colleges in patterned ways. Feldman and Newcomb explained this finding in terms of a two-step process. The prominence of certain entering characteristics suggests a readiness for many of these students to change in directions compatible with these characteristics. This readiness to change is then strengthened by social reinforcement from the peers who share the same characteristics. Although this process is not necessarily uniform it appears to account for a major portion of colleges' differential impacts.

One has only to read Astin (1975), Chickering (1972), Feldman and Newcomb (1973), Wilson, Gaff, Dienst, Wood, and Bavry (1975), and others to understand that, indeed, something personally significant happens to students when they attend college; and what happens to them appears to be influenced both by student characteristics and the characteristics of the college environment. Logically, therefore, to understand the process of student development throughout college, the college environment must be studied as carefully as the student.

Interaction in Theory

Traditional counseling, psychology, and college student personnel work largely have been concerned with only one aspect of the interaction: the assessment of persons (i.e., students), services, and programs to facilitate change in them. The pre-eminent psychological theories supporting this work have espoused the trait model: describing persons in terms of stable dispositions (traits) that determine their behavior and make it consistent across situations. Therefore, to understand behavior, it is necessary only to examine the strengths of various traits within a person and measure them by personality scales (Endler & Magnusson 1976). Because behavior was assumed to be consistent across situations, regardless of differing situational characteristics, the dynamic role of the environment in shaping and being shaped by individuals has inspired little systematic work. However, the theoretical basis for this work was laid years ago. Both Murray's (1938) conceptualization of the interaction between personal needs and environmental press, and Lewin's (1936) classic formula, "Behavior results from both the Person and Environment," or $B = f(P, E)$ have laid dormant until recently.

Since the mid-1960s, however, theory and research in person/ environment interactions have increased tremendously. Psychologists have begun to look more seriously at theories of personality that move away from a static trait approach and embrace, instead, an interactional approach that deals with both persons and situations. Mitchell (1969) stated "that the determinants of behavior need to be sought more often in the characteristics of the environmental context and that the interaction of these characteristics with individual traits and abilities, and a search for individual characteristics *in vacuo* can lead only to partial understanding or no understanding at all" (p. 696). Interest in improving this knowledge base is apparent. The first international conference on this approach was held in Sweden in June 1975; a recent text for advanced undergraduate and graduate classes in personality is titled, *Interactional Psychology and Personality* (Endler & Magnusson 1976).

In some theories, interest has shifted from reconceptualizing personality to examining the person/environment interaction. Much of this work focuses on the college student. A solid base primer by Walsh (1973) includes five major approaches ranging from Barker's (1968) theory of behavior settings, which takes the stance that environments select and shape the behavior of people who inhabit them, to Pervin's (1968) theory which indicates that for each individual there are interpersonal and noninterpersonal environments that tend to match or fit the individual's perception of self.

Hunt (1975) suggested that Lewin's *BPE* formula is the appropriate paradigm for studying person/environment interactions: identifying each major component—behavior, person, and environment—in a specific situation and viewing the behavior as jointly determined by the person and environment. Hunt stressed the careful identification of each component as an essential prelude to coordinating their interactive effects. He considered the paradigm to be a valuable way of accounting for *differential* behavioral effects. Pervin (1976) stated the same objective. He wrote, "In terms of conceptual approach, the goal is a more differentiated understanding of the interactions and transactions between people and situations as opposed to an emphasis purely on persons, purely on situations, or on a global Person X Situation interaction effect" (p. 466).

One of the more eclectic approaches to person/environment interaction is offered by Insel and Moos (1974). They applied the term "social ecology" to their study of the social environment and its interaction with the physical milieu. Their goal, by integrating ideas from ecology, human ecology, psychology, sociology, and medicine, is to develop a more complete conception of the person's interactions with both the physical and social environment. They believe that social ecology has a unique and explicit value orientation in that it is concerned with maximizing effective human functioning. To organize and assess the psychosocial characteristics of environments, they looked at eight different environments (including university student residences) and found three broad common environmental dimensions: relationship dimensions, personal development or goal orientation dimensions, and system maintenance and change dimensions. Insel and Moos stressed the importance of the environment to individual functioning and to affecting a person's satisfaction, mood, self-esteem, and personal growth.

Undoubtedly, the study of person/environment interactions has a theoretical basis. Now we have some terminology and basic methodology to use in developing and assessing a new type of student development program. We are ready to adopt what Banning and Kaiser (1974) labeled the "ecological perspective" to student personnel activities and campus design: considering the interdependent influences of environments on persons and of persons on environment. This perspective would, at least, double our potential for impact, as compared with looking at students alone. In fact, carefully developed environmental redesigns may well be as productive for student growth as redesigns addressed to students themselves. The perspective has revolutionary implications for the way we conceptualize and implement student-services programs.

The greatest change implied in the adoption of this new perspective, perhaps, comes as a natural outgrowth of our new professional role as facilitators of student development. Programs no longer can be developed strictly to help individual students adjust to the demands of college life and to grow into productive adulthood, as in the past. This old approach implied our automatic acceptance of the environmental status quo—the nature of the campus environment—as satisfactory for encouraging student development. Unfortunately, the environment was not often satisfactory. As Aulepp and Delworth (1976) noted, "students were adjusted, but rarely were their environments" (p. viii). Now we must begin to view the environment as mutable and to examine systematically ways to modify it, so that the two-way interaction between student and environment can be maximally growth producing.

INTERACTION MOVING TOWARD PRACTICE

Interest in exploring the implications of the interactive models for practice is evident by the research these models have stimulated Studies using a social ecology approach, one of the person/ environment fit theories described by Walsh, or other approaches conceptualizing environments and/or person/environment interaction, have proliferated since 1972. An annotated bibliography that lists many of the studies relevant to students and campus environments can be found in Kaiser and Sherritz (1976).

Several models have focused on the development of processes which are tentatively designed to enhance student growth through environmental change. The Western Interstate Commission for Higher Education (WICHE) uses the term "ecosystems" to define an approach that addresses assessment and the redesign of college environments. This model makes a number of assumptions about students and the college environments: (1) The campus environment consists of all the stimuli that impinge upon students' sensory modalities and includes physical, chemical, biological, and social stimuli. (2) A transactional relationship exists between college students and their campus environment; that is, the students shape the environment and are shaped by it. (3) For purposes of environmental design, the shaping properties of the campus environment are focused upon students; however, the students are still viewed as active, choice-making agents who may resist, transform or nullify environmental influences. (4) Every student possesses the capacity for a wide spectrum of possible behaviors. A given campus environment may facilitate or inhibit any one or more of these behaviors. The campus should be intentionally designed to offer opportunities, incentives, and reinforcements for growth and development. (5) Students will attempt to cope with any educational environment in which they are placed. If the environment is not compatible with the students, the students may react negatively or fail to develop desirable qualities. (6) Because of the wide range of individual differences among students, fitting the campus environment to the students requires the creation of a variety of campus subenvironments. There must be an attempt to design environments for the wide range of individual characteristics among students. (7) Every campus has a design, even if the administration, faculty, and students have not planned or are not consciously aware of it. A design technology for campus environments, therefore, is useful both for the analysis of existing campus environments and the design of new ones. (8) Successful campus design is dependent upon participation of all campus members, including students, faculty, staff, administration, and trustees or regents (Western Interstate Commission for Higher Education, 1973, p. 6).

The ecosystem model's process is used to identify shaping properties in the campus environment in order to design *out* dysfunctional features and to design *in* features that facilitate student educational and personal growth. For example, a physical space might be altered or a policy changed; in other instances, a service might be offered to help a specific group of students to cope with stress or to reach higher stages in a model of cognitive or affective development.

A major feature of this model that invites creative applications to diverse campus problems is its flexibility. It can be applied at a macrolevel to study person/environment interaction and redesign for the entire campus community. Applied at a microlevel, it permits study of and redesign for specific groups within the campus community. Finally, it can be used to affect individual students on a personal level by routing them to a physical environment, service, or program that should provide a positive match with the student's needs and/or developmental level.

Whatever the purpose or level of the intervention, there are basic steps in such a design process. These steps have been reconceptualized by the present authors, based on the WICHE material, as follows: (1) Select educational values. (2) Translate values into specific goals. (3) Design environments that contain mechanisms to reach the goals. (4) Select students whose characteristics show potential for matching with the environmental opportunities. (5) Assess interaction between students and environment in terms of positive matches and negative matches. (6) When positive matches are found, make the environment more available to students whose characteristics are similar to those of students showing a successful match. (7) When negative matches are found, redesign in terms of (a) environmental changes (e.g., policy, organization, programs), (b) student changes (e.g., counseling, skill training programs), and (c) changes in both areas. (8) Evaluate redesigns.

The process is not linear. Steps 3 and 4 are closely interchangeable and, possibly, they work best if they are done concurrently. When they are, the characteristics of probable students can be addressed in the planning process at the same time that the environment is being built. Thus, planners can avoid mistakes such as building a very high-powered, heavily academic environment that ends up admitting students from noncompetitive high schools and community colleges.

Of course, the ideal is to be able to anticipate and correct for potential interaction problems even before they exist by specifying certain types of students and environments in order to guarantee the attainment of desirable educational goals. Very few planners, however, have the power to start before step 5. Most of us arrive in institutions that have a design (clear or not) and a set student body. As the process proceeds through steps 5-8, then, we have a chance to question what was done (even if not systematically) in steps 1-4. We may discover incongruities (mismatches) between any combination of educational values, goals, environments, and students. For example, we may discover that values, goals, and environments match but are mismatches with student characteristics; or, that the values of the institution appear very different from some environments (e.g., academic programs or residence hall policy) within it. As always, the challenge of developing good programs is in determining the places where impact is desirable and possible.

In this sense, then, the process steps become cyclical and ongoing, with no necessarily "best" starting place and no specific ending place. Studying the interaction of students and their academic environments demands constant work over time if successful redesign is to be achieved.

A training manual (Aulepp & Delworth 1976), published by WICHE, presents some specific processes to use in this work with heavy emphasis on the use of student reports of satisfaction with various campus environments. The process looks at student characteristics in terms of demographic (e.g., major age, sex) rather than developmental variables but it can be adapted to look at the latter as well.

Thus, the ecosystem model bridges our interest in student development processes with the growing available knowledge on person/environment interaction. We can consider institutional characteristics and development as well as student characteristics and development. More important, we can look at the dynamic interrelations of students and their environments. Our potential for effecting significant changes on the college campus has suddenly multiplied.

PUTTING INTERACTION MODELS INTO PRACTICE

To be able to use some of the current opportunities, we must become knowledgeable in the theory and methodology of person/environment interaction. Courses on person/environment interaction should become part of the graduate curriculum in college student personnel and psychology. Enough is known for us to teach; and the field is wide open for what we and our students can do to develop effective ways to study student/environment fit and to redesign in ways to enhance student development.

We must add several caveats at this point, however.

1. This work cannot be carried on productively by student personnel staff alone, although the staff certainly can provide much expertise and initiate limited projects to develop and try out models and processes. In fact, using this approach in a small way is often the method of choice in building support for a more comprehensive effort. The work that has the best potential for real change in students' lives on campus, however, is that which includes all levels and functions in the campus community. All groups—governing boards, administrators, faculty, staff, and stu-

dents—are needed for their specific points of view, sanction, and support, and some are also needed for their special expertise or skills in assessment and redesign.

Participation by other units in the campus community is not only practical but required by the theory underlying the interactional model. In the past, different functions in the campus community were assumed to be handled by discrete groups, and the influence of each on the others was only dimly recognized. The new interactional model stresses consideration of the mutual dependencies and influences that are present in a complex institution. Information from other groups and offices in the campus community is essential for the estimation of the probable far-reaching consequences of projects and for the determination of the most appropriate method of intervention. The work is clearly *interdisciplinary* in the traditional academic sense and *interactive* in the sense of including the variety of persons with differing roles and functions in the university.

2. In a similar vein, we must insure that redesign is done *with* students, not *for* them. We have begun to speak of students as our colleagues. The actualization of such a role holds the most promise for the successful implementation of change in higher education because students are legitimate and extremely influential participants in the interaction process. As Endler and Magnusson (1976) pointed out, "Behavior is determined by a continuous process of interaction between the individual and the situation he encounters (feedback). The individual is an intentional, active agent in this interaction process" (p. 12). The student's ideas about desirable changes and reactions to proposed redesigns are essential to insure that the redesigns will have maximum positive impact.

3. We must be willing to put aside the laboratory physical-science model for our research. A variety of useful methods for applied behavioral research is available (Goldman 1977; Proshansky 1976) and we must both explore the use of available technology and risk the development of new methods. We must accept with Proshansky (1976) that "our research is slow and ponderous because we are not only new at it but we have given ourselves a set of requirements that do not permit it to be otherwise" (p. 309).

4. We ask our readers to take very seriously a fear we have of

the work being done in developmental programming and in the person/environment fit approaches. Part of the excitement engendered by this work is the feeling that we are finally beginning to take a broader, more realistic, and widely applicable view of student development and campus life in general. Yet, as we read, as we attend meetings, such as the Minnesota Conference, and as we talk to colleagues, we are struck with the reality that most of the pioneering in thought, research, and action is taking place on certain types of campuses. Many of them are private colleges and among the best known in the country; others are public, usually large, prestigious institutions with solid resources. The students who typically attend these schools are "traditional" students in American higher education—aged eighteen to twenty-two, Anglo, middle class, and academically able, However, such a view blinds us to the needs of the large number of "new students" (Cross 1971) who are less academically able, white or members of various ethnic minorities, and from working-class backgrounds. Their impact has been strongly felt on our campuses, yet it has been both recent and relatively peripheral. Certainly, these students are not typical of the ones on whom our new theoretical and programming approaches are based. What is known about development and person/environment fit for students who attend large, urban, community colleges? Small colleges without resources in remote rural areas? These campuses rarely have seen a "traditional" student. New students are their reality. And what of the "college without walls," the experiments in life-long learning? Are we not concerned about these students as well?

A major assumption underlying the ecosystem model is that different people respond differently to different types of environments (WICHE 1973). We may eagerly adopt the model to create campus environments in order to encourage student development. However, if we fail to consider the unique characteristics and needs of the large numbers of new students and do not design environments with them in mind, we will be taken back to where we started: focusing our interventions on behalf of a select minority.

The danger, in our enthusiasm, is that we will work where it is easiest and where the work usually has been done—in the traditionally elitist institutions which have been the core of American higher education. To do so would diminish our intentions, our work, and our potential impact. On the theoretical level, if we base our new theories on observations of a highly select sample, we run the risk of limiting their validity and applicability. Philosophically, however, the problem is much more acute. The "other higher education" that deals every day with overwhelming problems of student development and the fit between student and college needs our help desperately. In such settings we can find the colleagues we need to develop a fuller understanding of how various types of college environments fit with various kinds of students. Resources, people, understanding, and tremendous effort are necessary for such a venture. To do less, however, portends a future in which the college experience is even more "separate and unequal" for those whom we term students. Rather than "easing them out" or "adjusting" them to our specifications, we will be ignoring some of them. This possibility is certainly not progress toward a realistic, humanistic concern but, perhaps, an even more painful nonrecognition of students' legitimate needs.

REFERENCES

Astin, A. W. *Preventing students from dropping out.* San Francisco: Jossey-Bass, 1975.

Aulepp, L., & Delworth, U. *Training manual for an ecosystem model.* Boulder, Colo.: Western Interstate Commission for Higher Education, 1976.

Banning, J. H., & Kaiser, L. An ecological perspective and model for campus design. *Personnel and Guidance Journal,* 1974, 52, 370-375.

Barker, R. G. *Ecological psychology: concepts and methods for studying the environment of human behavior.* Stanford, Calif.: Stanford University Press, 1968.

Chickering, A. W. *Education and identity.* San Francisco: Jossey-Bass, 1972.

Cross, K. P. *Beyond the open door.* San Francisco: Jossey-Bass, 1971.

————. Lesson in ecology: you can't change the student body without changing the system. *NASPA Journal,* 1975, 13(2), 2-8.

————. *Accent on learning.* San Francisco: Jossey-Bass, 1976.

Endler, N. S., & Magnusson, D. *Interactional psychology and personality.* Washington, D.C.: Hemisphere, 1976.

Feldman, K. A., & Newcomb, T. M. *The impact of college on students.* Vol. 1. San Francisco: Jossey-Bass, 1973.

Goldman, L., ed. *Research methods for counselors.* New York: Wiley, 1977.

Hunt, D. E. Person-environment interaction: a challenge found wanting before it was tried. *Review of Educational Research,* 1975, 45, 209-230.

Insel, P. M., & Moos, R. H. Psychological environments: expanding the scope of human ecology. *American Psychologist*, 1974, 29, 179-188.

Kaiser, L., & Sherritz, L. *Designing campus environments: a review of selected literature.* Boulder, Colo.: Western Interstate Commission for Higher Education, 1976.

Kohlberg, L. Stage and sequence: the cognitive-developmental approach to socialization. In D. Goslin, ed., *Handbook of socialization theory and research.* New York: Rand McNally, 1969.

Lewin, K. *Principles of topological psychology.* New York: McGraw-Hill, 1936.

Loevinger, J., & Wessler, R. *Measuring ego development.* Vols. 1 & 2. San Francisco: Jossey-Bass, 1970.

Mitchell, J. V. Education's challenge to psychology: the prediction of behavior from person-environment interactions. *Review of Educational Research*, 1969, 39, 695-721.

Murray, H. A. *Exploration in personality.* New York: Oxford University Press, 1938.

Pervin, L. A. Performance and satisfaction as a function of individual-environment fit. *Psychological Bulletin*, 1968, 69, 56-68.

———. A free-response description approach to the analysis of person-situation interaction. *Journal of Personality and Social Psychology*, 1976, 34(3), 465-474.

Proshansky, H. M. Environmental psychology and the real world. *American Psychologist*, 1976, 31(4), 303-330.

Walsh, W. B. *Theories of person-environment interaction: implications for the college student.* ACT Monograph 10. Iowa City: American College Testing Program, 1973.

Western Interstate Commission for Higher Education. *The ecosystem model: designing campus environments.* Boulder, Colo.: 1973.

Wilson, R. C.; Gaff, J. G.; Dienst, E. R., Wood, L.; & Bavry, J. L. *College professors and their impact on students.* New York: Wiley, 1975.

Theorists Are Persons, Too:
On Preaching What You Practice

David E. Hunt

What comes to mind when one hears the conference title, "Developmental Theory and Student Development?" Ordinarily, we might expect the theorist to lead off by describing how development occurs and then to prescribe the general conditions required for its occurrence. Guided by these general prescriptions, the practitioner would discuss his specific programs which are designed to enhance student development. This developmental theory-to-practice sequence is exemplified by the influence of Piagetian theory on British infant schools and of Kohlberg's theory on moral education programs. Practitioners find developmental theories attractive because the general principles of development are stated in objective, abstract terms surrounded by an aura of scientific respectability. To describe a new program as derived from a developmental theory lends it a persuasive general rationale and directs attention away from the specific features of the program to the validity and value of the theory. But this theory-to-practice approach is based on an illusion, as I have suggested in my specific reactions to the "cases" presented.

My major assumption in this paper is that developmental theory does not and cannot directly lead to the derivation of specific programs. The traditional theory-to-practice approach is an illusion both because of its assumption that psychological ideas can be expressed in abstract, impersonal principles without regard to persons, times, and places, and because of the corollary that such abstract knowledge can be directly "applied" to the impure world of practice. Not only are these beliefs wrong, but they have seriously misdirected psychologists from trying to understand the basic phenomenon of psychology, persons-in-relation. Therefore, I discuss how the relation between theory and practice can be reconstrued so that practice can improve and theory can be enriched. A more balanced view of the relation between psychological theory and practice must be based on three assumptions: (*a*) that practitioners are also psychologists, (*b*) that theorists are persons, and (*c*) that the relation between theory and practice is best considered as persons-in-relation, that is, between theorist and practitoner.

Some of my work is used to illustrate the shift from the traditional theory-to-practice approach to a more balanced view. Following Lewin's well-known motto, "There is nothing so practical as a good theory," I used to believe that if theories were developed and verified through empirical research, the resulting knowledge could be directly applied to the world of practice. Some earlier titles exemplify this belief: "A conceptual systems change model and its application to education" (Hunt 1966), and "From psychological theory to educational practice: implementation of a matching model" (Hunt, Greenwood, Brill, & Deneika 1972). More recent titles reflect the shift in my view: "Teachers' adaptation to students: from implicit to explicit matching" (Hunt 1975b); "The problem of three populations: students, teachers, and psychologists" (Hunt 1976a); "Teachers are psychologists, too" (Hunt 1976b); "There is nothing so theoretical as good practice" (deCharms & Hunt 1976); and in another recent paper (Hunt 1976c) I proposed reversing the traditional sequence to read: student → teacher → researcher → theorist. In case you have not already noticed, I should warn you that there is a danger in all this setting of things straight by reversing them. It smacks of the flip-flop reversal in thinking by a true believer that simply reverses all the problems. I have tried to be aware of this danger and, in occasionally overstating the case, for example, practice-to-theory, I do so to set the stage for advocating the more balanced reciprocal relation which is required.

In the remainder of this paper I will convey this shift to reciprocation by describing the theory-practice relation in terms of the persons engaged in the process. First, however, I consider the three participants—theorist, practitioner, and client—as their roles and relations would be seen in the traditional theory-to-practice approach. Next, I describe how each of the three participants may be viewed as a *person* and how the process may be considered as persons-in-relation. I use the term "theorist" here in both its usual sense and its broad application to researchers and developers; "practitioner" refers to teachers, therapists, counselors, treatment workers, and the like; "clients" are students, patients, counselees, or others who are the recipients of educational or psychological "services." I realize that one person may at times play two roles, for example, both theorist and therapist, and such combinations of function may be very desirable. Here I emphasize the distinctions among the three participants in order to consider how their distinct functions may be related in a more reciprocal fashion.[1]

Traditional Theory-to-Practice View

In the traditional view, the three participants are seen in terms of abstract functions which are arranged in a unilateral hierarchy. The theorist describes and then prescribes to the practitioner who, in turn, delivers the services to the client who is the passive recipient. This telegraphic summary is exaggerated, of course, but it is also surprising how much our thinking is colored by this one-way view. Let us consider it in more detail by noting the function of each participant and the relations among them.

THEORIST

Traditionally, the developmental theorist formulates or hypothesizes a description of the developmental process in terms of developmental stages, usually. Next, he describes the development process more specifically by stating the "transition rules," that is, the necessary combinations of environmental influence and developmental stage to facilitate developmental change (Kessen 1962). All of these descriptive formulations are produced by logical deductions which are to be evaluated by criteria of logical consistency. The theorist may cite some practical examples, but if so they serve to clarify the idea, not to support its validity.

Now that the developmental theory has been described in terms of stages, environmental conditions, and transition rules, the next step is to verify the theory through empirical investigation. For example, Turiel (1966) "verified" Kohlberg's theory by an analogue in which children's developmental change varied as a function of theoretically derived forms of training. It is important to note that this empirical phase is not really too important because only positive instances of verification are reported. Developmental theories are never or, at least, hardly ever, influenced by empirical evidence in a self-corrective fashion (imagine what would happen if Erikson were forced on the basis of empirical data to reverse the order of stage 3 and stage 4!).

Once the theory has been verified, the next step (conducted by a program developer or consultant) is to prescribe the appropriate training or environment, as dictated by the developmental theory. Specifically, such prescriptions are derived by translating the transition rules into practical terms; for example, if a student is at stage 1 and requires environment X, then a specific program based on environment X is prescribed. Therefore, in its final form the program consists of prescriptions for the delivery of services which are derived from the developmental theory. Note that all of these activities and functions have been conducted in an abstract, impersonal fashion in which the theorist is not reflexive (does not see himself as a person to which his theory applies), and the personal qualities of the practitioner are also ignored. The personal qualities of the client are acknowledged insofar as they fall under the rubric of the developmental theory.

PRACTITIONER

In the traditional view, the practitioner "implements" or "applies" the theory through "delivering the program." Perhaps the most telling term to describe the practitioner's role is that of intervention, which is defined as "any interference that may effect the interest of others." The detached role assigned to the practitioner as he mediates between theory and client is probably the most misguided feature of the traditional view. His reliance on his being a person is restricted on both sides: He should "apply" the program as prescribed without variation and he should not respond to variations in clients except as prescribed.

The practitioner's role as automatic dispenser of a program reached its height with the proliferation of "teacher-proof" programs a few years ago. There certainly is a place for automated nonresponsive programs in both education and counseling, but it would seem to make more sense to "deliver" them through a computer. Good practitioners are skilled performers who respond adaptively to clients in ways that cannot possibly be planned in advance. Therefore, it may be better to speak of "teacher-proven" rather than "teacher-proof" programs.

Another way to identify the practitioner's role in delivering a program in an unwavering, objective, detached fashion is to note all the terms for describing practitioner variation through (God forbid!) responding to the client as a person: expectancy effects, Hawthorne effects, halo effects, and so on. All of these "sources of error" assume the practitioner to be an automatic dispenser of service. Elsewhere (Hunt 1976b), I compared the application process to applying a coat of paint, with the theorist providing the paint and brush and the practitioner applying it; the analogy can be carried further by considering the "program" as a "paint-by-numbers" kit; in this sense, any practitioner variation is viewed as an "error." There is a need to evaluate the effects of practitioner bias but, certainly, we should begin by understanding the practitioner's intentions in a *positive* sense before considering these sources of error.

Finally, it is worth re-emphasizing that the central unit in the traditional view is the *program*, not the persons (practitioners) who are applying it. This point is most clearly demonstrated in program evaluation. Does the program work? Is it successful? If so, we will adopt the program. All of this misdirected emphasis on the abstraction, "program," leads us away from the most vital ingredient — the persons working with that program and their characteristics. The reasons for emphasizing programs rather than persons can be understood, perhaps, but they do not excuse the wrong-headed thinking. The characterization of programs must take account of the persons (practitioners) working in the program, specifically, their experience, attitudes, and intentions, which are described in a later section.

CLIENT

In the application of developmental theories, clients are usually viewed in terms of some "developmental deficit"; that is, the target of intervention is to increase their development. In the traditional view, a client is the recipient or beneficiary of the "program" which is designed to increase his developmental growth. He is usually not informed about the nature of the theory or program so such issues as his wishes to "be developed" are rarely considered. For example, so-called objective evaluation of "program effects" often involves administering tests to clients in a manner that is similar to taking their temperature or an X-ray. The client wonders, What are they going to do with these results? How will they be used? What will I learn from this? Will I receive any feedback from filling out these questionnaires? In the traditional view, the client is seen as an organism, not as a person. Persons are organisms, of course, but those features are the least important ones in characterizing clients. If we wish to learn about clients as persons, we must treat them as persons.

THEORIST → PRACTITIONER

In the traditional view, the theorist/consultant relates to the practitioner through some form of in-service training. The practitioner is expected to acquire the nonresponsive skills prescribed in the program in much the same fashion as a subject in a learning experiment memorizes nonsense syllables. Just as in learning to a criterion, so the practitioner must reach a specified level of "going through the program" before the training is complete. In the traditional view, the practitioner is trained to deliver services, that is, "programmed," entirely on the basis of the prescriptions derived from the theory. The practitioner's attitudes and past experience are irrelevant. If the program prescription is in disagreement with the practitioner's beliefs or experience, the disagreement is seen as "resistance to adoption." There is no way to negotiate such disagreements.

In emphasizing the dangers of prescribing specific practitioner behavior, I do not intend to deny the value of explicating ideas for practitioners. However, ideas should be seen as guides which are

continually open to revision and transformation through reciprocal interchange with the practitioner.

PRACTITIONER → CLIENT

The first concern is with how well the practitioner delivers the
program to the client. Programs are monitored by observing practitioners in terms of the objective, nonresponsive dispensing of the
program as prescribed. Therefore, the success of the practitioner is
gauged by how well he functions as an organism and how much he
avoids being a person. The practitioner's transformation of program prescriptions on the basis of personal responsiveness to the
client is viewed as faulty application or slippage. Note that the
monitoring is based entirely on a fixed, nonresponsive blueprint
that does not consider the practitioner's views. Monitoring what
happens between practitioners and clients certainly has a place,
particularly in detecting "non-events" (Charters & Jones 1973),
but monitoring should be conducted in a framework that acknowl-
edges both the practitioner's skilled performance in providing a responsive environment and the practitioner-client interaction as
persons-in-relation.

The other concern with the unilateral practitioner to client relation is to evaluate the program effects. Note that neither the practitioner nor client is involved in developing the evaluative criteria.
One of the more frequently employed methods in evaluating the
effect of developmentally derived programs is to administer a measure to assess client stage before and after the program. Program
effects are then expressed in terms of units of stage increase, for
example, $+\frac{1}{3}$ stage. I mentioned earlier some of the questions that
arise when clients are not informed of the nature of the evaluation. In addition, one can ask what "$+\frac{1}{3}$ stage" means. If development is viewed in discontinuous stages, then a fractional increase
means very little. If one were to consider small units of growth
such a $+\frac{1}{3}$ stage it would seem more sensible to reconsider the
developmental dimension as a continuum. Apart from this methodological nit-picking, the effects of practitioner-client interaction
should be characterized by a variety of methods, for example, interview, observations, and unobtrusive measures applied to client
and practitioner.

THEORIST → CLIENT

It is striking that in the traditional view there is no relation between theorist and client. Their only relation is indirect and mediated by the practitioner. As discussed in the next section, this absence of theorist-client relation is as unfortunate as the theorist's nonreflexiveness about his being a person.

Theory-Practice as Persons-in-Relation

Figure 1 summarizes the theory-practice process as seen in the traditional view and as persons-in-relation. In order to reconceptualize the theory-practice process as in reciprocation of persons-in-relation, it is first necessary to develop an adequate conception of the person. In characterizing persons, I follow the suggestions of Ossorio (1973); he proposed five features as the minimum necessary features: (1) Who is the person? (identity); (2) What does

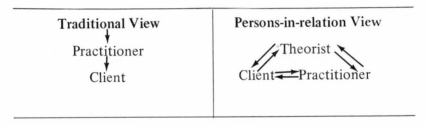

Figure 1. Two Views of Theory-Practice Process

the person want? (intention); (3) What does the person know? (knowledge); (4) What does the person know how to do? (competence); (5) What is the person trying to do? (action).

These features seem intuitively reasonable and deceptively simple. Ossorio emphasized that the five features are the minimum necessary to give a complete description; any characterization that omits one or more feature, therefore, is incomplete. He did not maintain that all must be understood fully at the same time but that each, at least, must be acknowledged. For example, to consider only a person's knowledge completely out of context with intention and competence yields an incomplete picture that is similar to the emphasis of the Gestalt psychologists; this emphasis has been dismissed as suggesting that everything must be studied simultaneously. The importance of viewing a feature (part) in context (whole) is nicely clarified by Sarason (1976): "how you approach and deal with the part is influenced mightily by where you see it in relationship to the whole; that is, what you hope to do and the ways in which you go about it are consequences of how you think it is imbedded in the larger picture" (pp. 323-24).

Therefore, I abbreviate Ossorio's notions as follows:

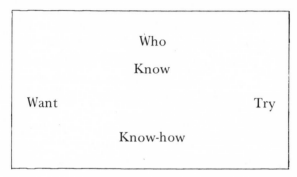

Each participant can be considered as a person by characterizing him or her in terms of these features. Such a characterization sets the foundation for describing persons-in-relation.

THEORIST-AS-PERSON

A theorist often is viewed incompletely by considering only what he knows and not his wants, know-how, and action. Therefore, it is useful to try to characterize a developmental theorist's ideas within this context. Like all persons, theorists have implicit theories about other persons, and it is valuable to know how well a theorist's explicit theories match his implicit, intuitive notions. Not only are psychological theorists also persons, but all persons are, in a sense, psychologists (Kelly 1955) in that they develop implicit theories about persons in their interpersonal world. Does this mean that every person's theory is as good as the next or, especially, as good as the explicit theory of the developmental theorist? Sarason (1976) observed that every person is also a community psychologist, but he reaffirms a distinction originally suggested by

Becker in "Every man his own historian." Acknowledging similarities between the psychologist and Mr. Everyman, the psychologist differs in his "more conscious and expert application" (Sarason 1976, p. 328) of the principle. This is the subtle yet important difference between the theorist's explicit formulation and Mr. Everyman's implicit psychological theory.

Although the formulations of the developmental theorist may be expected to be more conscious and expert, it is nonetheless true, as observed earlier, that a psychological theorist should be reflexive first and should acknowledge himself as a person. Once acknowledged, the theorist becomes the object of his own theory as well as its formulator. Such self-reflection should be of both theoretical and personal benefit to a theorist.

PRACTITIONER-AS-PERSON

What are the implications of characterizing practitioners in terms of the features proposed by Ossorio? To take account of a practitioner's *intention* is to emphasize the personal motives and concerns—images, hopes, and wishes—underlying what the practitioner does. To look for the personal, positive intentions of teachers and counselors shifts the emphasis from the "biasing" effects described earlier to how such factors as expectancy effects can serve constructive purposes.

To consider a practitioner's knowledge is to ask about his implicit psychological theories. If "Teachers are psychologists, too" (Hunt 1976b), then it is important to understand their theories—specifically, what is the practitioner's conception of development and how it occurs.

Once the practitioner's intentions, knowledge, and competence are acknowledged, then his action can be seen in relation to these features. The practitioner's action in "applying" the theory can be viewed then as a transformation process rather than an automatic inflexible application.

CLIENT-AS-PERSON

Since the major aim of the application of developmental theory to educational and counseling programs is to enhance the personal development of the client, it may seem unnecessary to consider the issue of client-as-person. However, the traditional theory-to-practice view rarely considers the client's intentions in regard to his development, only a limited version of the client in terms of developmental stage. Taking account of a client as person puts the client's developmental stage (knowledge and competence) into the context of his intentions. Perhaps the most important implication is to understand the client's motives for change and his perception of how it might occur. Also, taking account of the client's intentions is more likely to emphasize the importance of self-matching procedures in which the client is an active participant in the decision-making process.

THEORIST ⇆ PRACTITIONER AS PERSON-IN-RELATION

Rather than view the theorist-practitioner relation as objective in-service training, it is important to note that the reciprocal process between theorist and practitioner should exemplify the reciprocal process between practitioner and client. Reppucci and Saunders (1974) put it another way in noting that the process of acquainting practitioners with the "program" should be based on the same principles as the program itself. They referred to this as the "problem of two populations" (i.e., practitioners being the first population and clients, the second). I recently extended their analysis to describe three populations (Hunt 1976a, Table 1), in which theorists would be the third population.

One implication of the "problem of three populations" is that the theorist can best communicate an approach to a practitioner by letting the practitioner experience it. Thus, the theorist becomes the practitioner and the practitioner, the client, during this phase. For example, the theorist should be responsive to "practitioner pull" just as the practitioner or teacher is expected later to be responsive to "student pull" (Hunt 1975b). It is also especially important that the theorist be aware of the practitioner's knowledge or implicit theory in working with him since, as I noted elsewhere,

Assuming that the matching principle is sufficiently well established, it seems probable that one of the major determinants of its acceptability will be the degree to which it is congruent with the teacher's own ideas of matching. If so, then the task of implementing a matching model should begin with an investigation of what implicit matching model the educational decision maker is now using. From what we know of attitude change and adoption of new procedures, the proposed matching prescriptions should not be too far out of line with those held by the person implementing them. [Hunt 1971, p. 49.]

PRACTITIONER ⇆ CLIENT AS PERSON-IN-RELATION

Stated in terms of the five features of a person, the practitioner should have knowledge of all five features of the client: identity, intention, knowledge, competence, and actions. The knowledge will be continually shifting as the practitioner "reads" and "flexes" (Hunt 1976c) to the client. Another way to emphasize the practitioner-client reciprocation in the teacher-learning process is to emphasize the teacher's openness to "student pull."

THEORIST ⇆ CLIENT AS PERSON-IN-RELATION

To suggest that a theorist should preach what he practices is to acknowledge the importance of the theorist's competence in relating to the client in the way that he prescribes for the practitioner. Earlier, I suggested that the practitioner might learn through taking on the role of client; an equally valuable means of learning is to observe the theorist acting as practitioner with the client. The theorist who can demonstrate his theory by direct involvement with the client will have much more credibility with practitioners than one who simply states the prescriptions which the practitioner must learn. A theorist's preaching what he practices not only enhances practitioner credibility but also enriches the theorist's concepts through his exposing them to the client in a framework of persons-in-relation (compare with Madison's practices). Figure 2 summarizes the reciprocal relations among theorist, practitioner, and client as persons.

Another implication of viewing the three participants as persons is to emphasize the importance of considering how each views the program, as shown in Figure 3.

An Example

Perhaps the nature of this thought can be illustrated by using my experience in attempting to "apply" the idea of conceptual level (CL) matching (Hunt 1971).

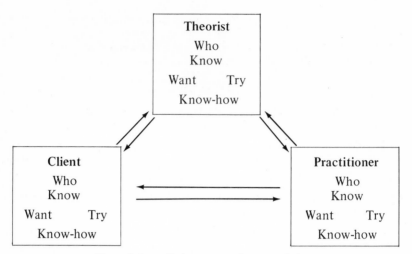

Figure 2. Interrelations among three populations.

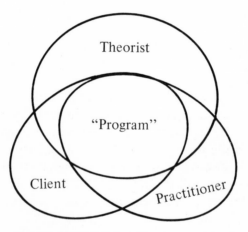

Figure 3. "Program" viewed by three participants.

The basic CL matching principle is that "low CL learners profit more from high structure, and high CL learners profit more from low structure, or in some cases, being less affected by variations in structure" (Hunt 1971, p. 44). In the theory-to-practice view, the "implication" would be that low CL students would profit from programs high in structure while high CL students would either do well in all programs or profit from low-structured programs.

We have had experience with using the idea at different levels of arrangements: within-class, between-classes, and between schools (Hunt 1975a). However, we proceeded by explaining the idea to teachers (who request that we do so) and discussing what it might mean for their own teaching. We did not provide a step-by-step program for them to follow; but I tended to view this work in terms of the degree to which the teacher took account of student CL and adapted his teaching approach accordingly. In all cases, the goal was to encourage development in student CL.

In one of these applications that involved homogeneous grouping by learning style (educational translation of CL), we discovered a surprising and gratifying effect on the teachers. As they worked with students who were clearly different in needs or learning styles, they became aware of what adaptation really meant. The old John Dewey idea of meeting student needs took on a new meaning; for the first time, the teachers realized that they could do something about meeting student needs by adapting their teaching approaches. Thus, the major effect of the homogeneous grouping was to sensitize the teachers to student needs and how to meet them.

Now let us take a look at this work from the point of view of the three populations. For me, this shift in perspective was very stimulating because I suddenly realized that the specific CL matching principle was not the major idea that accounted for what all three of us were doing. The psychological principle that described each person and the relations among us was the idea of adaptation in interpersonal communication or, more specifically, a communicator's reading and flexing to a listener.

For the student (client), we hoped that he would become more interpersonally sensitive and flexible in communicating because these are features of higher CL persons. For the teacher (practitioner), I emphasized their "tuning in" to the students and at-

tempting to adapt their approach, linguistic as well as instructional, to the student or group of students. For me (theorist), I tried
to read and flex in my interaction with the teacher (Hunt 1976c),
a process facilitated by considering the theorist-as-person. Figure 4
shows how the "application" of the CL matching model looks
when viewed in terms of persons-in-relation.

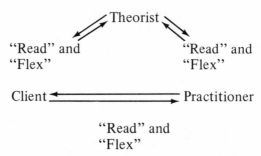

Figure 4. CL matching model as persons-in-relation.

Note in Figure 4 that the theorist is in reciprocal relation with
the client as well as with the practitioner. As theorist, I must be
able to relate directly to a client in the way I hope that the practitioner will learn to relate. Thus, I preach what I practice.

Implications

At this point my ideas probably seem either boringly obvious or
so complicated that they are unrealistically impractical. Let us
consider some of the specific implications for a psychologist who
takes this view seriously.

The clients themselves will be much more active in the process.
The purposes of the experience will be made clear to them, and
they will have an opportunity to modify and change the nature of
their experience. In matching terms, they are more likely to work
toward self-matching.

"Program evaluation" takes a very different appearance. Rather
than measuring the "degree of implementation" by comparing actual practice with the ideal model, the characterization will take
account of what a practitioner was doing initially and then focus

on the nature of the *persons* —their intentions, skills, and conceptions of goals and how to obtain them—and the process of their
interaction as persons. Such a characterization will likely take the
form of case studies emphasizing person descriptions. Characterizing program effects will also take account of the change in participating persons—practitioners and theorists as well as clients—as a
result of their interactions.

This recentering will focus the attention of psychologists where
it belongs—on the study of persons. Also, this focus, which aban-
dons the theory-practice dichotomy, should permit a more comprehensive understanding of how it is that practitioners acquire
the competence for skilled performance.

A consideration of the psychology of persons should provide
some understanding of the mysteries of the world of the practitioner. What makes him go? Why does he "burn out"? Why does
he change? What makes him feel good? In short, a range of un-
answered (and sometimes unasked) questions will come under
consideration, and with the invigorating effects of we theorists'
reacceptance of us as persons, some of these questions will be
better understood.

NOTE

1. In formulating some of these ideas I have been stimulated by discussions with
Richard deCharms, and I am especially grateful for his bringing to my attention the
ideas of Peter Ossorio (1973).

REFERENCES

Charters, W. W., & Jones, J. E. On the risk of appraising non-events in program evalua-
    tion. *Educational Research*, 1973, 2(November), 5-7.
deCharms, R., & Hunt, D. E. There is nothing so theoretical as good practice. Manuscript.
    Ontario Institute for Studies in Education, 1976.
Hunt, D. E. A conceptual systems change model and its application to education. In
    O. J. Harvey, ed., *Experience, structure, and adaptability*. New York: Springer,
    1966.
———. *Matching models in education*. Toronto: Ontario Institute for Studies in Educa-
    tion, 1971.

———. The B-P-E paradigm for theory, research, and practice. *Canadian Psychological Review*, 1975, 16, 185-197. (a)

———. Teachers' adaptation to students: from implicit to explicit matching. In B. R. Joyce, D. E. Hunt, & M. Weil, eds., *Teacher decision making.* Research Memorandum 139. Stanford, Calif.: SCRDT, 1975. (b)

———. The problem of three populations: students, teachers, and psychologists. Invited paper given to Ontario Psychological Association, London, Ont., February 1976. (a)

———. Teachers are psychologists, too: on the application of psychology to education. *Canadian Psychological Review*, 1976, 17, 210-218. (b)

———. Teachers' adaptation: "reading" and "flexing" to students, *Journal of Teacher Education*, 1976, 27, 268-275. (c)

Hunt, D. E., Greenwood, J.; Brill, R.; & Deneika, M. From psychological theory to educational practice: implementation of a matching model. Paper presented at American Education Research Association meeting, Chicago, 1972.

Kelly, G. A. *The psychology of personal constructs.* Vol. 1. New York: Norton, 1955.

Kessen, W. H. Stage and structure in the study of children. *Monographs of the Society for Research in Child Development*, 1962, 27, 65-82.

Ossorio, P. G. Never smile at a crocodile. *Journal of Theory of Social Behaviour*, 1973, 3, 121-140.

Reppucci, N. D., & Saunders, J. T. Social psychology of behavior modification. *American Psychologist*, 1974, 29, 649-660.

Sarason, S. B. Community psychology, networks, and Mr. Everyman. *American Psychologist*, 1976, 31, 317-328.

Turiel, E. An experimental test of the sequentiality of developmental stages in the child's moral judgments. *Journal of Personality and Social Psychology*, 1966, 3, 611-618.

Sharing in the Costs of Growth

William G. Perry, Jr.

During my visits to the conference groups and workshops, I had a feeling that developmental this and that (e.g., Perry's Scheme, whatever *that* might be) had been pushed onto people a bit these three days. In one group, a person suddenly broke into the conversation to say, "I don't know what's going on! I wish I knew what this conference was all about. All I'm doing is sitting wondering all the time whether I should sell my house. I shouldn't worry so about such a thing. My parents bought and sold lots of houses when I was young and never thought anything about it. I don't see why I'm so upset about it, but I am. And I can't seem to see how this fits into the Perry Scheme."

I am not about to fit such an experience into anything, much less the Perry Scheme. However, I want to put that experience up on the shelf, for a minute, because I think it may help us to understand something important about development, no matter whose scheme one uses to look at development—something we have not mentioned at this conference.

First, let me review three or four of those little discoveries of the obvious that we all make in life. When we first come into this world, it is obvious that there are authorities and that they know what they are doing, or at least so it seems. They tell us what to do and what not to do, and so they know what they are doing. That is discovery 1.

Discovery 2 is that they do not know what they are doing after all. And since they do not seem to know what they are doing and do not have all the answers, we think, "Hurray! As soon as I can get out from under their tyranny I'm free, and any opinion is as good as any other, mine included."

Discovery 3 is that when I get out from under their tyranny I walk smack into a plate-glass wall and find that I am still subject to a tyranny, not of *they*, but of *fact*. And in that tyranny of reality I discover that, although there are a lot of differences of opinion among reasonable people, not every opinion is as good as any other, including some which I have that are no good at all. And then I have to get to work and start thinking about all these things. I think about various ways in which very reasonable people disagree very reasonably in wide areas. For instance, I am told that all the Euclidian geometry I learned was just a nice little game with its own rules. Of course, one can be right or wrong within the rules of Euclidian geometry, but the chances that Euclidian geometry conforms to anything in this universe, I am now told, are only about one in three billion; there are other geometries that have a better probability of conforming to something in the universe. I also find that in such important matters as religion very reasonable people disagree very intensely. I examine various religions and I find that some of them have as much claim to be more than superstitution as anything I believe. Suddenly I realize that it is a little questionable to go around killing other people to the glory of the particular god I believe in. So I have discovered the obvious 3.

Then I make one more discovery, another obvious one, that I am faced with the challenge of affirming myself and my life as a person. Given so many differences of opinion among reasonable people, differences which reason alone cannot resolve, I see that I can never be sure I am making the "right" decisions in life. And yet I must decide. Oh, I have been told never to make a wrong decision lest I regret it all my life, but now I see I have no protection against regret. Unless I am going to weasel out of really living, I must choose what I believe in and own the consequences, and never know what lay down the roads I did not take. I have discovered what Robert Frost meant, and what it means to commit.

Why have I just rehearsed these four obvious discoveries? There has been all this talk at this conference about the Perry Scheme, and if some of you are in doubt about what it is—that is it. I mean, students reported to us about making these discoveries, and that is what the Perry Scheme is, nothing more. It took thirty of us, listening to students for fifteen years to make these obvious discoveries, and then we looked at each other and said, "Fifteen years for *this*?"

So the next questions are, "What's so good about advancing along such a series of discoveries (or any other scheme of development we have been considering)? Why should we educators devote ourselves to promoting discoveries like that? Why should we push or entice or seduce people to go along with discoveries like that?" I know of one reason, and that is that since the world is, indeed, complicated, it is better to have a matching set of complicated ideas to deal with it than to try to use a simple idea that does not fit. Perhaps something more can be said for these discoveries, however. One is that by a considerable study of the different ways in which reasonable people see things, we are put in the position to learn that the most valuable of all the qualities of maturity of which Doug Heath talked this morning is compassion.

I am not about to expand on the social utility of compassion. I want to ask some special questions about this conference: "If development is all so obvious, then *why is it so hard*? If it's all that simple and all that obvious, then what in the world are we here for? Why *is* it so hard to grow? Why is it even harder to help *other* people grow? What have we been talking about for three days?"

Over the past several months, some of the staff in our little office have been asking students about how they learn. We just ask, "Tell us about how you experience learning." The usual response is, "You mean *really* learning?" There seems to be a distinction between "just" learning and "really" learning, which is what the students want to talk about. "Really" learning invariably refers to experiences in which one sees the world and onself in a new and broader light—in short, to those very discoveries that mark the major steps into maturity I have been talking about.

I want to share with you the response of a young woman, a freshman. She said that so far she had been just learning more things at Harvard—"kind of flat"—and that the last time she had really learned was back in high school. She had a social science teacher whom she admired and he introduced to the class one of the Ames experiments with the revolving window. (You know it: There is this odd-shaped window that revolves on an axis and you see it revolve and you *know* it revolves; but then the lighting is changed and the window does not revolve; it oscillates from side to side, and you *know* it oscillates; and then the lighting is changed back and there the window is, revolving.) She said her teacher looked around and said to no one in particular, "So what do you make of *that*?" and no one said anything. "And all of a sudden I *saw*. I mean I saw how much we bring with us to our perception of things, how much we construct our worlds. And I realized that if this was true of windows, how about people? parents? myself, too? The whole world opened up to me, sort of, how everybody makes their own meanings, how different things can look in a different light, so to speak."

She then went on to say how the same experiment had been demonstrated at Harvard as just one more gimmick of perceptual illusion. The interviewer, bored with this complaint, brought her back to that moment in high school: "How did you feel then?" "Oh it was awful. I mean, my world was shattered. I guess it's sort of naive to use a word like this here, but it was like I lost my innocence. I mean nothing could ever be for sure—like it seems—I mean, again."

Our interviewer then asked, "How come you stayed with it instead of just laughing it off and forgetting it?"

"Oh, that was because of the teacher! You see, I trusted him, and I knew he knew. I mean, we didn't talk about it really, but he just looked at me and I knew he knew—what I'd learned—and what I'd lost! I guess because he knew what I'd lost, I could stay with what I'd seen."

So what I am talking about is something that we have left out in our talk of promoting development: What do we do about the house we leave when we go to a new place? When we leave the way we saw the world, in which everything was just so and just as we thought, and we see it all differently, we move into a world where all of what was solid and known is crumbling. And the new is untried. What do we do about the house we just sold out of? What do we do about the old simple world? It may be a great joy to discover a new and more complex way of thinking and seeing, but what do we do about all the hopes that we had invested and experienced in those simpler terms? When we leave those terms behind, are we to leave hope, too?

Does the teacher have a responsibility here, not only to promote growth and development, but to help people to do something with the losses?

I want to go back to the words: "Because he knew what I'd lost, I could stay with what I'd seen." If a loss has been known, if a pain of mine has been known and shared by somebody, if somebody has been aware of one of my pains, then I can go on. I can let that pain die in some way and go on to reinvest the hope. (Not that I ever really get entirely over it, you understand. What happens to the wounds of the past? Theodore Reik was asked that question, you remember. He said, "Well, they ache in bad weather.") But still, if these things have been known and shared, then somehow it is possible for me to do a strange thing called grieving, which I do not pretend to understand. It seems all right to let it hurt.

But if it is not allowed to grieve or to hurt, I have to deny the truth to have my chin up. If my loss has never "lived," socially, then I must keep it alive myself, protect it like a responsibility, even. Then I do not know why it is that I get stuck. It comes to me as a sort of theorem, that when you have taken one step in development, you cannot take another until you have grieved the losses of the first. I wonder how that hypothesis would look in testing. Jessie Taft, who was a therapist, wrote, "The therapist becomes the repository of the outworn self." So too, this teacher of social sciences became the repository of this young woman's innocence.   •

What about the losses in what we have been calling "career development"? In good times, when there is a world of plenty out there, students can be butcher, baker, candlestick maker; they can be anything. All they have to do is choose. It feels like a narrowing down. It feels as if you are losing all the other selves that you could have been. So I have always wanted to write vocational theory all over again; not about how you choose what you are going to do, but about how you give up all the other selves you are not going to be.

Nowadays, of course, fewer of those opportunities are available out there. So, in the last few years, we have had a different kind of feeling, one of desperation. In order to make it in this competitive world everything becomes contingent on what I do right now. It is an unbroken chain. If I slip any place, I have had it. My whole life rests on this one sentence that I am trying to write, so I cannot finish the sentence.

I do not know what to say about grieving and the teaching of grieving, because I do not understand it. I know it goes by waves. I know that when you take youself off someplace, and say, "Now I will face this, and grieve," nothing happens. But when you open up a bureau drawer and see something there that reminds you of something, then you have had it. I do not understand it, but I know that we do not allow it enough in our culture and we do not have the legitimizing rituals for the experience; therefore our people cannot grow well. They have to leave parts of themselves behind. Although I do not know how to teach people how to grieve, I have found that the teacher or counselor can make it clear that the pain is legitimate.

Such, then, is surely our responsibility: to stay, as it were, with the student's past and to the very extent that we invite the student to grow beyond it. It is a challenging task. Yet, just as our students can tell us why the obvious is so difficult (were we only to listen), so they may also tell us how we can help them to learn that the pain of growth is not a shame of youth that separates them from us.

I am reminded of a privileged moment I was given recently. A young woman had given me a lovely time all year. This woman, a freshman, is very accomplished; she was the president of her class in school and captain of the swimming team, and she had straight As in one of the most challenging schools in the country. But something was all wrong at college. She came to see me, we chatted, and she worked things out. I found that it was not only my privilege but my duty to enjoy her and to appreciate the trip she gave me on the roller coaster of adolescence. It was marvelous and sometimes very painful, but always somehow beautiful. Of course, she sometimes scared me by carrying too much sail. But I was enjoying it; I knew who I was supposed to be—the good uncle who listened. Then there came a day when she seemed profoundly moved, so I fastened my seatbelt. She had decided to transfer, she said, and she was feeling sad about leaving friends she had taken so long to make. There was a pause. Then she said, "Yesterday I was walking to class, and all of a sudden it came over me, that my days are numbered." I did my best not to stir. She looked at me. "Then it came to me that these days with you are numbered, too. Like, there comes a time when you have to move over and make room for others who need the time more." And then I thought of her as an older sister with her four younger sisters. And I said, "Well, gee, yeh, I know. And I've been thinking how I'll *miss* you." And she said, "Oh, really? Have you been thinking that way, too?" And so she just kept looking at me. It was one of those silences that went on for about fifteen minutes. About every five minutes or so she said softly, "Yes." Now I realized that she was a bright person and was putting things together. One of the things she was looking at was a guy whose days also were numbered, and by a lot smaller number than hers, and she looked me right in the eye for a long time. After a long time we got up. Somehow I decided it was time to say something, and I heard my voice say, "Growing is so bitter, so *bittersweet.*"

I did not hear the condescension in that remark until too late, and my inner critic turned on me in fury. "There you go, ruining the most beautiful moments again with your sappy platitudes." Well, I have learned that when I have made a mistake I am not the best person to try picking up the pieces, so I bit my tongue and waited. She looked at me without wavering and said gently, "And bittersweet for you, too." With that she touched my hand and left.

I have been finding that growing at this conference is bitter, bittersweet, and if I may let that young woman speak for all of us, I think she would say, gently, "And for you, too."

List of Contributors

List of Contributors

CLYDE A. PARKER is a counseling psychologist whose major interest for many years has been the psycho-social development of college students. He has served as the director of a college counseling center, assistant dean of students and chairman of two academic departments. His research and publications span a broad range of topics related to the development of students including changes in religious beliefs, differential effects of counseling modalities, organizational structures in student affairs and psychological consultation. His current research attempts to understand ways of increasing the ability of faculty to adapt the individual learning characteristics of college students. He is chairman of the Department of Social, Psychological and Philosophical Foundations in the College of Education at the University of Minnesota.

CAROLE WIDICK received her doctorate in counseling psychology from the University of Minnesota. She served as assistant professor, Faculty of Special Services, Ohio State University from 1974 to 1977. Currently, she is assistant professor of psychology at St. John's University, Collegeville, Minnesota. Her work has focused upon the use of developmental theory in the design of counseling and instructional programs. DEBORAH SIMPSON is a student personnel worker in higher education whose major research focus has been the cognitive and affective development of the college student in the classroom setting. In pursuing these interests, she has recently become involved in an examination of the role of faculty as facilitators of student development, while enrolled in a doctoral program in educational psychology at the University of Minnesota. She is a 1976 graduate of the Ohio State University.

PETER MADISON is a diplomate in clinical psychology and professor at the University of Arizona where he teaches in the clinical and personality programs of the Department of Psychology. He is also a part-time staff member both at the University's Counseling Service and at the Southern Arizona Mental Health Center. His current interest is in working at the interface between education and psychotherapy. He sees psychotherapy as a generative matrix for concepts and methods in personal learning that are potentially adaptable to teaching through the development of laboratory methods that teach the cognitive content of psychology while encouraging personal development using methods that are emotionally safe. He received his PhD degree in clinical psychology from Harvard University in 1953 and taught at Swarthmore College and Princeton University (where he also served as director of the Counseling Service) before coming to Arizona in 1963. He has published books on Freud's repression theory, on personality, and on personality development in college.

JAMES C. HURST is dean of students, assistant vice president for student affairs, and associate professor of counseling psychology at the University of Texas at Austin. Following his graduation from Brigham Young University in 1966, he completed his internship at Duke University, served a year on the staff of the Psychology Department and Counseling Center at Oregon University and was director of the University Counseling Center at Colorado State University. His professional and research interests include service and delivery systems for counseling psychology for remedial preventative and developmental purposes.

L. LEE KNEFELKAMP is assistant professor of counseling and personnel services and faculty associate for research and student development, Division of Student Affairs at the University of Maryland. She received her MA and PhD from the University of Minnesota. She currently serves as chairperson of the college student personnel specialty area in her department. Her research and teaching are in the areas of college student development theory and its application to the practice of the student affairs profession. She collaborated with Carole Widick on the creation of Developmental Instruction, an instructional methodology based on the Perry Scheme, and with Ronald A. Slepitza on the adaptation of the scheme to career development. RONALD A. SLEPITZA is the coordinator of rights and responsibilities for the resident life system at the University of Maryland. His responsibilities include staff training, program development, and crisis intervention in handling behavioral problems in the residence halls. He is also involved in the development of community development programs and organizational redesign efforts. Currently, he is completing requirements for his doctorate in student personnel administration at the University of Maryland. His research interests include the cognitive development of college students, community and organizational design, and the impact of the community on individual development.

JUDITH G. TOUCHTON is staff associate with the American Council on Education's Office of Women in Higher Education in Washington, D.C. Before joining the council in 1977, she spent five years as an administrator and counselor in the Career Development Center, University of Maryland, College Park. She received her MA degree in counseling and student personnel services from the University of Maryland in 1974 and will receive the PhD degree from the same institution in 1978. Her research interests lie in career development, cognitive development, and the career paths of academic women. LORETTA C. WERTHEIMER is affiliated with the Career Development Center of the University of Maryland, College Park. Her primary responsibility is the supervision of career planning and decision-making courses that are offered to undergraduates at the university. She received her MA degree in counseling and personnel services from the University of Maryland in 1976 and is currently completing her doctoral studies at the same institution. Her research interests have focused on the application of cognitive developmental principles to various phases of career counseling with college students. JANET L. CORNFELD is currently completing an internship at the Counseling Center of the University of Maryland, College Park. She has also served on the staffs of that university's Department of Counseling and Personnel Services, Career

Development Center, and Office of Resident Life. She received her MA degree in counseling from the University of Maryland in 1975 and will receive the PhD degree from that institution in 1978. Her research interests have emphasized the application of cognitive development, student development, and career development theories to the design of learning environments of both undergraduate and graduate students. KAREN H. HARRISON is now training administrator with the Providence National Bank in Philadelphia, Pa. Before joining the bank in 1978, she spent five years as a career counselor, first at the University of Maryland, College Park, and then at Temple University in Philadelphia. At Providence National Bank she is responsible for conducting training and educational programs for employees at all levels, including middle and upper management. She received her MS degree in counseling and guidance from Indiana University in 1973.

ROGER A. MYERS is professor of psychology and education at Teachers College, Columbia University, where he has been coordinator of the program in counseling psychology since 1966. He is currently chairman of the Department of Psychology and director of the Division of Psychology and Education. He received a PhD in counseling psychology from the Ohio State University in 1959 and directed the Counseling Center at the University of North Dakota from 1959 to 1963. He has been a conculting editor of the *Journal of Counseling Psychology*, the *Rehabilitation Counseling Bulletin*, and the *Journal of College Student Personnel*. For the past twelve years he has been engaged in designing computer-assisted systems for the promotion of career development.

DOUGLAS H. HEATH is professor of psychology at Haverford College. He is also a consultant and lecturer to schools and colleges about student development and its implications for educational change. The focus of his research has been the maturing process from adolescence to middle age. He has reported his work on vocational, educational, parental, and sexual development in the professional journals. His books include *Explorations of Maturity*, *Growing Up in College*, *Humanizing Schools*, and *Maturity and Competence: A Transcultural View*, the latter reporting the results of the first international study of the meaning of positive mental health. He received his PhD from Harvard University, secured post-doctoral training on a National Science Faculty Fellowship at the University of Michigan, and is currently a Fellow of the American Psychological Association.

ROY HEATH is a clinical psychologist in Amherst, Massachusetts. His longtime interest has been the development of individual students in higher education. He received an AB from Princeton University in 1939 and the PhD in psychology from the University of Pennsylvania in 1952. His first book, *The Reasonable Adventurer*, published in 1964, was a study of the temperament and development of thirty-six Princeton undergraduates, a sample of the class of 1954, during their four years of college. He is currently engaged in a follow-up study of these men and others from the class of 1954 to obtain an evaluation of their college education after the passage of some twenty-five years.

URSULA DELWORTH is director, University Counseling Service, and professor, counseling psychology and college student development, at the University of Iowa. She was previously director of an NIMH training grant with the Western Interstate Commission for Higher Education (WICHE). In this position, she worked with colleges and universities in the west to develop processes for program development, training of paraprofessionals, and assessment and redesign of campus environments. Dr. Delworth received her PhD in counseling psychology from the University of Oregon in 1969 and has held positions at Colorado State University and in a variety of consultation activities with Peace Corps, women's centers, and community groups. Her current scholarly interests and publications are largely in the area of assessment and redesign of college environments. ELLEN PIEL is assistant professor of educational psychology at the University of Nebraska-Lincoln. She received her PhD in counseling psychology from the University of Iowa in 1977. Her scholarly interests focus on person-environment interactions and issues of career development.

DAVID E. HUNT is a professor in the Department of Applied Psychology at the Ontario Institute for Studies in Education, University of Toronto, where has been for ten years. Before that he worked at Syracuse University and Yale University after completing graduate work at Ohio State University. His current interests are understanding what educational approaches are most appropriate for different students and how teachers can provide such approaches as well as reconceptualizing the relation between psychological theory and educational practice.

WILLIAM G. PERRY, JR. is director of the Bureau of Study Counsel and professor of education at Harvard University. For thirty years he and his staff have acted as consultants to students in the adventures of a liberal education. Perry made his own explorations of liberal education at Harvard in classics (he co-authored a translation of the *Iliad*) and in English, in which he holds an MA. How he became a psychologist he does not reveal, but he has published various articles and a book, *Forms of Intellectual and Ethical Development in the College Years* (Holt, Rinehart & Winston, 1970) to prove that he is one. He teaches the arts of counseling and says he aspires to become a good learner.

Index

Index

285